PEARL OF GREAT PRICE COMMENTARY

PEARL OF GREAT PRICE

COMMENTARY

A SELECTION FROM THE REVELATIONS,
TRANSLATIONS, AND NARRATIONS OF

JOSEPH SMITH

FIRST PROPHET, SEER AND REVELATOR TO
THE CHURCH OF JESUS CHRIST OF
LATTER-DAY SAINTS

COMMENTARY
BY
MILTON R. HUNTER
OF THE
FIRST COUNCIL OF THE SEVENTY

BOOKCRAFT

SALT LAKE CITY, UTAH

PREFACE

For many years the General Authorities of the Church of Jesus Christ of Latter-day Saints, and probably the majority of its members, have felt a definite need for a *Pearl of Great Price* commentary. This scripture is not only one of the standard works of the Church, but it is also one of the great books of the world. Heretofore comparatively little has been written about it and no definite effort has been made to explain each of the doctrines contained in it. For these reasons the First Council of the Seventy assigned the task to the author to prepare such a volume. With the foregoing purposes in mind and a prayer in his heart that God would sustain him in preparing a volume which would be useful to Church members, the author humbly and diligently accepted the assignment. The volume, entitled *Pearl of Great Price Commentary*, represents the result of said efforts.

Its first eight chapters are devoted to a discussion of the story of the origin of each of the four component parts of the *Pearl of Great Price* with a brief description of their contents. The remainder of the book is devoted to a discussion of the history and doctrine contained in that scripture. The doctrine has been classified according to subject-matter; and the subjects, as far as possible, are arranged chronologically. The first chapter on doctrine presents the ancient prophets' belief in God. This is followed by a discussion of the pre-existence of man. Then chapters are devoted to such subjects as the Grand Council in heaven, the creation of the world, and other topics in their appropriate order.

The entire *Pearl of Great Price* is reproduced in this commentary, being printed in double columns, while the author's discussion about the doctrines contained therein is printed in single column. This is done in order that the material quoted from the *Pearl of Great Price* might be very accessible to the readers. A definite and appropriate reference is given to every passage of scripture which is quoted throughout the entire book.

This also will make it easy for the readers to know the sources of the material that they are studying. The book also contains an appropriate index.

The writer expresses sincere and deep gratitude to Elder Joseph Fielding Smith, Elder Bruce R. McConkie, and Elder A. William Lund for their careful perusal of the manuscript and for their kind and helpful suggestions throughout the time that this volume was being prepared for publication.

Appreciation is also expressed to all of the members of the First Council of the Seventy who have generously made it possible for the writer to have sufficient time to complete the assignment; and the writer expresses a sincere hope that he has completed the job in accordance with their desires.

Deep appreciation is expressed to Dr. Sidney B. Sperry of the Brigham Young University for supplying the plates on the ancient Egyptian writings and also for granting his permission to the author to make use of his book, *Ancient Records Testify in Papyrus and Stone.*

The writer also expresses deep and sincere appreciation to Ferne G. Hunter who gave valuable assistance throughout the entire preparation of this book for publication and many helpful suggestions. Also, appreciation is expressed to June F. Oblad for typing the manuscript, proof-reading it, and offering many valuable suggestions.

The writer wishes to dedicate this volume to all faithful members of the Church of Jesus Christ of Latter-day Saints who are in search of eternal truth and are desirous of helping to teach the Gospel of Jesus Christ both at home and throughout the world. It is prayerfully and humbly hoped that those who study this book will gain a stronger testimony and a more thorough knowledge of the Gospel of Jesus Christ and that this book will help the work of the Lord to be advanced.

MILTON R. HUNTER

Salt Lake City, Utah
October 25, 1948

CONTENTS

ILLUSTRATIONS

Explanation Regarding Footnotes
and Abbreviations

ibid. From the Latin *ibidem,* meaning "the same
         reference as last cited."

op. cit. From the Latin *opere citato,* meaning "the
            work cited more than one note pre-
            viously."

e. g. From the Latin *exempli gratia,* meaning
         "for example."

ff. From the German *folgende,* meaning "and
       the pages following."

f. Meaning "and the page following."

pp. Meaning "pages."

p. Meaning "page."

2a. Meaning the first portion of verse two.

5b. Meaning the latter portion of verse five.

3:10; 4:6, 10, 16-20. Meaning "chapter three, verse
              ten; chapter four, verses six, ten, sixteen
              to twenty."

Chapter 1

INTRODUCTION TO THE STUDY OF THE PEARL OF GREAT PRICE

HOLY SCRIPTURES

The Church of Jesus Christ of Latter-day Saints accepts as holy scripture four books, which are termed the "four standard works of the Church." These books are as follows: the *Bible;* the *Book of Mormon;* the *Doctrine and Covenants;* and the *Pearl of Great Price.* By "scripture" is meant the writings which have been accepted by the Church as having been divinely inspired, hence authoritative, and binding upon each of the Saints.

BIBLE

The Church accepts, with certain reservations, the *Bible* to be the word of God. In the words of the Prophet Joseph Smith: "We believe the *Bible* to be the word of God as far as it is translated correctly." This holy book was inherited and adopted as scripture by the Latter-day Saints as it was by the other Christian groups. As is well known, the Old Testament was a contribution of the ancient Hebrews and the New Testament a contribution of the early Christian writers. Since the New Testament deals with the life and teachings of Jesus Christ and His associates, it is regarded by church members as a valuable and reliable scripture which holds a paramount position among the standard works of the Church.

BOOK OF MORMON

The *Book of Mormon,* as we all know, was translated by the Prophet Joseph Smith from some ancient records given to him by the Angel Moroni. It contains the history and religious

beliefs, doctrines, ordinances and practices of three groups of
people who inhabited the American continent in ancient times.
The first group was known as Jaredites. They came to America
from the Tower of Babel at the time of the confusion of tongues
and remained in this land for approximately 2,000 years. Their
history is told in the Book of Ether, which is an abridgment
made by Moroni from "twenty-four plates which were found
by the people of Limhi." The second group, known as Nephites,
came from Jerusalem under the leadership of Father Lehi and
his son Nephi; and for 1,000 years their descendants flourished
in America as a great people. The major portion of the historical account in the *Book of Mormon* deals with the Nephites
and the Lamanites (ancestors of the American Indians). The
doctrine in this book came directly from the Lord through His
holy prophets and also from Jesus Christ when He visited the
Nephites following His resurrection. The third people were
known as Mulekites. They came from Jerusalem fourteen years
after the Nephites, about 586 B.C. In approximately 200 B.C.
these people were discovered by the Nephites who, under the
leadership of Mosiah the first, had left their former home and
while migrating northward came upon the Mulekites living in
the city of Zarahemla. The two peoples merged together and
the Mulekites' identity was lost in the Nephite group of people.

Without reservation the Church of Jesus Christ of Latter-
day Saints accepts the *Book of Mormon* to be the word of God.
As one of the articles of faith, the Prophet Joseph Smith wrote:
"We believe the *Book of Mormon* to be the word of God." In
modern revelation the Lord declared to the Prophet Joseph
Smith that "The *Book of Mormon* . . . contains the truth and
the word of God—which is my word to the Gentiles, that soon
it may go to the Jews, of whom the Lamanites are a remnant,
that they may believe the gospel and look not for a Messiah
to come who has already come."[1] As a further verification of
the divine nature of this holy book, the Angel Moroni showed
the "gold plates" to Oliver Cowdery, David Whitmer, and
Martin Harris. While they were examining those ancient
records, God spoke from heaven and declared unto them that
the teachings in those records were true and that they had
been "translated by the gift and power of God." Then the Lord
commanded them to bear testimony to the world of what they

---

[1]*Doctrine and Covenants* 19:26-27.

had seen and heard. Thereupon they wrote what is termed "the testimony of the three witnesses." This testimony has been published in every *Book of Mormon* that has come from the press to this day. The three special witnesses wrote: "The voice of the Lord commanded us that we should bear record of it; wherefore, to be obedient to the commandment of God, we bear testimony of these things."

DOCTRINE AND COVENANTS

The *Doctrine and Covenants,* the third of the Latter-day Saint scriptures, occupies a unique and highly important position among Latter-day Saint sacred literature. It is a volume containing 136 chapters, known as sections, which are primarily composed of revelations received from the Lord by the Prophet Joseph Smith between 1823 and 1844. The last two sections, however, deal with the period following the Prophet's death, between 1844 and 1847. This holy scripture contains the word and will of the Lord as they relate to the restoration of the Gospel of Jesus Christ in the latter days. The doctrines which had been corrupted as a result of the great apostasy are clearly set forth in their purity in this book, having been given to Joseph Smith by the voice of God. The covenants which the Lord made with His chosen people in ancient times are reaffirmed in these revelations; and also the covenants that He makes with the "seed of Israel" in the latter days are herein contained. In addition to its gospel doctrine, this scripture of modern revelation contains many predictions in which every nation in the world should be interested. These predictions are a "voice of warning to the nations." In them we hear the "voice of God declaring:" "Hear, O heavens, and give ear, O earth, for the Lord hath spoken." Therefore, the *Doctrine and Covenants* is accepted by the Church of Jesus Christ of Latter-day Saints as the voice of the Lord, the will of the Lord, and the mind of the Lord; and its teachings are binding upon each member of the Church. It is, therefore, one of the holy scriptures.

PEARL OF GREAT PRICE

The *Pearl of Great Price* is accepted by the Church of Jesus Christ of Latter-day Saints as being no less authoritative

and binding upon church members than the other three volumes of holy scripture. It is accepted as the will, the word, and
the mind of God—thus it is scripture.

It fits well with the other standard works, sustaining and
verifying the principles and ordinances of the Gospel of Jesus
Christ as recorded in them. In fact, there are several outstanding contributions to church doctrine proclaimed in the *Pearl
of Great Price* which cause it to hold a unique place among
the four standard works of the Church. For example, it holds
first place among the Latter-day Saints' scriptures in presenting an abundance of evidence that God revealed to Father
Adam the very same gospel plan of salvation that Jesus Christ
established while living in mortality and also the same that He
revealed to Joseph Smith in the latter days. Thus Father Adam
and the other ancient prophets observed the same principles
and ordinances of the gospel that we practice today.

The personality of God, His intimate relationship with
man, and His concern for the human family are all shown
clearly in the visions of Enoch, Abraham, and Moses. The
majesty of God's work, its eternal nature, and the purpose of
life, with a definite assurance of the eternal nature and destiny
of man, are also unfolded in simplicity in this great book.
Furthermore, in the *Pearl of Great Price* is recorded the greatest statement regarding the work and glory of God to be
found in any of the holy scriptures or teachings of the prophets.
This scripture is: *"For behold, this is my work and my glory—
to bring to pass the immortality and eternal life of man."*[2]

Another unusual contribution to church doctrine, presented in the Book of Moses, is the account of the spiritual
creation of all plants, animals, and people, preceding their
mortal creation. The Book of Abraham makes an equally important contribution to our understanding of gospel truths
wherein it reveals to the world the knowledge of our eternal
existence and also of the great council of the Gods,
known as the Grand Council in heaven. We learn that
at that council God the Eternal Father presented the gospel
plan to His spirit-children and chose Jesus Christ to be the
Messiah, the Savior of the world; and the Book of Moses adds
to Abraham's teachings the information that at the time of
the Grand Council, Satan and his followers revolted against

---
[2]Moses 1:39.

the Father and the Only Begotten Son and were cast out of heaven. They were eternally damned and assigned to dwell on this earth as spirit beings. Thus the most complete account available of the Grand Council and war in heaven are found in the *Pearl of Great Price*.

There is no scripture equal to the Book of Abraham in revealing to man a knowledge of the great heavenly bodies, including the mighty Kolob which is near the throne of God, whose daily revolution is a thousand years of time as measured here upon this earth. Thus with a study of these two great books—Moses and Abraham—we learn that God has revealed to earth again knowledge which the ancient prophets had, and, in the case of the Book of Abraham, records which had been hidden from mankind for 4,000 years. Therefore, in this book we shall discuss somewhat in detail the eternal gospel truths proclaimed by the ancient prophets of God, beginning with Father Adam, or "Michael, the Ancient of Days."

The *Pearl of Great Price* also gives the Prophet Joseph Smith's own story of the most important events connected with the restoration of the gospel in the latter days, in the dispensation of the fullness of times. Joseph gives an account of one of the greatest of all visions which mortal man has been privileged to behold—the visitation of God the Father and His Only Begotten Son to the boy-prophet in answer to his humble prayer. Also, Joseph tells of the appearance of the Angel Moroni, of the coming forth of the *Book of Mormon,* and the restoration of the Aaronic Priesthood under the hands of John the Baptist. This is modern scripture revealed in the latter days.

The last page of the *Pearl of Great Price* is a copy of the Articles of Faith. Although they have been printed on small cards and widely distributed by missionaries and others, yet—since they constitute part of the *Pearl of Great Price*—these articles are definitely regarded by the Church of Jesus Christ of Latter-day Saints as holy scripture.

Chapter 2

ORIGIN OF THE BOOKS OF ABRAHAM
AND JOSEPH

INTRODUCTORY STATEMENT

The account of the writing of two doctrinal records on papyrus by the ancient patriarchs Father Abraham and his great-grandson Joseph, the preservation of those records for nearly 4,000 years, and the unusual way in which they were brought forth in the latter days and delivered into the hands of the Prophet Joseph Smith is in itself a very startling and interesting story. It is certain that the directing hand of God is evident in all that happened. The ways of the Lord are not man's ways. In accordance with God's divine will, the ancient records were preserved to be brought forth at the time of the restoration of the Gospel of Jesus Christ in the latter days, in the Dispensation of the Fullness of Times when all the ordinances, principles and doctrines of the gospel that had ever been on the earth were to be revealed. The story of the discovery of these ancient records and their purchase by the Latter-day Saints will be told in this chapter; and also more details regarding these records and their contents will be presented in the chapters that follow. Surely "the Lord moves in a mysterious way his wonders to perform."

DR. SIDNEY B. SPERRY QUOTED

Dr. Sidney B. Sperry of the Brigham Young University wrote a course of study for the Adult Department of the Mutual Improvement Association which was used by that group in 1938-1939. The title of his book was *Ancient Records Testify in Papyrus and Stone.* In his book Dr. Sperry gave an excellent discussion of the story of the Book of Abraham. Wherever copies are available, they could be referred to profitably

6

in connection with the material presented in this *Pearl of Great Price Commentary*. In fact, the author of this book desires to express appreciation to Dr. Sperry for the help received from *Ancient Records Testify in Papyrus and Stone* in the preparation of this work.

In his book Dr. Sperry presented many excellent details from original sources regarding the coming forth of the Book of Abraham; and, by way of introduction, he made the following observation:

> If a manuscript were to be found in the sands of Egypt written in Egyptian characters with the title "Book of Abraham," it would cause a sensation in the scholarly world. Our people do profess to have a scripture containing but five chapters which was written by Abraham who came from Ur of the Chaldees and eventually went down into the land of Egypt.[1]

It is now our purpose to tell the story of the manner in which the Book of Abraham came into the hands of the Latter-day Saints.

ANTONIO SEBOLO (LEBOLO) EXCAVATES EGYPTIAN CATACOMBS

In 1828 a Frenchman named Antonio Sebolo or Lebolo, while traveling in Egypt, became interested in the ancient catacombs and monuments of that country. He procured license from Mehemet Ali, then viceroy of Egypt under the protection of Chevalier Drovetti, the French consul, to excavate the catacombs neare the place where the renowned city of Thebes once stood. Sebolo "employed four hundred and thirty-three men, four months and two days—Egyptian and Turkish soldiers—at from four to six cents per diem, each man,"[2] so the Prophet Joseph Smith reported. Finally, on June 7, 1831, Sebolo succeeded in opening a large catacomb which contained several hundred mummies. About a hundred had been embalmed after the first order and neatly placed in niches. Two or three hundred others had been embalmed after the second and third orders and laid upon the floor of the ground cavity. The first order of embalming was rather expensive, and so its use was limited primarily to the deceased members of the royal family or others of the Egyptian nobility. The second order could be afforded for a much larger group of people, and the third order of embalming cost practically

[1]Sidney B. Sperry, *Ancient Records Testify in Papyrus and Stone*, p. 39.
[2]Joseph Smith, *History of the Church*, Period I, vol. 2, p. 348.

nothing, since it consisted only of soaking the body of the deceased individual in a solution of salt water. All of the mummies found by Sebolo, with the exception of eleven of the first order found in the niches, were so badly decomposed that they could not be removed. Thereupon Sebolo took these eleven, which constituted his diligently sought-for treasure, and set sail for his homeland.

On his way from Alexandria to Paris he became very ill and was forced to stop off at Trieste. Thereupon he willed his mummies to his nephew, Michael H. Chandler, who, he supposed, was living in Ireland. Ten days later Sebolo died. Accordingly the treasures were sent to Dublin, but while his uncle had been in Egypt Mr. Chandler had left Ireland for America. Several accounts of how Mr. Chandler came into possession of the Egyptian mummies appear in the journals of the leaders of the Church and in the early publications. They all agree on the principal fundamentals, but one account has the mummies arriving at London by the Thames River while other accounts have them going to Dublin. It may have been that the mummies were shipped to each of these places in the hope that the rightful owner would receive them.

MICHAEL H. CHANDLER AND HIS EGYPTIAN MUMMIES

Eventually, however, the mummies arrived in the harbor of New York City during the winter or early spring of 1833. Mr. Chandler was notified that his uncle had willed him an Egyptian treasure; thereupon he came to New York to receive it at the customhouse. The Prophet Joseph Smith described Chandler's experience as follows:

In April of the same year, Mr. Chandler paid the duties and took possession of his mummies. Up to this time, they had not been taken out of the coffins, nor the coffins opened. On opening the coffins, he discovered that in connection with two of the bodies was something rolled up with the same kind of linen, saturated with the same bitumen, which, when examined, proved to be two rolls of papyrus, previously mentioned. Two or three other small pieces of papyrus, with astronomical calculations, epitaphs, etc., were found with others of the mummies. When Mr. Chandler discovered that there was something with the mummies, he supposed, or hoped that it might be some diamonds or valuable metal, and was no little chagrined when he saw his disappointment. "He was immediately told, while yet in the customhouse, that there was no man in the city who could translate his roll; but was referred, by the same gentleman (a stranger), to Mr. Joseph Smith, Jr., who, continued he, possesses some kind of power or gifts, by which he had previously translated similar characters."[3]

Then Joseph Smith continued his account as follows: "I was then unknown to Mr. Chandler, neither did he know that such a book or work as the record of the Nephites, had been brought before the public. From New York, he took his collection on to Philadelphia, where he obtained the certificate of the learned."[4]

Since Mr. Chandler did not receive any valuable treasures in the coffins with his mummies, it seems that he decided to make the best use of his new gift by going from town to town and from city to city, exhibiting them to the public at a nominal charge. In the *Millennial Star* we read that Chandler "everywhere heard mention of Joseph Smith and the *Book of Mormon,* but so generally associated [him] with something slanderous, that he could scarcely think seriously of applying to him."[5]

Oliver Cowdery confirms the statement made in the *Millennial Star.* To quote:

> While Mr. Chandler was in Philadelphia, he used every exertion to find someone who could give him the translation of his papyrus, but could not, satisfactorily, though from some few men of the first eminence he obtained in a small degree, the translation of a few characters. Here he was referred to Brother Smith. From Philadelphia he visited Harrisburg, and other places east of the mountains, and was frequently referred to Brother Smith for a translation of the Egyptian relic.[6]

Finally, however, after he had exhibited his mummies for more than two years, Mr. Chandler arrived at Kirtland, Ohio, on July 3, 1835, where the Prophet was residing.

THE SAINTS PURCHASED FOUR MUMMIES AND PAPYRUS SCROLLS

Thereupon "he called upon Mr. Smith, to inquire if he had a power by which he could translate the ancient Egyptian. Mr. Smith replied that he had, when Mr. Chandler presented the fragment which had been partially interpreted. Mr. Smith

[3]*Ibid.*, p. 349.
[4]*Ibid.*, pp. 349-350.
[5]Parley P. Pratt and T. Ward, *Millennial Star,* vol. 3, July, 1842, p. 46.
[6]Oliver Cowdery to William Frye, *Latter-day Saint Messenger and Advocate,* vol. 2, no. 3, Kirtland, Ohio, December, 1835, p. 235.

retired into his translating room, and presently returned with a written translation in English, of the fragment."[7]

Oliver Cowdery reports the foregoing event as follows:

The morning Mr. Chandler first presented his papyrus to Brother Smith, he was shown by the latter a number of characters like those upon the writings of Mr. Chandler which were previously copied from the plates, containing the history of the Nephites, or *Book of Mormon*. Being solicited by Mr. Chandler to give an opinion concerning his antiquities, or a translation of some of the characters, Brother Smith gave him the interpretation of some few for his satisfaction.[8]

But probably the most interesting statement made relative to what took place between Mr. Chandler and Joseph Smith was recorded by the Prophet in his journal: "On the 3rd of July [1835], Michael H. Chandler came to Kirtland to exhibit some Egyptian mummies. There were four human figures, together with some two or more rolls of papyrus covered with hieroglyphic figures and devices. As Mr. Chandler had been told I could translate them, he brought me some of the characters, and I gave him the interpretation, and like a gentleman he gave me the following certificate:

Kirtland, July 6, 1835

This is to make known to all who may be desirous, concerning the knowledge of Mr. Joseph Smith, Jun., in deciphering the ancient Egyptian hieroglyphic characters in my possession, which I have, in many eminent cities, showed to the most learned; and, from the information that I could ever learn, or meet with, I find that of Mr. Joseph Smith, Jun., to correspond in the most minute matters.

Michael H. Chandler,
Traveling with, and proprietor of,
Egyptian Mummies."[9]

The four mummies and the papyri which Mr. Chandler had in his possession when he arrived at Kirtland were purchased by the Latter-day Saints. One of these mummies was the body of a woman, and the other three were bodies of men. It seems that the papyri were preserved in the family of the Pharaohs "and afterwards hid up with the embalmed body of the female with whom they were found." One of the papyrus scrolls was written by Father Abraham and the other by Joseph who was sold into Egypt. Just how much money was paid for these valuable antiquities is not known, but a

[7]*Millennial Star*, vol. 3, p. 46.
[8]Oliver Cowdery to William Frye in *op. cit.*, p. 235.
[9]Joseph Smith, *op. cit.*, vol. 2, p. 235.

statement appeared in the *Alexandria Gazette* that they were purchased at the suggestion of Joseph Smith "for a large sum of money." Oliver Cowdery reported the purchase of Mr. Chandler's relics as follows:

You will have understood from the foregoing, that eleven mummies were taken from the catacomb, at the time of which I have been speaking, and nothing definite having been said as to their disposal, I may, with propriety add a few words. Seven of the said eleven were purchased by gentlemen for private museums, previous to Mr. Chandler's visit to this place, with a small quantity of papyrus, similar, (as he says), to the astronomical representation, contained with the present two rolls, of which I previously spoke, and the remaining four by gentlemen resident here.

Though the mummies themselves are a curiosity, and an astonishment, well calculated to arouse the mind to a reflection of past ages, when men strove, as at this day, to immortalize their names, though in another manner, yet I do not consider them of much value compared with those records which were deposited with them.[10]

Thus God preserved the writings of Abraham and Joseph for approximately 4,000 years; and when the time came for celestial light to burst forth in full brilliance in the latter days in the restoration of the Gospel of Jesus Christ, the ancient records were taken from the Egyptian tomb. They were carried from land to land until they were finally deposited in the hands of the Prophet of God who had been foreordained to be the instrument of the Father and the Only Begotten Son through whom the true Church would be established on earth again. Therefore, the reception of these ancient records by Joseph the Prophet constituted a partial fulfillment of the predictions of the ancient prophets of God. Paul had predicted "that in the Dispensation of the Fullness of Times he [God] might gather in one all things in Christ, both which are in heaven, and which are on earth; even in him;"[11] and Nephi had declared that "all things which have been revealed unto the children of men shall at that day be revealed."[12]

[10]Oliver Cowdery to William Frye in *op. cit.*, pp. 236-237.
[11]Ephesians 1:10.
[12]2 Nephi 30:18.

Chapter 3

EVIDENCE THAT JOSEPH SMITH POSSESSED
THE PAPYRUS SCROLLS

INTRODUCTORY STATEMENT

The story was told in the last chapter of how the Prophet
Joseph Smith and his associates came into possession of the
papyrus scrolls which contained the writings of Father Abraham and his great-grandson Joseph who was sold into Egyptian
bondage. This chapter will present evidence that Joseph
Smith possessed the papyrus scrolls.

TESTIMONY OF THE PROPHET JOSEPH SMITH

Since more than a hundred years have elapsed since the
Prophet translated the writings taken from the Egyptian
papyri, and neither the mummies nor the original records are
now available, the serious-minded student is now concerned
with the problem of the evidence sustaining the fact that
Joseph Smith had in his possession the previously discussed
Egyptian relics. In other words, what is the evidence which
sustains the story of the origin of the Book of Abraham?

First, from time to time after the Saints had purchased
the four Egyptian mummies and the writings of the ancient
patriarchs from Michael H. Chandler in July, 1835, Joseph
Smith frequently made mention in his journal of incidents
connected with exhibiting these ancient relics to various people
and also of his work in translating the Egyptian characters
which were written on the scrolls. For the purpose of illustrating this point, we shall quote extracts from the Prophet's
journal:

Monday, 19, [October, 1835]. At home. Exhibited the records of
antiquity to a number who had called to see them.

Saturday, 24, [October, 1835]. Mr. Goodrich and wife called to see the ancient records, and also Dr. Frederick G. Williams to see the mummies.

Thursday, 29, [October, 1835]. . . . While at the doctor's, Bishop Edward Partridge came in in company with President Phelps. I was much rejoiced to see him. We examined the mummies, returned home, and my scribe commenced writing in my journal a history of my life.

Tuesday, 17, [November, 1835]. Exhibited the alphabet of the ancient records to Mr. Holmes, and some others. Went with him to Frederick G. Williams', to see the mummies.

Monday, 30, [November, 1835]. . . . Henry Capron, an old acquaintance from Manchester, New York, called on me. I showed him the Egyptian records.

Saturday, 12, [December, 1835]. . . . About twelve o'clock a number of young persons called to see the Egyptian records. My scribe exhibited them. One of the young ladies who had been examining them, was asked if they had the appearance of antiquity. She observed, with an air of contempt, that they had not. On hearing this, I was surprised at the ignorance she displayed, and I observed to her, that she was an anomaly in creation, for all the wise and learned that had examined them, without hesitation pronounced them ancient. . . .

Monday, 14, [December, 1835]. A number of brethren from New York called to visit me and see the Egyptian records. . . .

Wednesday, 16, [December, 1835]. . . . Elders William E. McLellin, Brigham Young, and Jared Carter, called and paid me a visit with which I was much gratified. I exhibited and explained the Egyptian records to them, and explained many things concerning the dealings of God with the ancients, and the formation of the planetary system.

Wednesday, 23, [December, 1835]. In the forenoon, at home, studying the Greek language. And also waited upon the brethren who came in, and exhibited to them the papyrus. . . .

Tuesday, 12, [January, 1836]. . . . This afternoon, a young man called to see the Egyptian manuscripts, which I exhibited. . . .

Saturday, 30, [January, 1836]. Attended school as usual, and waited upon several visitors, and showed them the record of Abraham. Mr. Seixas, our Hebrew teacher, examined it with deep interest, and pronounced it to be original beyond all doubt. He is a man of excellent understanding, and has a knowledge of many languages which were spoken by the ancients, and he is an honorable man, so far as I can judge yet.[1]

TESTIMONY OF OTHER LATTER-DAY SAINT LEADERS

The second evidence comes from the journals and articles of other Latter-day Saint leaders who were closely associated with the Prophet Joseph Smith. Many of them not only saw

---

[1]Joseph Smith, *History of the Church,* Period I, vol. 2, pp. 290, 291, 293, 316, 322, 327, 328, 329, 330, 331, 334, 344, 364, 388.

the ancient relics but also helped the Prophet in the work of translating the Egyptian characters and preparing the writings of Abraham for publication. For example, on February 19, 1842, the following entry was made by Wilford Woodruff—a member of the Quorum of the Twelve Apostles—in his daily journal:

Joseph the Seer has presented us some of the Book of Abraham which was written by his own hand but hid from the knowledge of man for the last four thousand years but has now come to light through the mercy of God. Joseph has had these records in his possession for several years but has never presented them before the world in the English language until now, but he is now about to publish it to the world or parts of it by publishing it in the *Times and Seasons*, for Joseph the Seer is now the editor of that paper and Elder Taylor assists him in the writing while it has fallen to my lot to take charge of the business parts of the establishment. I have had the privilege this day of assisting in setting the *tipe* for printing of the first piece of the Book of Abraham that is to be presented to the inhabitants of the earth in the last days.[2]

Another member of the Quorum of the Twelve, Parley P. Pratt, and his assistant T. Ward published two editorials in the *Millennial Star* in England in the summer of 1842 in which they told the story of the coming forth of the Book of Abraham.[3]

Oliver Cowdery, who was the assistant president of the Church and very closely associated with Joseph Smith during the early rise of Mormonism, was of course intimately acquainted with the circumstances connected with the purchase of the Egyptian mummies and with the conditions under which the papyri found with them were translated by the Prophet. Cowdery wrote a letter to William Frye (who lived in Gilead, Calhoun County, Illinois) in which he told in some detail the events connected with the discovery of the Egyptian mummies, their purchase by the Saints, and the translation of the writings on the papyrus scrolls. His letter was published in the *Latter-day Saint Messenger and Advocate*. Oliver's letter verifies the statements made by Joseph Smith in regard to the Latter-day Saints purchasing the mummies and the papyrus scrolls and also gives much information regarding the contents of the same. This letter is a valuable evidence that the Prophet possessed the mummies and the papyrus scrolls.

[2]Wilford Woodruff, *Daily Journal and History*, February 19, 1842.
[3]*Millennial Star*, vol. 3, no. 3, July 1, 1842, pp. 46-47; no. 4, August 1, 1842, pp. 70-71.

Oliver began his letter by telling William Frye the story of Mr. Chandler's coming into possession of the Egyptian mummies and the scrolls. Then he explained that Chandler had spent two years exhibiting his mummies east of the Appalachian Mountains and that on many occasions he was referred to Joseph Smith as being the only man in America who might be able to translate the ancient writings. Then, to quote directly from the letter, Oliver explained the following to William Frye:

It would be beyond my purpose to follow this gentleman in his different circuits to the time he visited this place the last of June, or the first of July, at which time he presented Brother Smith with his papyrus. Till then neither myself nor Brother Smith knew of such relics being in America. Mr. Chandler was told that his writings could be deciphered, and very politely gave me a privilege of copying some four or five different sentences or separate pieces, stating, at the same time, that unless he found some one who could give him a translation soon, he would carry them to London. . . .

If Providence permits, I will, ere long, write you again upon the propriety of looking for additions to our present scriptures, according to their own literal reading.[4]

TESTIMONY OF NON-MORMONS

Statements made by the Mormon Prophet and the other church leaders who were his associates are accepted by members of the Church of Jesus Christ of Latter-day Saints as being completely trustworthy and true; therefore, we accept such statements as the foregoing which have been quoted from the Prophet's and Wilford Woodruff's journals, from Parley P. Pratt's editorials, and from Oliver Cowdery's letter to William Frye as being the most reliable kind of evidence sustaining the story of the Book of Abraham. The non-Mormon, however, may object to such evidence since it is submitted entirely by church members. But Dr. Sidney B. Sperry, in his M. I. A. Manual, *Ancient Records Testify in Papyrus and Stone,* has presented a number of excellent statements and accounts of experiences of Gentiles who had the privilege of viewing the Egyptian mummies and the ancient writings on the papyrus rolls. For the purpose of illustrating this point, the following excellent extracts from *The Quincy Whig,* which were apparently copied from the *Alexandria Gazette,* are given:

---

[4]Oliver Cowdery to William Frye in *Latter-day Saint Messenger and Advocate,* vol. 2, no. 3, Kirtland, Ohio, December, 1835, pp. 235, 237.

It was a beautiful morning towards the close of April last, when the writer of the foregoing sketch, accompanied by a friend, crossed the Mississippi River, from Montrose, to pay a visit to the Prophet. As we approached his house, we saw him ride up and alight from his beautiful horse; and handing the bridle to one of his followers in attendance, he waited in front of his gate to receive us. A number of principal men of the place soon collected around, apparently anxious to hear the words which fell from his lips. His bearing towards them was like one who has authority; and the deference which they paid him convinced us that his dominion was deeply seated in the empire of their consciences. To our minds, profound knowledge of human nature had evidently taught him that, of all principles, the most omnipotent is the religious principle, and to govern men of certain classes, it is only necessary to control their religious sentiments.

After he had shown us the fine grounds around his dwelling, he conducted us, at our request, to an upper room, where he drew aside the curtains of a case, and showed us several Egyptian mummies, which we were told that the church had purchased, at his suggestion, some time before, for a large sum of money.

"The embalmed body that stands near the center of the case," said he, "is one of the Pharoahs, who sat on the throne of Egypt, and the female figure by it was probably one of the daughters."

"It may have been the Princess Thermutis," I replied, "the same that rescued Moses from the waters of the Nile!" (See the Works of Josephus.)

"It is not improbable," answered the Prophet, "but time has not yet allowed fully to examine and decide that point."

"Do you understand the Hebrew language?" said he, raising his hand to the top of the case, and taking down a small Hebrew grammar of Rabbi Seixas.

"That language has not altogether escaped my attention," was the reply.

He then walked to a secretary, on the opposite side of the room, and drew out several frames, covered with glass, under which were numerous fragments of Egyptian papyrus, on which, as usual, a great variety of hieroglyphical characters had been imprinted.

"These ancient records," said he, "throw great light on the subject of Christianity. They have been unrolled and preserved with great labor and care. My time has been hitherto too much taken up to translate the whole of them, but I will show you how I interpret certain parts. There," said he, pointing to a particular character, "that is the signature of the patriarch Abraham."

"It is indeed a most interesting autograph," I replied, "and doubtless the only one extant. What an ornament it would be to have these ancient manuscripts handsomely set, in appropriate frames, and hung up around the walls of the temple which you are about to erect at this place."

"Yes," replied the Prophet, "and the translation hung up with them."[5]

---

[5] *The Quincy Whig*, vol. 3, no. 25, Quincy, Illinois, October 17, 1840, p. 1.

On May 14, 1844, only a little over one month before the martyrdom of the Phophet Joseph Smith, Josiah Quincy, "the sophisticated mayor of Boston," in company with Charles Francis Adams, the illustrious son of John Quincy Adams, visited Nauvoo. Mr. Quincy described in his journal his impressions of the Mormon Prophet and recorded the following significant facts regarding the Egyptian mummies and the papyrus which they were shown:

> "And now come with me," said the Prophet, "and I will show you the curiosities." So saying, he led the way to a lower room, where sat a venerable and respectable-looking lady. "This is my mother, gentlemen. The curiosities we shall see belong to her. They were purchased with her own money, at a cost of six thousand dollars;" and then, with deep feeling, were added the words, "And that woman was turned out upon the prairie in the dead of night by a mob."
>
> There were some pine presses fixed against the wall of the room. These receptacles Smith opened, and disclosed four human bodies, shrunken and black with age.
>
> "These are mumies," said the exhibitor. "I want you to look at that little runt of a fellow over there. He was a great man in his day. Why, that was Pharaoh Necho, King of Egypt!"
>
> Some parchments inscribed with hieroglyphics were then offered us. They were preserved under glass and handled with great respect. "That is the handwriting of Abraham, the Father of the Faithful," said the Prophet. "This is the autograph of Moses, and these lines were written by his brother Aaron. Here we have the earliest account of the Creation, from which Moses composed the First Book of Genesis."
>
> The parchment last referred to showed a crude drawing of a man and woman, and a serpent walking upon a pair of legs. I ventured to doubt the propriety of providing the reptile in question with this unusual means of locomotion.
>
> "Why, that's as plain as a pikestaff," was the rejoinder. "Before the Fall snakes always went about on legs, just like chickens. They were deprived of them, in punishment for their agency in the ruin of man." We were further assured that the prophet was the only mortal who could translate these mysterious writings, and that his power was given by direct inspiration. . . .
>
> The exhibition of these august relics concluded with a similar descent into the hard modern world of fact. Monarchs, patriarchs, and parchments were very well in their way; but this was clearly the nineteenth century, when prophets must get a living and provide for their relations. *"Gentlemen,"* said this *bourgeois* Mohammed, as he closed the cabinets, *"those who see these curiosities generally pay my mother a quarter of a dollar."*[6]

CONCLUSION

The statements quoted in this chapter from Joseph Smith, Wilford Woodruff, Parley P. Pratt, Oliver Cowdery, and from non-Mormons furnish sufficient evidence to prove beyond a shadow of a doubt in any court of the land the validity of the story of the origin of the Book of Abraham.

[6]Josiah Quincy, *Figures of the Past,* pp. 286-287.

Chapter 4

ANCIENT EGYPTIAN WRITING AND LANGUAGE

INTEREST OF SAINTS IN THE WRITINGS OF ANCIENT EGYPT

No people should be more interested in the story of the language and writings of ancient Egypt than members of the Church of Jesus Christ of Latter-day Saints, because the Book of Abraham and also the *Book of Mormon* records were written in certain types of Egyptian characters. The former writings were recorded in those characters that were used in Father Abraham's day, while the Nephites wrote their records in what they termed *reformed Egyptian.*[1]

The Nephites brought with them to America in 600 B.C. a scripture quite similar to our Old Testament down to the Prophet Jeremiah. It was written in Egyptian characters engraved on brass plates. They secured the plates from a man named Laban; therefore, this scripture was known as "the brass plates" or "the plates of Laban." The Egyptian characters served as the pattern for the ancient Americans to record their own history on metal plates. Nephi, the first historian of his people, wrote: "Yea, I make a record in the language of my father, which consists of the learning of the Jews, and the language of the Egyptians."[2] Four hundred years later King Mosiah the second explained to his son the origin of their language and the purpose for which the "brass plates" had been used. To quote his exact words:

> For it were not possible that our father, Lehi, could have remembered all these things, to have taught them to his children, except it were for the help of these plates [the brass plates]; for he having been taught in the language of the Egyptians, therefore he could read these engravings, and teach them to his children, that thereby they could teach them to their children, and so fulfilling the commandments of God, even down to this present time.[3]

[1]Mormon 9:32.
[2]1 Nephi 1:2.
[3]Mosiah 1:4.

As time passed, the Nephites modified many of the characters, resulting in what they termed "reformed Egyptian." Near the close of Nephite history, after those people had flourished as a great nation in America for approximately 1,000 years, Mormon, the next to last great prophet and writer on the records, was commanded by the Lord to make an abridgment of all of the records of his people. Toward the close of his writings he made the following comment regarding the type of script which was used on the *Book of Mormon* record:

> And now behold, we have written this record according to our knowledge of the characters, which are called among us the reformed Egyptian, being handed down and altered by us, according to our manner of speech. And if our plates had been sufficiently large, we should have written in Hebrew; but the Hebrew hath been altered by us also; and if we could have written in Hebrew, behold, we would have had no imperfection in our record.[4]

Dr. Sidney B. Sperry of the Brigham Young University made the following comment regarding the type of writing used by the Nephites:

> Just what is meant by reformed Egyptian? Opinions may vary, but the writer believes that reformed Egyptian was a kind of shorthand devised by the ancient Nephites from Egyptian characters and certain Hebrew characters, and used by them to express Hebrew words. To make the explanation a little clearer: modern shorthand cannot be read by the ordinary person, nevertheless it may express English words. In the same way reformed Egyptian was used to express Hebrew words. It was used rather than Hebrew because it occupied less space.[5]

The photograph inserted is a copy of the characters taken from the plates of the *Book of Mormon* and just below it appear three lines of the Egyptian demotic, the type of Egyptian characters being used at the time Lehi left Jerusalem, and therefore, similar to that found on the brass plates. In making a comparison of the three lines taken from the Nephite record and the three lines of ancient Egyptian demotic, one can observe a resemblance but also a very marked difference in the two scripts. During a thousand years of Nephite history, one would expect to find a marked divergence made from the Egyptian characters, especially when one recalls the testimony of the last Nephite historian that his people had altered the Egyptian characters to fit their own needs as well

[4]Mormon 9:32-33.
[5]Sidney B. Sperry, *Ancient Records Testify in Papyrus and Stone*, p. 24.

as altering the Hebrew way of expressing ideas and that they had termed this modified writing the reformed Egyptian.

Ancient Egyptian Writings

In order that we may have an understanding regarding the type of language used by Father Abraham in making his record and also the problems confronting Joseph Smith in translating that record, a brief description of the ancient Egyptian writings or language will be given. The language went through three general steps from the beginning of Egyptian history down to the time Lehi left Jerusalem; namely, the hieroglyphic, the hieratic, and the demotic.

First—The Hieroglyphic:

Probably as early as 3,000 B. C. the Egyptians knew how to read and write. They used a picture-writing known to us as hieroglyphic. By this term is meant "sacred" (Greek *hieros*) inscriptions "sculptured" (Greek *glupho*). The ancient Egyptians used the hieroglyphs for two principal purposes: first, to record events and sacred teachings; and, second, to decorate their temples and public monuments. Therefore, those people either chiseled or painted hundreds of pictures or hieroglyphs on the stone surface of their temples, tombs, public buildings, and monuments. Sometimes they were inscribed on papyrus, and, in many cases, were buried in the dry sands of Egypt and preserved there for ages to come forth in modern times under the searching eye of the archeologist. Naturally this type of language required a great deal of time to write and was difficult to read. As time passed and commerce became an important factor in Egyptian life, there was a need for a simpler, more concentrated type of writing.

Second—The Hieratic:

This new style of writing gradually evolved out of the hieroglyphic. It is known to us as hieratic, receiving "its name from the fact that in the Graeco-Roman age (100 B. C.) it was the usual writing used by the Egyptian priests (Greek *hieratikos,* 'priestly').["6] Hieratic is a shorthand of the Egyptian hieroglyphic; therefore, it was superior for commercial purposes. It was also extensively used by the Egyptian priests for writing religious texts on papyrus.

---

[6]*Ibid.,* p. 26.

PLATE I

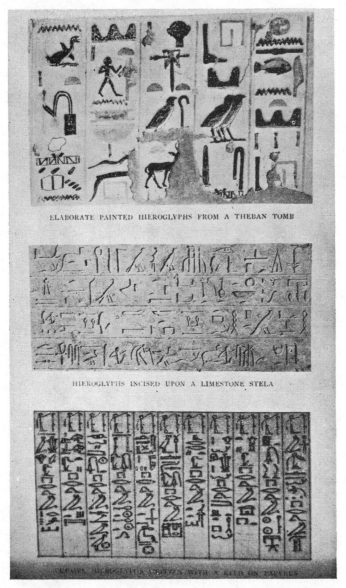

ELABORATE PAINTED HIEROGLYPHS FROM A THEBAN TOMB

HIEROGLYPHS INCISED UPON A LIMESTONE STELA

CURSIVE HIEROGLYPHS WRITTEN WITH A REED ON PAPYRUS

DIFFERENT STYLES OF HIEROGLYPHIC WRITING
From Allan H. Gardiner, *Egyptian Grammar*
Reproduced from *Ancient Records Testify in Papyrus and Stone,*
Courtesy of Dr. Sidney B. Sperry, Brigham Young University.

—20a—

PLATE II

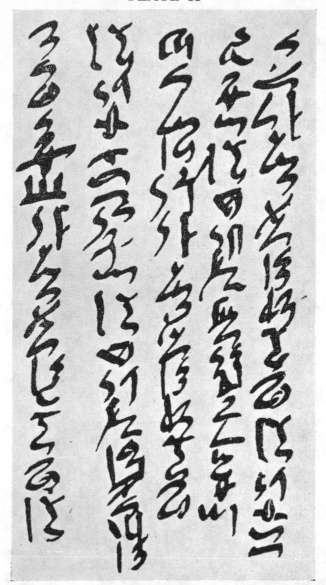

HIERATIC WRITING
From Erman, *The Literature of the Ancient Egyptians,*
trans. by A. M. Blackman.
Reproduced from *Ancient Records Testify in Papyrus and Stone,*
Courtesy of Dr. Sidney B. Sperry, Brigham Young University.

PLATE III

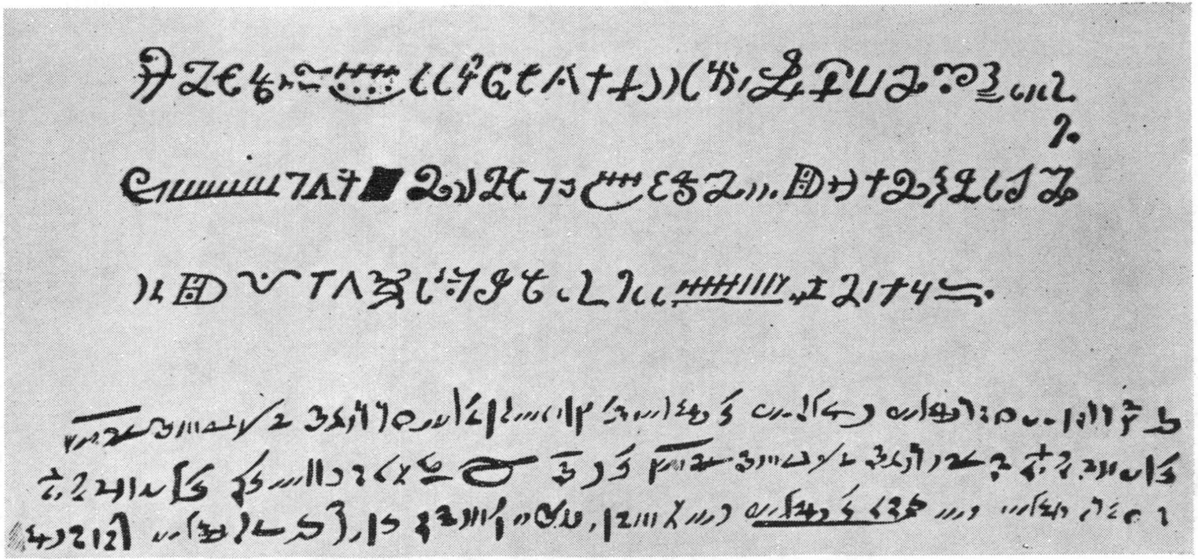

THREE LINES OF DEMOTIC (*bottom*)

COMPARE WITH CHARACTERS TAKEN FROM THE PLATES
OF THE BOOK OF MORMON (*top*)

Reproduced from *Ancient Records Testify in Papyrus and Stone,*
Courtesy of Dr. Sidney B. Sperry, Brigham Young University.

PLATE IV

The Rosetta Stone

Reproduced from *Ancient Records Testify in Papyrus and Stone*,
Courtesy of Dr. Sidney B. Sperry, Brigham Young University.

Third—The Demotic:

The third state in the development of the Egyptian language was the demotic (Greek *demotikos,* "popular"). According to Dr. Sperry:

> This was a very rapid or shortened form of hieratic used in the books and the documents written from about 700 B. C. to A. D. 470. During much of this period demotic was the ordinary writing of daily life, but is occasionally found chiseled even upon stone. From the dates given, it will be apparent that if Lehi and Nephi knew Egyptian they may have been familiar with this very shortened form of Egyptian. Demotic in itself was a sort of reformed Egyptian.[7]

GENERAL SUGGESTIONS

It would be advisable at this point for the readers to observe the three facsimiles which have been taken from the Book of Abraham and printed in this chapter and make a comparison of them with the Egyptian hieroglyphic and hieratic writings as shown on Plate I and Plate II.

The material found in this chapter and the one that follows is given much more completely in the M. I. A. Adult Manual for 1938-1939, written by Dr. Sidney B. Sperry of the Brigham Young University faculty. As previously mentioned, the manual, called *Ancient Records Testify in Papyrus and Stone,* is helpful, and is the most complete study that has been made of the background of the Book of Abraham. It is out of print now but anyone who has a copy of that manual can use it to good advantage in studying this introductory material to the *Pearl of Great Price.*

---

[7]*Ibia.*

A FACSIMILE FROM THE BOOK OF ABRAHAM

No. 1

EXPLANATION OF THE ABOVE CUT

Fig. 1. The Angel of the Lord. 2. Abraham fastened upon an altar. 3. The idolatrous priest of Elkenah attempting to offer up Abraham as a sacrifice. 4. The altar for sacrifice by the idolatrous priests, standing before the gods of Elkenah, Libnah, Mahmackrah, Korash, and Pharaoh. 5. The idolatrous god of Elkenah. 6. The idolatrous god of Libnah. 7. The idolatrous god of Mahmackrah. 8. The idolatrous god of Korash. 9. The idolatrous god of Pharaoh. 10. Abraham in Egypt. 11. Designed to represent the pillars of heaven, as understood by the Egyptians. 12. Raukeeyang, signifying expanse, or the firmament over our heads; but in this case, in relation to this subject, the Egyptians meant it to signify Shaumau, to be high, or the heavens, answering to the Hebrew word, Shaumahyeem.

A FACSIMILE FROM THE BOOK OF ABRAHAM

No. 2

EXPLANATION OF THE FOREGOING CUT

Fig. 1. Kolob, signifying the first creation, nearest to the celestial, or the residence of God. First in government, the last pertaining to the measurement of time. The measurement according to celestial time, which celestial time signifies one day to a cubit. One day in Kolob is equal to a thousand years according to the measurement of this earth, which is called by the Egyptians Jah-oh-eh.

Fig. 2. Stands next to Kolob, called by the Egyptians Oliblish, which is the next grand governing creation near to the celestial or the place where God resides; holding the key of power also, pertaining to other planets; as revealed from God to Abraham, as he offered sacrifice upon an altar, which he had built unto the Lord.

Fig. 3. Is made to represent God, sitting upon his throne, clothed with power and authority; with a crown of eternal light upon his head; representing also the grand Key-words of the Holy Priesthood, as revealed to Adam in the Garden of Eden, as also to Seth, Noah, Melchizedek, Abraham, and all to whom the Priesthood was revealed.

Fig. 4. Answers to the Hebrew word Raukeeyang, signifying expanse, or the firmament of the heavens; also a numerical figure, in Egyptian signifying one thousand; answering to the measuring of the time of Oliblish, which is equal with Kolob in its revolution and in its measuring of time.

Fig. 5. Is called in Egyptian Enish-go-on-dosh; this is one of the governing planets also, and is said by the Egyptians to be the Sun, and to borrow its light from Kolob through the medium of Kae-e-vanrash, which is the grand Key, or, in other words, the governing power, which governs fifteen other fixed planets or stars, as also Floeese or the Moon, the Earth and the Sun in their annual revolutions. This planet receives its power through the medium of Kli-flos-is-es, or

Hah-ko-kau-beam, the stars represented by numbers 22 and 23, receiving light from the revolutions of Kolob.

Fig. 6. Represents this earth in its four quarters.

Fig. 7. Represents God sitting upon his throne, revealing through the heavens the grand Key-words of the Priesthood: as, also, the sign of the Holy Ghost unto Abraham, in the form of a dove.

Fig. 8. Contains writing that cannot be revealed unto the world; but is to be had in the Holy Temple of God.

Fig. 9. Ought not to be revealed at the present time.

Fig. 10. Also.

Fig. 11. Also. If the world can find out these numbers, so let it be. Amen.

Figures 12, 13, 14, 15, 16, 17, 18, 19, and 20, will be given in the own due time of the Lord.

The above translation is given as far as we have any right to give at the present time.

A FACSIMILE FROM THE BOOK OF ABRAHAM

No. 3

Explanation of the Above Cut

1. Abraham sitting upon Pharaoh's throne, by the politeness of the king, with a crown upon his head, representing the Priesthood, as emblematical of the grand Presidency in Heaven; with the scepter of justice and judgment in his hand.

2. King Pharaoh, whose name is given in the characters above his head.

3. Signifies Abraham in Egypt—referring to Abraham, as given in the ninth number of the *Times and Seasons*. (Also as given in the first facsimile of this book.)

4. Prince of Pharaoh, King of Egypt, as written above the head.

5. Shulem, one of the king's principal waiters, as represented by the characters above his hand.

6. Olimlah, a slave belonging to the prince.

Abraham is reasoning upon the principles of Astronomy, in the king's court.

Chapter 5

DECIPHERING OF THE ANCIENT
EGYPTIAN LANGUAGE

ROSETTA STONE

The ancient Egyptian language, which was used through-out the entire country of Egypt as the dominant tongue and mode of writing until after the conquest of Alexander the Great during the early part of the fourth century B. C., was eventually forgotten, and it was not until comparatively recent times that a knowledge of it was revived. Egyptian had become one of the dead languages of antiquity.

During the latter part of the eighteenth century, many Europeans visited Egypt and observed the numerous hiero-glyphs which covered the walls of the ancient public buildings and temples. These pictures or hieroglyphs were either chiseled on the walls of the Egyptians' public buildings or at times painted there. They had the appearance of great antiquity. Although it was generally understood that they represented the writings of the early inhabitants of that land, no one in the world could read them. Try as they would, not a scholar in any land was able to decipher the Egyptian characters until after the discovery of the Rosetta Stone in 1798 by Napoleon's soldiers.

Napoleon was on a military campaign in Egypt when some of the French soldiers, while working on a fortress at a place called Rosetta, came across a large black stone of basalt covered with three sections of inscriptions, written in hiero-glyphic, demotic, and Greek, respectively. Dr. Sperry described the stone as follows:

This stone eventually became famous as the Rosetta Stone. It measures three feet, nine inches, by two feet, four and one-half inches. There are fourteen lines of hieroglyphic, thirty-two lines of demotic, and fifty-four lines of Greek upon it. The stone, after being found, was removed to Cairo, there to be examined by learned men. Napoleon was sufficiently interested to order the inscriptions copied and sent to scholars and learned societies in Europe.[1]

The stone itself, however, was captured from the French by the English and placed on exhibition in the British Museum. There it has remained most of the time during more than a hundred years.

The reader probably observed that there were more lines of the demotic on the Rosetta Stone than there were of the hieroglyphic characters. The reason for that was that the latter writing was on the top of the stone and a part of that end of the stone was broken off before its discovery.

DECIPHERING OF THE EGYPTIAN LANGUAGE

The knowledge of Greek had never been lost to mankind, but hundreds of years had passed since there was even one man left in the entire world who could read hieroglyphic or demotic symbols. The scholars readily deciphered the Greek on the Rosetta Stone and guessed correctly that the two other sections of writing contained the same information as did the Greek section. Therefore, they believed that if they, aided by the Greek section, could decipher the Egyptian characters on the Rosetta Stone, they would henceforth have a key to the Egyptian language.

Scholar after scholar, representative of the best paleographers in the world, diligently worked for a period of over twenty-three years to discover the key to the unknown tongue. About the time that the heavens were opened in the latter days and celestial beings were visiting the Prophet Joseph Smith, light penetrated the mind of a great European scholar and he succeeded in translating the Rosetta Stone. His name was Jean François Champollion. This brilliant and ambitious young French scholar had acquired a knowledge of Greek, Coptic, Hebrew, and Arabic. Having steeped himself in things Oriental, in 1818 he began an intensive study of the Rosetta Stone. Regarding Champollion, Dr. Sperry wrote the following:

> During this period a young French scholar by the name of Jean Francois Champollion took up the problem and was destined to win immortal fame as a decipherer of hieroglyphs. Champollion was born

[1]Sidney B. Sperry, *Ancient Records Testify in Papyrus and Stone*, pp. 31-32.

in France on the twenty-third of December, 1790. Oddly enough the day of the month, though not the year, in which he was born corresponds with the Prophet Joseph Smith's anniversary. It is of further interest that his decipherment of the hieroglyphs took place at about the time that the Prophet Joseph Smith was receiving his first visions. He died in the year 1832, just three years before the papyri from which the Book of Abraham was translated came into the hands of the Prophet. It is one of the strange facts in the history of the Mormon people that the decipherment of Egyptian was accomplished at about the same time that the Prophet became interested in Egyptian manuscripts and in the *Book of Mormon* which, as we have seen, has interesting connections with Egyptian.[2]

Champollion succeeded in deciphering the Egyptian writings on the Rosetta Stone, and in 1824 the results of his marvelous accomplishments were published in his *Précis du systéme hiéroglyphique* (Summary of the Hieroglyphic System). That was a year after the Angel Moroni had appeared to the Prophet Joseph Smith and had informed him of the *Book of Mormon* records, written in reformed Egyptian, which he was to receive and, through the power of God, translate. Three years later the Prophet received the Nephite records (1827), and less than two years passed before he had completely translated a large volume from these ancient characters. (We are discussing Joseph Smith's achievements as translator of the *Book of Mormon* records, as well as that of the Book of Abraham, since both ancient records were written in certain styles of Egyptian and both, therefore, have a certain relationship to the problem under consideration.)

Joseph Smith As A Divinely Inspired Translator

Just how much help could Joseph Smith have received from all the scholars of the world if he had solicited their assistance in deciphering the Nephite writings? Practically none. Champollion was virtually the only renowned scholar, if not the only one, who knew anything in particular regarding the Egyptian characters, and he was in the very midst of his work. According to Dr. Sperry:

After the death of Champollion at the early age of forty-one many scholars were dubious of the accuracy of his interpretation of Egyptian. However, new impetus was given to the study of hieroglyphs by Richard Lepsius, a great German scholar, in one of his publications at Rome in 1837. Lepsius had submitted Champollion's principles of decipherment

---
[2]*Ibid.*, p. 34.

to a penetrating re-examination and pronounced the foundations to be sound.[2]

The Prophet Joseph Smith's source of inspiration and information was more potent than all the human scholarship on the ancient Egyptian language which existed in the world at that time. It is of interest to note that the greatest paleographer of the world spent over twenty years translating only one page of Egyptian hieroglyphic and demotic symbols while the Prophet of God translated enough reformed Egyptian characters from the Nephite records to make a book of over five hundred printed pages, and he had the record in his possession only one year and ten months when this mammoth job was completed and the book ready for the printer. In fact, during the last ninety days of this period, Joseph Smith, assisted by Oliver Cowdery, began on the small plates of Nephi and translated and recorded the entire *Book of Mormon*. It should be remembered, however, that before Oliver Cowdery began on April 7, 1829, to serve as Joseph Smith's scribe, the Prophet had the Nephite records in his possession for a year and a half. During that time he had been instructed by divine teachers, and had spent much time studying the ancient records; therefore, he was prepared to translate the records rapidly when Oliver was his assistant.

The secret of Joseph Smith's astounding degree of success as a translator was the fact that God gave unto him "the gift and power" to translate ancient languages and the Urim and Thummim to aid him in the work. All of these facts proclaim the Latter-day Saint Prophet to be a divinely inspired translator of ancient scriptures; and they also show that man plus God is more powerful than all the learned men in the world combined.

[2]*Ibid.*, p. 36.

Chapter 6

TRANSLATING AND PUBLISHING OF
THE BOOK OF ABRAHAM

TRANSLATION BY JOSEPH SMITH

Although Joseph Smith never prepared the writings of Joseph for publication, he did translate and publish the Book of Abraham. As was pointed out in an earlier chapter, it was on July 3, 1835, when the Saints who resided at Kirtland, Ohio, purchased the mummies and two papyrus scrolls. The Prophet immediately devoted attention to translating the Book of Abraham and also reading some of the characters on the Book of Joseph, as we will find to be true from his own statement. It seems from the comments made by Joseph Smith in his journal that during the first two or three months that he had the papyrus scrolls in his possession he devoted considerable time to working upon them; thereafter the task of translating had to be worked in piecemeal among his other numerous activities. He probably did little work upon these ancient manuscripts during August and September, 1835, but in October and November he began work upon them. On October 7, 1835, he recorded in his journal as follows: "This afternoon I re-commenced translating the ancient record."[1] About six weeks later, November 19, 1835, the Prophet recorded in his journal: "I returned home and spent the day in translating the Egyptian record."[2] Five days later he wrote in his journal: "In the afternoon we translated some of the Egyptian record;" and the following day he wrote, "Spent the day in translating."[3]

BOOK OF ABRAHAM ALPHABET AND EGYPTIAN GRAMMAR

One of the first tasks that Joseph Smith did when working on the Book of Abraham was to prepare, or, as he termed it,

[1]Joseph Smith, *History of the Church*, Period I, vol. 2, p. 289.
[2]*Ibid.*, p. 318.
[3]*Ibid.*, p. 320.

translate an alphabet or grammar of the Egyptian language. Several times in his journal he made mention of this activity. The following quotations will give the Prophet's own words regarding this task:

The remainder of this month [July, 1835], I was continually engaged in translating an alphabet to the Book of Abraham, and arranging a grammar of the Egyptian language as practiced by the ancients.

October 1, [1835]. This afternoon I labored on the Egyptian alphabet, in company with Brothers Oliver Cowdery and W. W. Phelps, and during the research, the principles of astronomy as understood by Father Abraham and the ancients unfolded to our understanding, the particulars of which will appear hereafter.[4]

Of this activity, Dr. Sidney B. Sperry of the Brigham Young University made the following comment:

For many years the writer has been intrigued by the statement of the Prophet that he was "translating an alphabet to the Book of Abraham." Just what is meant by this phrase? A little by way of explanation— evidence leads us to the conclusion that the Prophet found it anything but easy to translate the Abrahamic records. The Lord did not reveal the substance of the Book of Abraham to the Prophet without considerable effort on the part of the latter. The Seer would of course receive the interpretation of all new and unknown signs or hieroglyphics, but after their meaning had been given to him it is not likely that the Lord would repeat the process when the same characters appeared again. (See D. & C. 9:7-9.) Possibly for that reason the Prophet decided to make a sign list in which would be recorded the meanings of each new symbol as it appeared upon the papyrus of Abraham. Once recorded it could be consulted as often as the Prophet needed to refresh his mind. It seems therefore quite probable that the alphabet was arranged very much as follows. On the extreme left of the page the signs in question would be written down in a vertical column. To the right of this column would appear the sounds of the Egyptian sign or hieroglyphic in English letters together with an interpretation of the character in question. We could readily imagine that some grammatical phenomena of the language would be revealed in the notes which the Prophet wrote down. It would seem rational to suppose that after the Prophet had written down many pages of these signs with their meanings he would become more and more competent to read them as they appeared on the papyri. This mention of an alphabet to the Book of Abraham and the grammar of the Egyptian language reminds us of the fact that the Prophet dictated his translations to Elders W. W. Phelps and Oliver Cowdery who acted as his scribes.[5]

―――――――
[4]*Ibid.,* pp. 238, 286.
[5]Sidney B. Sperry, *Ancient Records Testify in Papyrus and Stone,* pp. 68-69.

Joseph Smith the Translator

It is quite certain that the translation of these ancient records was not a mere mechanical process. The Prophet had to be living an almost perfect life in order to retain communion with God. Faith in God and purity of soul were prime requisites. The fitness of Joseph Smith, or any other prophet, to be an instrument in God's hand is not entirely a gift of the Lord, but it is a result of a growth of the spiritual portion of man—a life of godliness.

Among the great prophets who have lived, it seems that Joseph Smith ranks high as one who could practically at all times conform to the law by which he communed with God and received revelations and numerous personal visitations from the heavens. Thus his superb faith and purity of soul were paramount in making possible his translating of ancient records.

As Dr. Sperry suggested, it is quite certain that the Prophet had to exert all of his mental and spiritual energies in studying the characters in order that he might receive the interpretation of them. Certainly God would not do the job for him, but when Joseph exerted his energies and devoted his mind in deep study to the characters, through the power of God he was given the interpretation of them. The Prophet Joseph Smith has told us very little regarding how he translated either the ancient Book of Abraham records or the *Book of Mormon* records. Regarding the latter, however, he did leave this statement: "Through the medium of the Urim and Thummim I translated the record by the gift and power of God."[6]

Since the Egyptian language was extremely difficult to decipher and also a dead language, Joseph Smith, the Latterday Saint Prophet, was dependent entirely upon the same source for help which he had used previously in translating the *Book of Mormon* records: namely, inspiration and revelation from God.

[6]Joseph Smith, "The Wentworth Letter," *op. cit.*, vol. 4, p. 537.

PUBLISHING THE BOOK OF ABRAHAM

During the winter of 1842, Joseph Smith was exerting his last efforts upon translating the Book of Abraham and preparing it for publication. Elder Wilford Woodruff and some of the other leading brethren were assisting the Prophet. The Saints had established at Nauvoo a periodical known as the *Times and Seasons*. It was in the *Times and Seasons* that the Book of Abraham was first published.

As was previously mentioned, Wilford Woodruff, on February 19, 1842, recorded in his *Daily Journal and History* the facts that the Prophet had had the writings of Father Abraham in his possession for a number of years and that they had not as yet been published in the English language. Then he said: "But he is now about to publish it to the world or parts of it by publishing it in the *Times and Seasons.*" Then he continued by pointing out the fact that he had the privilege that day of setting the type for printing the first portion of the Book of Abraham.

A week later, February 27, Elder Woodruff recorded in his journal that between February 21st and the 27th he had spent most of the time each day in the printing office and that he and his associates had prepared a plate for making a cut which was to be used "at the commencement of the Book of Abraham which is to be published in the 9th No. of the 3 vol. of the *Times and Seasons* which will be interesting to many of the inhabitants of the earth."

The Prophet Joseph Smith also makes mention several times in his journal early in March, 1842, of the progress and preparation being made on publishing the Book of Abraham. On March 1, he recorded the following:

During the afternoon I was at my office and the printing office, correcting the first plate or cut of the records of Father Abraham, prepared by Reuben Hedlock, for the *Times and Seasons,* and in council in my office in the afternoon; and in the evening with the Twelve and their wives at Elder Woodruff's at which time I explained many important principles in relation to progressive improvement in the scale of intelligent existence.

I commenced publishing my translation of the Book of Abraham in the *Times and Seasons* as follows:[7]

---

[7]Joseph Smith, *op. cit.,* vol. 4, pp. 519-520.

In the next twenty pages of the *History of the Church* appears a publication of the entire Book of Abraham preceded by the three facsimiles. During the following week the Prophet made these entries in his journal regarding the publishing of the Book of Abraham:

> *Friday, 4,* [March, 1842]. At my office exhibiting the Book of Abraham in the original to Brother Reuben Hedlock so that he might take the size of the several plates or cuts, and prepare the blocks for the *Times and Seasons;* and also gave instruction concerning the arrangement of the writing on the large cut, illustrating the principles of astronomy, with other general business.
>
> *Tuesday, 8,* [March, 1842]. Re-commenced translating from the Records of Abraham for the tenth number of the *Times and Seasons,* and was engaged at my office day and evening.
>
> *Wednesday, 9,* [March, 1842]. Examining copy for the *Times and Seasons,* presented by Messrs. Taylor and Bennett, and a variety of other business in my office, in the morning; in the afternoon continued the translation of the Book of Abraham, called at Bishop Knight's and Mr. Davis', with the recorder, and continued translating and revising, and reading letters in the evening, Sister Emma being present in the office.[8]

On March 19, 1842, Elder Wilford Woodruff recorded in his journal the fact that he had spent the day in the printing office and that day they had printed about 500 copies of the 10th number of volume 3 of the *Times and Seasons* which contained the latter portion of the Book of Abraham. Brother Woodruff expressed his delight with its contents, saying: "The truths of the Book of Abraham are truly edifying, great and glorious which are among the rich treasures that are revealed unto us, in the last days."

From the information that has been presented it is clear that the Book of Abraham was first published in the *Times and Seasons* in two numbers: volume 3, numbers 9 and 10, March 1 and March 15, 1842, respectively. It is also evident from the statements made by Joseph Smith and Wilford Woodruff that each of these two issues came off the press a few days later than the dates indicated.

JOSEPH THE EDITOR OF TIMES AND SEASONS

On February 19, Elder Wilford Woodruff recorded in his journal the fact that at the time of the preparing of the Book of Abraham for publication in the *Times and Seasons,* "Joseph

Ibid., pp. 542, 543, 548.

the Seer is now the Editor of that paper and Elder [John] Taylor assists him in writing while it has fallen to my lot to take charge of the business part of the establishment." The Prophet confirms the statement made by Wilford Woodruff in the following entry in his journal regarding the publishing of the Book of Abraham:

> *Wednesday, 2,* [March, 1842]. I read the proof of the *Times and Seasons,* as editor for the first time, No. 9, Vol. III, in which is the commencement of the Book of Abraham.[9]

In fact, the Prophet Joseph Smith made a definite announcement of his editorial responsibility in number 9 of volume 3, page 710 of the *Times and Seasons* and recorded the same statement in his journal as follows:

The Prophet Becomes Editor of the Times and Seasons

> This paper commences my editorial career; I alone stand responsible for it, and shall do for all papers (i.e. Nos. of the Times and Seasons,) having my signature henceforward. I am not responsible for the publication or arrangement of the former paper; the matter did not come under my supervision.
>
> [Signed]   Joseph Smith[10]

The foregoing fact is very important, for it certainly stamps the approval of the Prophet Joseph Smith on the Book of Abraham as being correct and authoritative. Thus all the statements and doctrines contained in the Book of Abraham were approved by the Prophet of the Lord and accepted by the Church as scripture; hence they are authoritative and binding upon the Church of Jesus Christ of Latter-day Saints.

PUBLISHED IN THE MILLENNIAL STAR

Shortly after the Book of Abraham was published in the *Times and Seasons* at Nauvoo, Illinois, it was published in the *Millennial Star* in England under the editorship of Parley P. Pratt and T. Ward. The first of the *Book of Abraham* to appear in the *Star* was printed in volume 3, number 3, July, 1842, (pp. 33-36). The number 1 facsimile from the Book of Abraham preceded the story of Abraham. The editors told the story of the discovery of the papyrus scrolls and the mummies by Sebolo and the bringing of those ancient relics to Kirtland,

[9]*Ibid.,* p. 542.
[10]*Ibid.,* p. 551.

Ohio, and the procuring of four of the mummies and two of the papyrus scrolls by the Saints. They also pointed out, as previously mentioned, that Abraham and Joseph wrote those two scrolls.[11]

Some more of the Book of Abraham was published in the *Millennial Star* the following month.[12] In this issue Elders Pratt and Ward made the following comment:

> When we read the Book of Abraham with the reflection that its light has burst upon the world after a silence of three or four thousand years, during which it has slumbered in the bosom of the dead, and been sealed up in the secret archives of Egypt's moldering ruins; when we see there unfolded our eternal beings—our existence before the world was—our high and responsible station in the councils of the Holy One, and our eternal destiny; when we there contemplate the majesty of the works of God as unfolded in all the simplicity of truth, opening to our view the wide expanse of the universe and showing the laws and regulations, the times and revolutions of all worlds, from the celestial throne of heaven's King, or the mighty Kolob, whose daily revolution is a thousand years, down through all the gradations of existence to our puny earth, we are lost in astonishment and admiration, and are led to exclaim, What is man without the key of knowledge? Or what can he know when shut from the presence of his Maker, and deprived of conversation with all intelligences of a higher order? Surely the mind of man is just awakening from the deep slumber of many generations, from his thousand years of midnight darkness. The morning of celestial light has dawned upon a benighted world—"the opening seals announce the day by prophets long foretold."[13]

Thus we see that the first two places that the Book of Abraham was published were in the *Times and Seasons* (March, 1842) and the *Millennial Star* (July and August, 1842). Also, at about the time of the publication of the Book of Abraham in the *Times and Seasons*, the contents of this ancient book were copied in the Prophet's journal and hence published later as part of the *History of the Church*, Period I, volume 4, pages 520 to 534.

---

[11]Parley P. Pratt and T. Ward, *Millennial Star*, vol. 3, no. 3, July 1, 1842, p. 47.
[12]*Millennial Star*, vol. 3, no. 4, August, 1842, pp. 49-53.
[13]*Ibid.*, vol. 3, no. 4, August 1, 1842, pp. 70-71.

Chapter 7

BOOK OF JOSEPH

Joseph Smith's Statement

As was suggested in an earlier chapter, there were two papyrus rolls in addition to the four mummies purchased by the Latter-day Saints from Mr. Chandler. One was written by Father Abraham and the other by his great-grandson Joseph, who was sold into Egyptian bondage. Since the Prophet did not completely translate nor publish the writings of Joseph, we do not know the details of what that book contains. However, we do have a statement from the Prophet to the effect that one of the papyrus scrolls contained the writings of Joseph. To quote his exact words:

> Soon after this, some of the Saints at Kirtland purchased the mummies and papyrus, a description of which will appear hereafter, and with W. W. Phelps and Oliver Cowdery as scribes, I commenced the translation of some of the characters or hieroglyphics, and much to our joy found that one of the rolls contained the writings of Abraham, another the writings of Joseph of Egypt, etc., —a more full account of which will appear in its place, as I proceed to examine or unfold them. Truly we can say, the Lord is beginning to reveal the abundance of peace and truth.[1]

Oliver Cowdery's Letter

Fortunately Oliver Cowdery wrote a letter to William Frye in which he pointed out some of the important items presented by Joseph, the ancient patriarch and ruler of Egypt. This letter furnishes us our best source of information and practically the only comprehensive manuscript statement available. Oliver Cowdery pointed out that the record of Joseph contained at least the following four items: first, the correct doctrine of the Godhead; second, an excellent presentation of the fall; third, a copy of Enoch's Pillar; and fourth, a vivid

[1]Joseph Smith, *History of the Church*, Period I, vol. 2, p. 236.

description of the final judgment. To quote from Oliver
Cowdery's letter in regard to the Book of Joseph:

The language in which this record [writings of Joseph] is written
is very comprehensive, and many of the hieroglyphics exceedingly strik-
ing. The evidence is apparent upon the face, that they were written by
persons acquainted with the history of the creation, the fall of man, and
more or less of the correct ideas or notions of the Deity. The representation of the Godhead—three, yet in one, is curiously drawn to give simply,
though impressively, the writer's views of that exalted personage. The
serpent, represented as walking, or formed in a manner to be able to
walk, standing in front of, and near a female figure, is to me, one of the
greatest representations I have ever seen upon paper, or a writing substance; and must go far towards convincing the rational mind of the cor-
rectness and divine authority of the holy scriptures, and especially that
part which has ever been assailed by the infidel community, as being a
fiction, as to carry away, with one mighty sweep, the whole atheistical
fabric, without leaving a vestige sufficient for a foundation stone. Enoch's
Pillar, as mentioned by Josephus, is upon the same roll. True, our present
version of the Bible does not mention this fact, though it speaks of the
righteousness of Abel and the holiness of Enoch—one slain because his
offering was accepted of the Lord, and the other being taken to the
regions of everlasting day without being confined to the narrow limits of
the tomb, or tasting death; but Josephus says that the descendants of
Seth were virtuous, and possessed a great knowledge of the heavenly
bodies, and, that, in consequence of the prophecy of Adam, that the world
should be destroyed once by water and again by fire. Enoch wrote a
history or an account of the same, and put two pillars one of brick and
the other of stone; and that the same were in being at his (Josephus')
day. The inner end of the same roll, (Joseph's record), presents a representation of the judgment: At one view you behold the Savior seated
upon his throne, crowned, and holding the scepters of righteousness and
power, before whom also, are assembled the twelve tribes of Israel, the
nations, languages and tongues of the earth, and kingdoms of the world
over which Satan is represented as reigning, Michael the arch-angel,
holding the key to the bottomless pit, and at the same time the devil as
being chained and shut up in the bottomless pit. But upon this last scene,
I am able only to give you a shadow, to the real picture. I am certain
that it cannot be viewed without filling the mind with awe, unless the
mind is far estranged from God. . . .

I might continue my communication to a great length upon the
different figures and characters represented upon the two rolls, but I
have no doubt my subject has already become sufficiently prolix for your
patience: I will therefore soon cease for the present. When the translation of these valuable documents will be completed, I am unable to say;
neither can I give you a probable idea how large volumes they will make;
but judging from their size, and the comprehensiveness of the language,
one might reasonably expect to see a sufficient to develop much upon the
mighty acts of ancient men of God, and of his dealing with the children
of men when they saw him face to face. Be there little or much, it must

be an inestimable acquisition to our present scriptures, fulfilling, in a small degree, the word of the prophet: For the earth shall be full of the knowledge of the Lord as the waters cover the sea.[2]

JOSEPHUS AND ENOCH'S PILLAR

During the period from 75 to approximately 100 A. D., a famous Jewish historian named Flavius Josephus wrote a voluminous account of the history of his people. In its present printed form, *The Works of Flavius Josephus* are nearly as extensive as the writings in the *Bible*. His account somewhat parallels the story told in the *Bible,* beginning with Father Adam and continuing down through the Old Testament period and forward to the coming of Christ. Josephus in his history tells also of John the Baptist, of the Savior, and of other Christians, and then carries forward the story of the Jews to near the close of the first century A. D. He also gives some very reliable information on the Greeks and the Romans, as their history parallels the latter portion of Jewish and Christian history as accounted in his book. The *Works of Flavius Josephus* are held today in high esteem by historians.

In his letter to William Frye, Oliver Cowdery pointed out that Josephus had declared that the descendants of Seth were virtuous and filled with wisdom; and then Oliver made mention of Enoch's pillars. According to William Whiston's translation of *The Works of Flavius Josephus,* the ancient Jewish historian merely stated that Seth's righteous descendants wrote on those pillars, without mentioning Enoch as being the one who did the writing. Regardless of who did the writing, Josephus made the following comment regarding those ancient ones:

They [the descendants of Adam through Seth] also were the inventors of the peculiar sort of wisdom which is concerned with the heavenly bodies, and their order. And that their inventions might not be lost before they were sufficiently known, upon Adam's prediction that the world was to be destroyed at one time by the source of fire, and at another time by the violence and quantity of water, they made two pillars; the one of brick, the other of stone: they inscribed their discoveries on them both, that in case the pillar of brick should be destroyed by the flood, the pillar of stone might remain, and exhibit those discoveries to mankind; and also inform them that there was another pillar of brick erected by them, now these remain in the land of Siriad today.[3]

---

[2]Oliver Cowdery to William Frye in *Latter-day Saints' Messenger and Advocate,* vol. 2, no. 3, Kirtland, Ohio, December, 1835, p. 236.
[3]Flavius Josephus, *The Works of Flavius Josephus,* translated by William Whiston, p. 27.

BOOK OF MORMON EVIDENCE

The *Book of Mormon* bears witness to the fact that Joseph who was sold into Egyptian bondage did write religious records. Father Lehi, while giving a blessing to his son, Joseph, made the following remarks:

And now, Joseph, my last born, . . . thou art the fruit of my loins; and I am a descendant of Joseph, who was carried away captive into Egypt and great were the covenants of the Lord which he made unto Joseph; wherefore, Joseph truly saw our day. And he obtained a promise of the Lord, that out of the fruit of his loins, the Lord would raise up a righteous branch unto the house of Israel; not the Messiah, but a branch which was to be broken off; nevertheless, to be remembered in the covenants of the Lord. . . .

For Joseph truly testified saying: A seer shall the Lord my God raise up who shall be a choice seer unto the fruit of my loins. Yea, Joseph truly said: thus saith the Lord unto me: A choice seer will I raise up out of the fruit of thy loins; and he shall be esteemed highly among the fruit of thy loins. And unto him will I give commandment that he shall do a work for the fruit of thy loins, his brethren. . . .

And he shall be great like unto Moses, whom I have said I would raise up unto you, to deliver my people, O house of Israel. And Moses will I raise up, to deliver thy people out of the land of Egypt.[4]

Throughout the remainder of Chapter 3 of 2 Nephi, Father Lehi continued to quote to his son prophecies which were made by Joseph who was sold into Egypt. Thus we see from the *Book of Mormon* that Joseph did write religious records and they were handed down from generation to generation to the time of Father Lehi. Joseph's writings, as quoted by Father Lehi, were a part of the writings that were on the brass plates of Laban.

WRITINGS OF JOSEPH NOT PUBLISHED

In this chapter we have learned a few facts regarding the many wonderful gospel doctrines which were written upon the record of Joseph and which the Latter-day Saint Prophet was privileged to peruse. However, the details of the contents of this book were never published to the Church. In discussing the reason for its not being made available to the Church, Dr. Sidney B. Sperry made the following observation: "It is possible that its contents were too sacred to be given to this generation. If so, the people of the Church can look forward

[4]2 Nephi 3:3-10.

to its coming at some future time."[5] The fact remains that we are not certain why Joseph Smith did not translate and publish the Book of Joseph; but if and when the Lord desires that the church members have the writings of Joseph of old, it certainly lies within the power of God to bring forth that record again.

MUMMIES AND THE PAPYRUS ROLLS

The problem of what became of the papyrus rolls and the Egyptian mummies has always been of interest to students of the *Pearl of Great Price*. At the time of Joseph Smith's death they were in his home in Nauvoo and were kept there for some time under the direction of Emma and the Prophet's mother. From a letter written by Almon W. Babbitt to President Brigham Young, dated Nauvoo, January 31, 1845, it seems that William Smith got possession of the Egyptian relics. To quote: "William Smith has got the mummies from Mother Smith and refuses to give them up." In regards to their whereabouts thereafter, Dr. Sperry stated: "It is reported that at a later time they found their way to a museum in St. Louis and were then transported to the museum in Chicago."[6] As far as is known, the mummies and probably the papyri also were burned in the great fire at Chicago in 1871.

---

[5]Sidney B. Sperry, *Ancient Records Testify in Papyrus and Stone*, p. 56.
[6]*Ibid.*, p. 66.

Chapter 8

THE PEARL OF GREAT PRICE

Publishing of the Pearl of Great Price

In 1851 while residing in England and presiding over the European Mission, President Franklin D. Richards, a member of the Quorum of the Twelve Apostles, collected together the four principal items which compose the *Pearl of Great Price*—namely, the Book of Abraham, the Book of Moses, the Writings of the Prophet Joseph Smith, and the Articles of Faith, and also some additional material—and published them in one volume. All of this material had been previously published at various times in separate publications; however, it was at that date that they were first collected, grouped together, and published in one volume under the name of the *Pearl of Great Price.*

The Name "Pearl of Great Price"

Franklin D. Richards not only collected the items that composed the first edition of the *Pearl of Great Price,* but he was also responsible for giving this fourth volume of the standard works of the Church its name. The following parable spoken by the Savior was undoubtedly the motivating force which inspired Franklin D. Richards to name this sacred scripture:

Again, the kingdom of heaven is like unto a merchant man, seeking goodly pearls: who, when he had found one pearl of great price went and sold all that he had, and bought it.[1]

Since the *Pearl of Great Price* contains valuable gospel doctrine—the plan of salvation as given to Father Adam and his descendants—it points the way into the kingdom of God; therefore, it is aptly named.

---

[1]Matt. 13:45-46.

41

Preface of the First Edition

In the preface of the first edition of the *Pearl of Great Price* Elder Fraklin D. Richards states:

The following compilation has been induced by the repeated solicitation of several friends of the publisher, who are desirous to be put in possession of the very important articles contained therein. Most of the Revelations composing this work were published at early periods of the Church, when the circulation of its journals was so very limited as to render them comparatively unknown at present, except to a few who have treasured up the products of the Church with great care from the beginning. A smaller portion of this work has never before appeared in print; and altogether it is presumed, that true believers in the Divine mission of the Prophet Joseph Smith, will appreciate this little collection of precious truths as a *Pearl of Great Price* that will increase their ability to maintain and to defend the holy faith by becoming possessors of it.

Although not adapted, nor designed, as a pioneer of faith among unbelievers, still it will commend itself to all careful students of the scriptures, and detailing many important facts which are therein only alluded to, or entirely unmentioned, but consonant with the whole tenor of the revealed will of God; and, to the beginner in the gospel, will add confirmatory evidence of the rectitude of his faith, by showing him that the doctrines and ordinances thereof are the same as were revealed to Adam for his salvation after his expulsion from the garden, and the same that he handed down and caused to be taught to his generations after him, as the only means appointed of God by which the generations of men may regain his presence.

Nor do we conceive it possible for any unprejudiced person to arise from a careful perusal of this work, without being deeply impressed with a sense of the Divine calling, and holy ordination, of the man by whom these revelations, translations, and narrations have been communicated to us. As impervious as the minds of men may be at present to these convictions, the day is not far distant when sinners, as well as Saints, will know Joseph Smith was one of the greatest men that ever lived upon the earth, and that under God he was the Prophet and founder of the dispensation of the fulness of times, in which will be gathered together into one all things which are in Christ, both which are in heaven and which are on earth.

The following is a reproduction of the title page of the first edition:

The

PEARL OF GREAT PRICE

Being a

CHOICE SELECTION

from the

REVELATIONS, TRANSLATIONS, AND NARRATIONS

of

JOSEPH SMITH

First Prophet, Seer, and Revelator to the Church
of Jesus Christ of Latter-day Saints

Liverpool:
Published by F. D. Richards, 15, Wilton Street
1851

PEARL OF GREAT PRICE ACCEPTED BY PRESIDENT YOUNG

As early as 1857, at least one copy of the first edition of the *Pearl of Great Price* had found its way to Salt Lake City and was placed by the President of the Church of Jesus Christ of Latter-day Saints among the important doctrinal works of the Church. A statement appears in the *Latter-day Saint Journal History* on August 13 of that year to the effect that "President Brigham Young, president, seer, and revelator of the Church of Jesus Christ of Latter-day Saints" had that day deposited in the temple at Salt Lake City a number of church books, pamphlets, and newspapers. A list was made of those publications and the *Pearl of Great Price* was included in that list.

MAKE-UP AND CONTENTS OF THE FIRST EDITION, 1851

A number of suggestions have been given in this book up to this point in regard to the contents of the *Pearl of Great Price,* but it now becomes advisable to make a definite study of the make-up and contents of the various editions that have been published.

The first edition of the *Pearl of Great Price* (published in 1851 in England) was not divided into verses, as is the book at the present time, nor was it divided into double columns. Also, it was a little larger than it is today, because it contained some of the material which is in the *Doctrine and Covenants*. To avoid duplications in our scriptures, that material was later deleted. The *Doctrine and Covenants'* material which appeared in the first edition of the *Pearl of Great Price* was the seventy-seventh section which was entitled at that time "A Key to the Revelation of St. John, written by Joseph Smith;" and also, "A Revelation and Prophecy by the Prophet Joseph Smith given on War, December 25, 1832."[2] In addition to these, it contained from the *Doctrine and Covenants* extracts from the commandments to the Church concerning baptism, the duties of members after they were baptized, methods of administering the sacrament of the Lord's supper, the duties of elders, priests, teachers, and deacons, a revelation on Priesthood, the calling and duties of the Twelve Apostles, the calling and duties of the Seventy, and extracts from the revelation which told of the rise of the Church of Jesus Christ.[3] In addition to the foregoing, the last page of the book contained the words to the song "O, Say What is Truth?" which were written by John Jaques.

FIRST AMERICAN EDITION, 1878

The first American edition of the *Pearl of Great Price* was published in Salt Lake City in 1878. It agreed in practically every detail with the first edition which was published by Franklin D. Richards in England in 1851. However, it contained the addition of "The Revelation on the Eternity of the Marriage Covenant, including Plurality of Wives, given through Joseph Smith, the Seer, in Nauvoo, Hancock County, Illinois, July 12, 1843." This revelation today is found as section 132 of the *Doctrine and Covenants*.

1902 EDITION

In 1902 an edition of the *Pearl of Great Price* was printed which omitted the material duplicating the *Doctrine and Covenants'* revelations. That edition, in contents, was exactly

---

[2]*Doctrine and Covenants* 87:1-8.
[3]*Ibid.*, 20:71, 37, 72-79, 38-44; 107:11; 20:45-59, 70; 107:1-10, 12-20, 23, 33-35, 93-100; 27:5-18.

like the *Pearl of Great Price* as we have it today. The 1902 edition was the first one to appear in print divided into chapters and verses with references; however, its pages were not divided into double columns. The study helps were prepared by Dr. James E. Talmage under the direction of President Joseph F. Smith. That edition was used for the following nineteen years without further changes being made.

1921 Edition

In 1921 more changes were made in the make-up of the *Pearl of Great Price*. This edition was the first one to be published in double-column pages with a comprehensive index. Elder James E. Talmage was primarily responsible for making this arrangement of the text and the index. The purpose of dividing the pages into double columns was to shorten the lines and thereby make reading of the scripture easier and more attractive. Also, the book followed the printing pattern used in the *Bible* and the other standard works of the Church. No further changes have been made in the make-up of the *Pearl of Great Price* since 1921; therefore, that edition is the one that the Church uses today.

It would be well to take a copy of the *Pearl of Great Price* published in 1921 or since that date and observe carefully the way in which it is composed. It is interesting to collect all of the editions that have been discussed and compare their make-up and contents with each other.

Editions in Foreign Languages

The *Pearl of Great Price* has also been translated and published in the following foreign languages: Welsh (1852, Wales); German (1882, Bern, Switzerland); Danish (1883, Salt Lake City); Dutch (1911, Rotterdam, Holland); Hawaiian (1914, Honolulu, Hawaii); Maori (1919, Auckland, New Zealand); Samoan (1944, Salt Lake City); Spanish (1948, Salt Lake City).

Contents of the Pearl of Great Price

The table of contents indicates that our present edition of the *Pearl of Great Price* is composed of four principal items:

first, the Book of Moses; second, the Book of Abraham; third, the Writings of Joseph Smith; and fourth, a copy of the Articles of Faith.

First—The Book of Moses:

Chapter one is a vision that Moses received approximately 3,000 years ago; and this vision was revealed to Joseph Smith, the Prophet, in June, 1830.

Chapters two to eight are the writings of Moses which were revealed to Joseph Smith in December, 1830. These writings are quite similar to chapters one to six of Genesis. Chapters two and three tell the story of the physical creation of the world with the declaration interpolated in that account of a spiritual creation of plants, animals and man. Chapter four gives the account of Lucifer's rejection at the Grand Council in heaven and the fall of Adam and Eve. Chapter five tells the story of early beginnings, such as the creation of mortals, Adam's and Eve's receiving of the Gospel of Jesus Christ, the first apostasy, Cain's sin and his posterity, Lamech and secret combinations, and a declaration that the gospel was preached from the beginning. Chapter six continues the account of Adam and his descendants' having the Gospel of Jesus Christ and tells the story of Enoch. The account of Enoch is continued in chapter seven. The last chapter in the book, number eight, gives a chronology from Enoch to Noah and then tells of Noah's preaching repentance to the wicked people of his day and predicting destruction through a flood.

Second—The Book of Abraham:

As has been pointed out in the several preceding chapters, the Book of Abraham was obtained from a papyrus scroll, which, in connection with some Egyptian mummies, was purchased by the Saints at Kirtland, Ohio, in July, 1835, from Michael H. Chandler and later translated and published by the Prophet Joseph Smith.

There are five chapters in the Book of Abraham. Chapters one and two give an account of the life of this great prophet until he arrived in Egypt. Chapter three is Abraham's account of astronomy and pre-existence, including the eternal nature of matter and the Grand Council in heaven. Chapters four and five give an account of the Gods making their plans regarding the creation of the world. The steps that They outlined in their plans that would be followed in the creative process are similar to the accounts of what actually transpired during the creation of the world as recorded in chapters one and two of Genesis and chapters two and three of the Book of Moses.

As we proceed throughout the remainder of this *Pearl of Great Price Commentary,* we shall have the opportunity to study and discuss in detail the contents of the books of Moses and Abraham.

Third—Writings of Joseph Smith:

1. *An extract from a translation of the Bible—Matthew* 23:39; 24:1-55.

This material gives an account of Jesus' description and predictions of the events that should transpire throughout the world prior to His second coming.

2. *Extracts from the History of Joseph Smith, the Prophet.*

The Prophet tells briefly of his birth and early history, then gives an account of the "First Vision" and the subsequent reactions. Following this is an account of the appearances of the Angel Moroni, of Joseph's obtaining the *Book of Mormon* records, and of Martin Harris' taking copies of the Nephite characters to Professor Charles Anthon at Columbia University, New York City. The story then tells of Oliver Cowdery's helping the Prophet translate, and of the restoration of the Aaronic Priesthood.

Fourth—The Articles of Faith:

An official copy of the thirteen Articles of Faith is the last item in the *Pearl of Great Price;* therefore, these thirteen articles are accepted by Latter-day Saints as being holy scripture.

Chapter 9

GOSPEL OF JESUS CHRIST AND THE GODHEAD

INTRODUCTION

The point has now been reached where the gospel doctrines contained in the *Pearl of Great Price* are to be studied, commented upon, and explained. The author of this book has outlined the complete contents of the *Pearl of Great Price* according to subject matter, and the subjects are presented in the following twenty-eight chapters. His comments concerning the various subjects presented, quotations from the scriptures other than the *Pearl of Great Price,* as well as quotations from the teachings of the holy prophets of God, are printed in a single column; but the entire contents of the *Pearl of Great Price* appears in smaller type and in double columns.

The *Pearl of Great Price* subject matter has been organized as far as possible in a chronological order. Since the concept of God held by a people is very basic in any religion, the doctrinal discussions begin with a study of God and the Godhead. That subject is followed by a discussion of the pre-existence of man. Then the accounts of the creation of this earth are presented, and the other subjects follow in as chronological an order as the author was able to place them.

The purpose in each of the following twenty-eight chapters is for the readers to obtain a clear understanding regarding the teachings of the *Pearl of Great Price* on the various principles and ordinances of the gospel. In the process of explaining, clarifying, and sustaining the gospel doctrine as presented in this holy scripture, the words of the prophets as given in any of the standard works were used as needed. The final result of perusing the contents of this book should be that the readers will know that the true Gospel of Jesus Christ, as proclaimed in the *Pearl of Great Price,* was known in ancient times and that the gospel principles and ordinances were the same as

48

were known and practiced by the holy prophets of God from age to age, down to and including the Dispensation of the Fullness of Times.

ADAM AND THE GOSPEL OF JESUS CHRIST

Father Adam, called by Daniel the Ancient of Days, and by the Lord, Michael, the Prince, the Archangel, received through divine revelation the Gospel of Jesus Christ—the same gospel with the same principles and ordinances that we have today.[1] There is only one Gospel of Jesus Christ; and it is the plan of salvation by which God the Father through His Only Begotten Son makes it possible for mortals to come back into His presence and receive eternal life. The Prophet Joseph Smith declared that God "set the ordinances to be the same forever and ever, and set Adam to watch over them."[2] The *Pearl of Great Price, Book of Mormon, Doctrine and Covenants,* teachings of the Prophet Joseph Smith and all the other presidents of the Church since his day, with a lesser amount of evidence in the *Bible,* attest the foregoing statement to be positively true. But of all the holy scriptures, the *Pearl of Great Price* tells the most complete story of the gospel's being given to Adam and Eve and their descendants; therefore, on this subject this scripture is our best source of information. However, such excellent statements as the following one made by Alma, wherein he explained the interest that God had in Adam and Eve after they had been driven from the Garden of Eden, appear in the *Book of Mormon:*

[God] saw that it was expedient that men should know concerning the things whereof he had appointed unto them; therefore, he sent angels to converse with them, who caused men to behold of his glory. And they began from that time forth to call on his name; therefore, God conversed with men, and made known unto them the plan of redemption, which had been prepared from the foundation of the world; and this he made known unto them according to their faith and repentance and their holy works.[3]

There are statements in the *Doctrine and Covenants* equally as definite regarding Father Adam's receiving the Gospel of Jesus Christ as the one just quoted from the *Book of*

[1]Daniel 7:13-14; 12:1-3; *Doctrine and Covenants* 107:54; 27:11; 78:16; 116:1.
[2]Joseph Fielding Smith, *Teachings of the Prophet Joseph Smith,* pp. 166-170.
[3]Alma 12:28-34.

Mormon. For example, the word of the Lord came to the Prophet Joseph Smith as follows:

Wherefore, I, the Lord God, caused that he [Adam] should be cast out of the Garden of Eden, from my presence, because of his transgression, wherein he became spiritually dead, which is the first death, even that same death which is the last death, which is spiritual, which shall be pronounced upon the wicked when I shall say: Depart, ye cursed.

But, behold, I say unto you that I, the Lord God, gave unto Adam and unto his seed, that they should not die as to the temporal death, until I, the Lord God, should send forth angels to declare unto them repentance and redemption, through faith on the name of mine Only Begotten Son.

And thus did I, the Lord God, appoint unto man the days of his probation—that by his natural death he might be raised in immortality unto eternal life, even as many as would believe; and they that believe not unto eternal damnation; for they cannot be redeemed from their spiritual fall, because they repent not; for they love darkness rather than light, and their deeds are evil, and they receive their wages of whom they list to obey.[4]

All of the presidents of the Church of Jesus Christ of Latter-day Saints have proclaimed that the gospel was given to Adam and to the other ancient prophets. President Joseph F. Smith declared: "Christ taught the gospel to Adam, and made known his truths to Abraham and the prophets."[5] In the words of President Wilford Woodruff:

Adam, our first great progenitor and father, after the fall, received the gospel, and he received the Holy Priesthood in all its power, and its keys and ordinances. He sealed these blessings upon his sons—Seth, Enos, Jared, Mahaleel, Enoch, and Methuselah. All of these men received this high and Holy Priesthood. They all professed to give revelation.[6]

President John Taylor taught the following:

As the gospel is a principle that emanates from God, like its author, it is "the same yesterday, today, and for ever,"—eternal and unchangeable. . . . It has been in the mind of God, and as often as developed it has been manifested as an eternal, unchangeable, undeviating plan by which to save, bless, exalt, and dignify man. . . .

How did Adam get his information of the things of God? He got it through the Gospel of Jesus Christ, and through this same Priesthood of which we have been speaking. God came to him in the Garden and talked with him. How was it that he obtained his knowledge of God? Through the gospel; and he was the first man upon this earth that had the gospel and the holy Priesthood; and if he had it not, he could not have known anything about God or his revelations.[7]

[4]*Doctrine and Covenants* 29:41-45; Smith, *op. cit.*, pp. 59-62, 168-169.
[5]Joseph F. Smith, *Gospel Doctrine*, p. 39.
[6]Wilford Woodruff, *Journal of Discourses*, vol. 16, pp. 263-264, October 8, 1873.
[7]G. Homer Durham, *The Gospel Kingdom*, pp. 87, 19.

In his terse way of speaking, Brigham Young declared:

God was once known on the earth among His children of mankind, as we know one another. Adam was as conversant with his Father, who placed him upon the earth, as we are conversant with our earthly parents. The Father frequently came to visit his son Adam, and talked and walked with him; and the children of Adam were more or less acquainted with Him, and the things that pertain to God and to heaven were as familiar among mankind in the first ages of their existence as our gardens are to our wives and children, or as the road to the western ocean is to the experienced traveler. *From this source mankind have received their religious traditions.*[8]

KNOWLEDGE OF GOD

Probably the most basic element in the Gospel of Jesus Christ is a true concept of the personality, attributes, and powers of God. The type of God in which a people believe determines their morals, attitudes of worship, and religious rituals. When men and women have conceived of God as being a person who possesses an abundance of love, justice, and kindness, and, as a person who had a direct and definite concern for and interest in them, they have made definite efforts to inculcate into their lives attributes similar to His. On the other hand, when mortals believed that God was an individual of caprice, who was unjust, easy to anger, and could be influenced by religious rituals and ceremonials, they resorted to magic and the offering of human sacrifices. And again, human beings in their man-made creeds and theological beliefs ofttimes have taken away from God His personal attributes, thereby robbing Him of all of His intimacy with mortals and His power to influence their lives. Under those conditions they were walking in darkness at noontime, having no light regarding the true nature and personality of Him whom they worshipped. When Jesus Christ was upon the earth He explained the great significance of knowing God as follows:

And this is life eternal, that they might know thee the only true God, and Jesus Christ, whom thou hast sent.[9]

In modern revelation, the Lord proclaimed the same doctrine to the Prophet Joseph Smith. To quote:

This is eternal lives—to know the only wise and true God, and Jesus Christ, whom he hath sent. I am he. Receive ye, therefore, my law.[10]

[8]John A. Widtsoe, *Discourses of Brigham Young*, p. 159.
[9]John 17:3.
[10]*Doctrine and Covenants* 132:24.

Thus there can be eternal life on no other principle than to know God; and we learn to know Him by thinking, acting, and living exactly as He thinks, acts, and lives. That great goal will be completely attained only by those who become as God is. The vital importance of having a knowledge of the Father and His Only Begotten Son was clearly pointed out by the Prophet Joseph. In his exact words:

> It is the first principle of the Gospel to know for a certainty the character of God, and to know that we may converse with him as one man converses with another, and that he was once a man like us; yea, that God himself, the Father of us all, dwelt on an earth, the same as Jesus Christ himself did.[11]

GODHEAD OR HOLY TRINITY

Whenever the true Gospel of Jesus Christ has been on the earth, faithful church members have had a knowledge of God the Father, His Only Begotten Son, and the Holy Ghost. In fact, in the very beginning, following the expulsion of Adam and Eve from the Garden of Eden, a true concept of all three members of the Godhead was revealed to our first parents. According to the *Pearl of Great Price,* that same knowledge and understanding of God was held by the great prophets who were the heads of gospel dispensations, such as Enoch, Abraham, Moses, and the others. The ancient prophets knew that the Godhead consisted of three separate and distinct personages, each of whom had a definite work to perform, and yet they all worked in perfect unity as one. The three Gods constituted the Holy Trinity. Thus the following scripture regarding the Godhead appears in the *Pearl of Great Price:*

Adam's knowledge of the Godhead:

6. And after many days an angel of the Lord appeared unto Adam, saying: Why dost thou offer sacrifices unto the Lord? And Adam said unto him: I know not, save the Lord commanded me.

7. And then the angel spake, saying: This thing is a similitude of the sacrifice of the Only Begotten of the Father, which is full of grace and truth.

8. Wherefore, thou shalt do all that thou doest in the name of the Son, and thou shalt repent and call upon God in the name of the Son forevermore.

9. And in that day the Holy Ghost fell upon Adam, which beareth record of the Father and the Son, saying: I am the Only Begotten of the Father from the beginning, henceforth and forever, that as thou hast fallen thou mayest be redeemed, and all mankind, even as many as will.   Moses 5:6-9.

God's commandment to Enoch, and the Trinity:

11. And he gave unto me a commandment that I should baptize in the name of the Father, and of the Son, which is full of grace and truth, and of

[11]Joseph Fielding Smith, *op. cit.,* pp. 345-346.

the Holy Ghost, which beareth record of the Father and the Son.

Moses 7:11.

Manifestations of all three members of the Godhead to Moses:

24. And it came to pass that when Satan had departed from the presence of Moses, that Moses lifted up his eyes unto heaven, being filled with the Holy Ghost, which beareth record of the Father and the Son;   Moses 1:24.

See also Moses 1:6, 15-17.

(The foregoing scriptures make a brief mention of the mission of Jesus Christ and of baptism. At this point these subjects will not be discussed. They will both be dealt with in later chapters.)

The emphasis regarding the Holy Ghost in each of the three foregoing passages of scripture is to the effect that His mission is to bear record of the Father and the Son. Another purpose mentioned in the *Pearl of Great Price* is for the Holy Ghost to be bestowed on believers of Christ at the time of baptism. Following the baptism of Father Adam, we read that the following occurred:

65. And thus he was baptized, and the Spirit of God descended upon him, and thus he was born of the Spirit, and became quickened in the inner man.

66. And he heard a voice out of heaven, saying: Thou art baptized with fire, and with the Holy Ghost. This is the record of the Father, and the Son, from henceforth and forever.

Moses 6:65-66.

In a later chapter the Holy Ghost will be mentioned again in connection with a discussion of the ordinance of baptism. Our principal purpose in this chapter, however, is to point out that even at the beginning of the populating of this earth God revealed to Father Adam and to the other prophets a true concept of the Godhead which was composed of the Father, the Son, and the Holy Ghost—the three constituting a Holy Trinity.

GODHEAD DESCRIBED IN THE OTHER SCRIPTURES

The fact should be mentioned that the other Latter-day Saint scriptures confirm the teachings of the *Pearl of Great Price* and give additional information regarding the Holy Ghost and the other two members of the Godhead.[12] For example, the *Book of Mormon* states:

I, Nephi, was desirous also that I might see, and hear, and know of these things, by the power of the Holy Ghost, which is the gift of God unto

---

[12]1 Nephi 11:27; 12:7, 18; 13:37; 2 Nephi 26:12-13; 28:4-5, 26; 31:6-21; Jacob 6:8; 7:11-13, 17; Alma 7:9-10; 8:30-32; 13:11-12; 34:37-38; 39:5-6; 3 Nephi 9:20; 12:1-2; 11:25-36; 18:36-37; 19:9-22; Moroni 2:1-3; 3:4; 6:4, 9; 8:7, 9, 26-28; 12:23; 10:4-7; 7:7, 10, 31-32; *Doctrine and Covenants* 25:8; 35:5-6; 36:2; 39:23; 49:14; 20:26-28, 35, 41-45, 60, 73; 33:15; 84-27, 64, 74; 6:21; 10:57; 11-28; 14:9; 35:2; 55:2; 11:21-23, 31; 21:1-7.

all those who diligently seek him. . . . For he that diligently seeketh shall find; and the mysteries of God shall be unfolded unto them, by the power of the Holy Ghost.[13] [And again], Do ye not remember that I said unto you that after ye had received the Holy Ghost ye could speak with the tongue of angels? . . . Angels speak by the power of the Holy Ghost; therefore, they speak the words of Christ.[14]

After the resurrected Lord appeared to the Nephites and established His Church among them, the conditions in the Church were as follows:

And their meetings were conducted by the church after the manner of the workings of the Spirit, and by the power of the Holy Ghost; for as the power of the Holy Ghost led them whether to preach, or to exhort, or to pray, so it was done.[15]

In modern revelation, the Prophet Joseph Smith gives to the world one of the most enlightening statements regarding the personality of the members of the Godhead to be found in any of the holy scriptures. The statement is as follows:

The Father has a body of flesh and bones as tangible as man's; the son also; but the Holy Ghost has not a body of flesh and bones, but is a personage of Spirit. Were it not so, the Holy Ghost could not dwell in us.[16]

And the ancient Prophet Nephi emphasized the unity of the Godhead as follows: "And now, behold, this is the doctrine of Christ, and the only true doctrine of the Father, and of the Son, and of the Holy Ghost, which is one God, without end. Amen."[17]

Thus the scriptures proclaim that the Godhead is composed of three separate and distinct persons, two of whom have passed through mortality and are now resurrected, glorified, celestialized beings, and the third remaining a spiritual being. Yet, all three of these personages are one in purpose and in unity; and they constitute the Holy Trinity. Therefore, all of the holy scriptures attest the teachings of the *Pearl of Great Price* regarding the Godhead.

---

[13]1 Nephi 10:17, 19.
[14]2 Nephi 32:2-3.
[15]Moroni 6:9.
[16]*Doctrine and Covenants* 130:22.
[17]2 Nephi 31:21.

Chapter 10

ATTRIBUTES AND PERSONALITY OF GOD

GOD A PERSONAL BEING

The *Pearl of Great Price* gives one a clear and comprehensive view of the conception of God held by the ancient prophets. As one reads the books of Moses and Abraham, he is impressed with the many personal attributes that God possessed and His nearness to and interest in human beings. In the creation story (which will be discussed in a later chapter) God or "the Gods" conversed with each other. They walked, talked, planned, worked, rested, and did numerous things which only personal beings are capable of doing. After Adam and Eve had partaken of the forbidden fruit and had become mortals, "they heard the voice of the Lord God, as they were walking in the garden, in the cool of the day."[1] A few verses later we read, "And I, the Lord God, said unto mine Only Begotten: Behold, the man is become as one of us to know good and evil."[2] Also, the record states, "For as I, the Lord God liveth, even so my words cannot return void, for as they go forth out of my mouth they must be fulfilled."[3] A voice, a mouth, and other similar organs and functions connote a personal being. Few places, if any, in the holy scriptures give a more definite and clear concept of God as a personal being than the following visitations received by Enoch, Abraham, and Moses:

Enoch's vision of God:

3. And it came to pass that I turned and went up on the mount; and as I stood upon the mount, I beheld the heavens open, and I was clothed upon with glory;

4. And I saw the Lord; and he stood before my face, and he talked with me, even as a man talketh one with another, face to face; and he said unto me: Look, and I will show unto thee the world for the space of many generations.

Moses 7:3-4.

Abraham's vision of God:

11. Thus I, Abraham, talked with the Lord, face to face, as one man talketh with another; and he told me of the works which his hands had made;

12. And he said unto me: My son, my son (and his hand was stretched out), behold I will show you all these.

Abraham 3:11-12a.

[1]Moses 4:14.
[2]*Ibid.*, 4:28.
[3]*Ibid.*, 4:30.

55

Moses' vision of God:

1. The words of God, which he spake unto Moses at a time when Moses was caught up into an exceedingly high mountain,

2. And he saw God face to face, and he talked with him, and the glory of God was upon Moses; therefore Moses could endure his presence. Moses 1:1-2.

CONCEPT SUSTAINED BY MODERN REVELATION

In the latter days God the Father and His Only Begotten Son appeared to the boy-prophet Joseph Smith, and one of the principal purposes of this glorious manifestation was to re-reveal to the world the doctrine that was so thoroughly understood by Father Adam and the other ancient saints—i.e., that the members of the Godhead are personal beings. The following is quoted from Joseph's account of the "First Vision:"

I saw two Personages, whose brightness and glory defy all description, standing above me in the air. One of them spake unto me, calling me by name, and said, pointing to the other—*This is My Beloved Son. Hear Him!*[4]

At the April conference of the Church in 1844, less than three months prior to his death, Joseph Smith made the following significant explanation regarding God as a personal being and an exalted man:

God himself was once as we are now, and is an exalted man, and sits enthroned in yonder heavens! That is the great secret! If the veil were rent today, and the great God who holds this world in its orbit, and who upholds all worlds and all things by his power, was to make himself visible, —I say, if you were to see him today, you would see him like a man in form—like yourselves in all the person, image, and very form as a man; for Adam was created in the very fashion, image and likeness of God, and received instruction from, and walked, talked and conversed with him, as one man talks and communes with another.[5]

GOD'S NAMES AND ETERNAL NATURE

The eternal nature and names of God the Father and the Son were proclaimed to the ancient prophets, Enoch and Moses, as the following scriptures attest:

God's declaration to Enoch:

35. Behold, I am God; Man of Holiness is my name; Man of Counsel is my name, and Endless and Eternal is my name, also.

57. . . . In the language of Adam, Man of Holiness is his name, and the name of his Only Begotten is the Son of Man, even Jesus Christ, a righteous Judge, who shall come in the meridian of time.   Moses 7:35; 6:57b.

God's declaration to Moses:

3. And God spake unto Moses, saying: Behold, I am the Lord God Almighty, and Endless is my name; for I am without beginning of days or end of years; and is not this endless?
Moses 1:3.

[4]*Pearl of Great Price,* "Writings of Joseph Smith," 2:17.
[5]Joseph Fielding Smith, *Teachings of the Prophet Joseph Smith,* p. 345.

All of the scriptures, including modern revelations, proclaim that God is an immortal, eternal, being. In the words of the Prophet Joseph Smith: "We say that God himself is a self-existent being. . . . It is correct enough."[6] In fact, Christians in general accept God as an eternal being; but the most important contribution in the restoration of gospel truths in the latter days found in the foregoing revelations to Enoch is the statement that one of Jesus Christ's names is the "Son of Man." Time and time again while living in mortality—as recorded in the New Testament—Jesus proclaimed Himself to be the "Son of Man." In their attempts to explain this statement, many modern scholars and *Bible* commentators have made the claim that when Jesus called Himself "the Son of Man" He was not making reference to His divinity, but, on the other hand, He was making mention of the fact that He was a mortal man.

But God's statement to Enoch as recorded in the foregoing quotation from the *Pearl of Great Price* gives to the world extra light and a new interpretation regarding what Christ meant when He claimed to be the "Son of Man." The *Eternal Father* declared to Enoch that *His name was "Man of Holiness"* and that *"the name of His Only Begotten is the Son of Man, even Jesus Christ." The Savior is, therefore, the Son of the Man of Holiness, or, in other words, the Only Begotten Son of God the Eternal Father. Thus when Jesus referred to Himself as the Son of Man, He was making mention of His Godhood.*

INTELLIGENCE, WISDOM, AND PRUDENCE OF GOD

God showed Abraham in vision the spirit world at the time of the Grand Council in heaven prior to the placing of mortals upon the earth. In the course of the vision, He explained to the ancient Patriarch that individual differences existed among the spirits in their pre-mortal existence just as they do here in mortality. Perhaps in the spirit world the range was from the very un-intelligent spirits to that of the high intelligence of Jesus Christ and God the Eternal Father. Just as each of us differ in talents one from another here in mortality, the revelation indicates that each of us differed from each other in talents and development in the spirit world. Our differences

---
[6]*Ibid.*, p. 352.

in the attributes and development in the pre-mortal life help to account for the differences in those respects here. The revelation Abraham received on this subject is as follows:

God's declaration to Abraham:

19. And the Lord said unto me: These two facts do exist, that there are two spirits, one being more intelligent than the other; there shall be another more intelligent than they; I am the Lord thy God, I am more intelligent than they all.

21. I dwelt in the midst of them all; I now, therefore, have come down unto thee to deliver unto thee the works which my hands have made, wherein my wisdom excelleth them all, for I rule in the heavens above, and in the earth beneath, in all wisdom and prudence, over all the intelligences thine eyes have seen from the beginning; I came down in the beginning in the midst of all the intelligences thou hast seen.

Abraham 3:19, 21.

The foregoing scripture also points out the fact that one of the principal attributes of God is His intelligence, as He is more intelligent than all of His sons and daughters combined (verse 19). Modern revelation adds the thought that the Divine Being's power to perform His great work—which gives Him His glory—is resident in His superior and supreme intelligence. To quote: *"The glory of God is intelligence."*[7] Elder B. H. Roberts made the following conclusion regarding the superior intelligence, wisdom, and prudence that God possessed:

It is the direct statement in the Book of Abraham—accepted by the Church as Scripture—that there are differences in the intelligences that exist, that some are more intelligent than others; and that God is "more intelligent than they all." I believe that this means more than that God is more intelligent than all of the other intelligences. It means that he is more intelligent than all of the other intelligences combined. His intelligence is greater than that of the mass, and that has led me to say in the second Year Book of the Seventies: —"It is this fact doubtless which makes this One, 'more intelligent than they all'," God. He is the All-Wise One! The All-Powerful One! What he tells other Intelligences to do must be precisely the wisest, fittest thing that they could anywhere or anyhow learn—the thing which it will always behoove them, with right loyal thankfulness and nothing doubting, to do. There goes with this, too, the thought that this All-Wise One will be the Unselfish One, the All-Loving One, the One who desires that which is highest, and best; not for himself alone, but for all: and that will be best for him too. His glory, his power, his joy will be enhanced by the uplifting of all, by enlarging them; by increasing their joy, power, and glory. And because this All Intelligent One is all this, and does all this, the other Intelligences worship him, submit their judgments and their will to his judgment and his will. He knows, and can do that which is best; and this submission of the mind to the Most Intelligent, Wisest—wiser than all—is worship. This is the whole meaning of the doctrine and the life of the Christ expressed in—"Father, not my will but Thy will, be done."[8]

[7] *Doctrine and Covenants* 93:36.
[8] B. H. Roberts, cited in Smith, *op. cit.,* p. 353.

JOSEPH SMITH'S STATEMENT

On June 16, 1844, only eleven days before his martyrdom, the Prophet Joseph Smith delivered a sermon to the Saints on the subject of the "Plurality of Gods." In that great discourse, he touched directly upon the scripture which we are considering in this topic (Abr. 3:19, 21). The ideas that he presented give an additional interpretation to the explanation made by Elder B. H. Roberts; therefore, we shall quote a portion of the Prophet's address:

I want to reason a little on this subject. I learned it by translating the papyrus which is now in my house. I learned a testimony concerning Abraham, and he reasoned concerning the God of heaven. "In order to do that," said he, "suppose we have two facts: that supposes another fact may exist—two men on the earth, one wiser than the other, would logically show that another who is wiser than the wisest may exist. Intelligences exist one above another, so that there is no end to them."

If Abraham reasoned thus—If Jesus Christ was the Son of God, and John discovered that God the Father of Jesus Christ had a Father, you may suppose that He had a Father also. Where was there ever a son without a father. And where was there ever a father without first being a son? Whenever did a tree or anything spring into existence without a progenitor? And everything comes in this way. Paul says that which is earthly is the likeness of that which is heavenly. Hence if Jesus had a Father, can we not believe that He had a Father also? I despise the idea of being scared to death at such a doctrine, for the Bible is full of it.

I want you to pay particular attention to what I am saying. Jesus said that the Father wrought precisely in the same way as His Father had done before Him. As the Father had done before. He laid down His life, and took it up the same as His Father had done before. He did as He was sent, to lay down His life and take it up again; and then was committed unto Him the keys, etc. I know it is good reasoning.[9]

CONCLUDING THOUGHT

Thus we have learned in this chapter that the *Pearl of Great Price* proclaimed that the ancient prophets—beginning with Father Adam—had as clear and as correct an understanding of the true personality, nature, and attributes of God as we have today as a result of the restoration of the Gospel of Jesus Christ. According to the understanding of the holy prophets, God the Father was a celestialized, glorified, personal being, and Jesus Christ was His Only Begotten Son. These Deities were eternal in nature and superior in intelligence, wisdom and prudence.

---

[9]Joseph Smith, *History of the Church*, Period I, vol. 6, pp. 476-477.

Chapter 11

MAJESTY, POWER AND GLORY OF GOD

MAJESTY AND POWER OF GOD

The following scriptures are quotations from the *Pearl of Great Price* in which God explained to Abraham, Enoch, and Moses certain facts regarding His majesty and power:

God declared His powers of omnipotence and omniscience to Abraham:

7. For I am the Lord thy God; I dwell in heaven; the earth is my footstool; I stretch my hand over the sea, and it obeys my voice; I cause the wind and the fire to be my chariot; I say to the mountains—Depart hence—and behold, they are taken away by a whirlwind, in an instant, suddenly.

8. My name is Jehovah, and I know the end from the beginning; therefore my hand shall be over thee.

Abraham 2:7-8.

God declared His universal power of sight to Enoch and His omnipresence to Moses:

36. Wherefore, I can stretch forth mine hands and hold all the creations which I have made; and mine eye can pierce them also.

35. . . . For behold, there are many worlds that have passed away by the word of my power. And there are many that now stand, and innumerable are they unto man; but all things are numbered unto me, for they are mine and I know them.

6. . . . All things are present with me, for I know them all.

Moses 7:36; 1:35b, 6b.

In the foregoing quotation from the Book of Abraham is recorded God's declaration to the "Father of the Faithful" regarding His attributes of omnipotence (all-powerfulness) and omniscience (all-knowingness). In the next quotation (Moses 7:36), Deity made an explanation to Enoch concerning His omnipresence, making special mention of His unlimited power of sight; and later He emphasized to the ancient Lawgiver (Moses 1:35b, 6b) the fact of His omniscience. It should be pointed out that both God the Father and God the Son possess the attributes of omniscience, omnipotence, and omnipresence.

CONCEPT OF MAJESTY AND POWER OF GOD CONFIRMED

The concept of God held today by the members of the Church of Jesus Christ of Latter-day Saints agrees in every detail with the revelations given to the ancient prophets as recorded in the *Pearl of Great Price*. For example, the Lord made the following declaration to the Prophet Joseph Smith:

> Thus saith the Lord your God, even Jesus Christ, the great I AM, Alpha and Omega, the beginning and the end, the same which looked upon the wide expanse of eternity, and all the seraphic host of heaven, before the world was made; the same which knoweth all things, for all things are present before mine eyes.[1]

Regarding the omnipresence, omniscience, and omnipotence of God, Dr. James E. Talmage wrote:

> *God is Omnipresent*: There is no part of creation, however remote, into which He [God] cannot penetrate; through the medium of the Spirit the Godhead is in direct communication with all things at all times. . . . The senses of God are of infinite power, His mind of unlimited capacity; His eye can penetrate all space, His ear can comprehend every sound; His powers of transferring Himself from place to place are not limited; plainly, however, His person cannot be in more than one place at any one time. . . .
>
> *God is Omniscient:* . . . His power and His wisdom are alike incomprehensible to man, for they are infinite. Being Himself eternal and perfect, His knowledge cannot be otherwise than infinite. To comprehend Himself, an infinite Being, He must possess an infinite mind. Through the agency of angels and ministering servants, He is in continuous communication with all parts of creation, and may personally visit as He may determine.
>
> *God is Omnipotent:* He is properly called the Almighty. Man can discern proofs of the Divine omnipotence on every side, in the forces that control the elements of earth, and that guide the orbs of heaven in their prescribed courses; all are working together for the common good. There can be no limits to the powers of God; whatever His wisdom indicates as fit to be done He can and will do. The means through which He operates may not be of infinite capacity in themselves; but they are directed by an infinite power. A rational conception of His omnipotence is power to do all that He may will to do.[2]

THE NAME "JEHOVAH"

In Abraham 2:8 (previously quoted), the Lord declared that His name was Jehovah. This is the name by which Jesus Christ was known during Old Testament days; therefore, the God who spoke to Father Abraham was none other than the Savior of the world. Dr. James E. Talmage explained the name "Jehovah" as follows:

> Jesus of Nazareth, who in solemn testimony to the Jews declared Himself the *I Am* or *Jehovah*, who was God before Abraham lived on earth,

---

[1]*Doctrine and Covenants* 38:1-2.
[2]James E. Talmage, *The Articles of Faith*, pp. 42-43.

was the same Being who is repeatedly proclaimed as the God who made covenant with Abraham, Isaac, and Jacob; the God who led Israel from the bondage of Egypt to the freedom of the promised land. . . .

Jehovah is the Anglicized rendering of the Hebrew, *Yahveh* or *Jahveh*, signifying the *Self-existent One*, or *The Eternal*. This name is generally rendered in our English version of the Old Testament as the Lord, printed in capitals. The Hebrew, *Ehyeh*, signifying *I am*, is related in meaning and thought derivation with the term *Yahveh or Jehovah*.[3]

GOD THE CREATOR OF HEAVEN AND EARTH

God's declaration to Moses:

1. And it came to pass that the Lord spake unto Moses, saying: Behold, I reveal unto you concerning this heaven, and this earth; write the words which I speak. I am the Beginning and the End, the Almighty God; by mine Only Begotten I created these things; yea, in the beginning I created the heavens, and the earth upon which thou standest.

30. And it came to pass that Moses called upon God, saying: Tell me, I pray thee, why these things are so, and by what thou madest them?

31. And behold, the glory of the Lord was upon Moses, so that Moses stood in the presence of God, and talked with him face to face. And the Lord God said unto Moses: For mine own purpose have I made these things. Here is wisdom and it remaineth in me.

32. And by the word of my power, have I created them, which is mine Only Begotten Son, who is full of grace and truth.

33. And worlds without number have I created; and I also created them for mine own purpose; and by the Son I created them, which is mine Only Begotten.   Moses 2:1; 1:30-33.

According to the foregoing scripture, God the Father and His Only Begotten Son worked together in creating the heavens and the earth. Through the power of the Son—that is, through the power of the Priesthood which was named after the Son— worlds without number were organized. In vol. 9, no. 21, of the *Millenial Star* (November 1, 1847) is published an important article "On Priesthood" which was written by President John Taylor. In regard to the power resident in the Priesthood, he declared:

As my time is limited, and I shall be necessitated to be brief, I shall commence by asking the question—What is Priesthood? Without circumlocution, I shall as briefly answer that it is the government of God, whether on the earth or in the heavens, for it is by that power, agency, or principle that all things are governed on the earth and in the heavens, and by that power that all things are upheld and sustained. It governs all things —it directs all things—it sustains all things—and has to do with all things that God and truth are associated with. . . . To define the power of the priesthood would be impossible, for, as stated before, it governs all things.

This *Pearl of Great Price* doctrine is confirmed in modern revelation. Jesus Christ made known to the Prophet Joseph Smith many facts regarding the majesty and power of the Godhead in regard to their creating and controlling the various

---

[3]Talmage, *Jesus the Christ*, pp. 38, 36.

bodies of matter throughout the universe. These revelations not only confirm the truthfulness of the doctrines revealed to the ancient prophets from Adam's day forward, but they also give to members of the Church of Jesus Christ of Latter-day Saints an enlarged concept and understanding of God. To quote from the *Doctrine and Covenants:*

Thus saith the Lord your God, . . . I am the same which spake, and the world was made, and all things came by me.[4]

John, the ancient apostle of the Master, wrote, and his writings were revealed to the Prophet Joseph as follows:

Therefore, in the beginning the Word was, . . . the light and the Redeemer of the world; the Spirit of truth. . . . The worlds were made by him; men were made by him; all things were made by him, and through him, and of him.[5]

The Lord revealed also to the latter-day Prophet that a divine substance emanated from the Godhead which is termed "light of truth." It is through this substance that the power of the Priesthood operates and that the Father and the Son created the heavens and the earth and set into operation the laws which control the various bodies which They organized. The following quotation is a portion of the revelation to Joseph Smith wherein the Lord explained the power by which He performs His creative work:

Verily, thus saith the Lord: . . . [Jesus Christ is] the light of truth; which truth shineth. This is the light of Christ. As also he is in the sun, and the light of the sun, and the power thereof by which it was made. As also he is in the moon, and is the light of the moon, and the power thereof by which it was made; as also the light of the stars, and the power thereof by which they were made; and the earth also, and the power thereof, even the earth upon which you stand.

And the light which shineth, which giveth you light, is through him who enlighteneth your eyes, which is the same light that quickeneth your understandings; which light proceedeth forth from the presence of God to fill the immensity of space—the light which is in all things, which giveth life to all things, which is the law by which all things are governed, even the power of God who sitteth upon his throne, who is in the bosom of eternity, who is in the midst of all things.[6]

GLORY OF GOD

Moses, Israel's ancient Lawgiver, had a vision in which God appeared unto him in His glory. Following that vision,

[4]*Doctrine and Covenants* 38:1-3.
[5]*Ibid.*, 93:8-10; John 1:1-4.
[6]*Doctrine and Covenants* 88:1, 6-13.

Satan appeared unto Moses, making it possible for the ancient Prophet to contrast the two personages from the unseen world. The purpose at this point in studying those two revelations in the *Pearl of Great Price* is to receive an understanding regarding the "glory of God."

(In those visions the facts that man is an eternal being and that he is "in the similitude of the Only Begotten Son of God" are mentioned; and also reference is made to the personality and work of Satan. However, those points will be discussed in later chapters; therefore, they need not be emphasized at this time. In fact, the purpose of presenting a portion of Moses' vision of Satan here is to show the contrast between his lack of light, truth and glory, and those attributes as possessed by the Lord.)

God's glory manifest to Moses:

4. And, behold, thou art my son; wherefore look, and I will show thee the workmanship of mine hands; but not all, for my works are without end, and also my words, for they never cease.

5. Wherefore, no man can behold all my works, except he behold all my glory, and no man can behold all my glory, and afterwards remain in the flesh on the earth.

6. And I have a work for thee, Moses, my son; and thou art in the similitude of mine Only Begotten; and mine Only Begotten is and shall be the Savior, for he is full of grace and truth; but there is no God beside me, and all things are present with me, for I know them all.

9. And the presence of God withdrew from Moses, that his glory was not upon Moses; and Moses was left unto himself. And as he was left unto himself, he fell unto the earth.

10. And it came to pass that it was for the space of many hours before Moses did again receive his natural strength like unto man; and he said unto himself: Now, for this cause I know that man is nothing, which thing I never had supposed.

11. But now mine own eyes have beheld God; but not my natural, but my spiritual eyes, for my natural eyes could not have beheld; for I should have withered and died in his presence; but his glory was upon me; and I beheld his face, for I was transfigured before him.   Moses 1:4-6, 9-11.

Moses compares God's glory with Satan's:

12. And it came to pass that when Moses had said these words, behold Satan came tempting him, saying: Moses, son of man, worship me.

13. And it came to pass that Moses looked upon Satan and said: Who art thou? For behold, I am a son of God, in the similitude of his Only Begotten; and where is thy glory, that I should worship thee?

14. For behold, I could not look upon God, except his glory should come upon me, and I were strengthened before him. But I can look upon thee in the natural man. Is it not so, surely?

15. Blessed be the name of my God, for his Spirit hath not altogether withdrawn from me, or else where is thy glory, for it is darkness unto me? And I can judge between thee and God; for God said unto me: Worship God, for him only shalt thou serve.

16. Get thee hence, Satan; deceive me not; for God said unto me: Thou art after the similitude of mine Only Begotten.

17. And he also gave me commandments when he called unto me out of the burning bush, saying: Call upon God in the name of mine Only Begotten, and worship me.

18. And again Moses said: I will not cease to call upon God, I have other things to inquire of him: for his glory has been upon me, wherefore I can judge between him and thee. Depart hence, Satan.   Moses 1:12-18.

A significant point in the foregoing revelation to Moses is the fact that the work that God accomplishes constitutes His glory. That work is eternal.

Also, in the same revelation the glory of God is used with another meaning. It denotes the brilliance of the light that attends the personage of God. Almost immediately after the visitation of the Lord, Satan appeared unto Moses, thereby making it possible for the ancient Lawgiver to become thoroughly aware of the great contrast between Deity and Lucifer. The one personage he described as possessing glory (light) and the other as expressing darkness.

Prophets Testify to the Glory of God

Moses' visions were in complete harmony with the experiences of the prophets of the Lord throughout the ages. For example, when Paul was on the road going to Damascus to persecute the Christians, "suddenly there shined round about him a light from heaven" and Jesus Christ, the resurrected Lord, appeared unto him.[7] However, Paul was not able to withstand the glory of the Savior and so he lost his eyesight for three days. It was through the power of the Priesthood and the mercy of God, however, that he was healed.

Alma's experiences somewhat resembled Paul's. The young Nephite was overcome by the glory of an angel and the voice of God and fell into a condition of unconsciousness. After he had experienced for three days and three nights the torments of a damned soul, he was blessed with a vision of God sitting upon His throne, surrounded with numberless concourses of angels, in the attitude of singing and praising their God.[8] Alma described the experience in the following words: "And oh, what joy, and what marvelous light I did behold; yea, my soul was filled with joy as exceeding as was my pain."[9]

The experiences of the boy-prophet Joseph Smith in the "Sacred Grove" bear testimony to Moses' visions—recorded in the *Pearl of Great Price*—of the glory of God and the darkness which attends Lucifer. To quote the words of the Prophet:

Thick darkness gathered around me, and it seemed to me for a time as if I were doomed to sudden destruction. . . . —not to an imaginary ruin, but to the power of some actual being from the unseen world, who

---

[7]Acts 9:3.
[8]Alma 36:22.
[9]*Ibid.*, 36:20.

had such marvelous power as I had never before felt in any being—just at this moment of great alarm, I saw a pillar of light exactly over my head, above the brightness of the sun, which descended gradually until it fell upon me.

It no sooner appeared than I found myself delivered from the enemy which held me bound. When the light rested upon me I saw two Personages, whose brightness and glory defy all description, standing above me in the air. One of them spake unto me, calling me by name, and said, pointing to the other—*This is My Beloved Son. Hear Him!*[10]

When Jesus Christ appeared unto Joseph Smith and Oliver Cowdery in the Kirtland Temple, April 3, 1836, the Prophet described the resurrected Lord as follows—and his description represents the efforts of a man to picture a glorified God:

The veil was taken from our minds, and the eyes of our understanding were opened. We saw the Lord standing upon the breastwork of the pulpit, before us, and under his feet was a paved work of pure gold, in color like amber. His eyes were as a flame of fire; the hair of his head was white like the pure snow; his countenance shone above the brightness of the sun; and his voice was as the sound of rushing of great waters, even the voice of Jehovah.[11]

Thus it is definite that the holy prophets throughout the ages who have experienced visitations from God and also from Lucifer testify to the fact that God is a personage of glory— radiant and attended by brilliant light. On the other hand, the devil is attended by darkness, accompanied by a feeling of depression and evil. Therefore, the teachings of the prophets attest the truthfulness of Moses' visions as recorded in the *Pearl of Great Price*.

---

[10]*Pearl of Great Price*, "Writings of Joseph Smith," 2:15-17.
[11]*Doctrine and Covenants* 110:1-3.

Chapter 12

THE GRAND COUNCIL IN HEAVEN

The Grand Council

God our Eternal Father called the leaders of His spirit-children together in a Grand Council in heaven prior to the organizing or creating of this world. Since God's spirit-children had progressed as far as they could in the spirit world and it would now be necessary for them to leave their heavenly home for a certain length of time and live in a mortal world in order that they might learn to walk by faith, the Gods held the Grand Council for the purpose of formulating plans for placing those spirit beings on this mortal earth. Those in attendance at that Council were the leading spirits in heaven, "the noble and great ones" whom God had chosen to be the "rulers." After the grand councilors completed their plans, an explanation of their decisions was made to all of God's sons and daughters throughout the spirit realm.

Some people are of the opinion that Jesus Christ called the Grand Council in heaven and presented to the assembled throng the gospel plan in regard to mortality. According to Joseph Smith, it was God the Father and not His Only Begotten Son who presided at that Grand Council. In fact, God had lived in accordance with the gospel plan of salvation when He was a mortal man prior to the time of His being exalted to Godhood; therefore, He was thoroughly familiar with all of the eternal laws of truth which constituted the gospel. Of this important problem, the latter-day Prophet declared: *"Thus the head God brought forth the Gods in the Grand Council."*[1] Then Joseph explained what he meant by saying: "The head, the Father of Gods, . . . "[2] "The head God called together the Gods and sat in Grand Council to bring forth the world. The grand councilors sat at

[1] Joseph Fielding Smith, *Teachings of the Prophet Joseph Smith*, p. 348.
[2] *Ibid.*, p. 349.

67

the head in yonder heavens and contemplated the creation of the worlds which were created at the time."[3] After explaining the problem a little more fully, the Prophet made the following statement: "In the beginning, the head of the Gods called a council of the Gods; and they came together and concocted a plan to create the world and people it."[4]

The two most complete accounts of what occurred at the Grand Council in heaven to appear in any of the scriptures are found in the *Pearl of Great Price*. The narrative in the Book of Abraham centers primarily on the selecting of the Only Begotten Son to be the Savior of the world; while the acount in the Book of Moses tells the story of Lucifer concocting a plan of salvation with himself as the one to be the Savior and his presenting that plan to the Eternal Father and His children.

The following scriptures will serve the purpose of comparing Abraham's and Moses' accounts of what occurred in the heavens as recorded in the *Pearl of Great Price:*

Abraham's vision of the Grand Council and the appointment of Jesus Christ to be the Savior:

24. And there stood one among them that was like unto God, and he said unto those who were with him; we will go down, for there is space there, and we will take of these materials, and we will make an earth whereon these may dwell;

25. And we will prove them herewith, to see if they will do all things whatsoever the Lord their God shall command them;

26. And they who keep their first estate shall be added upon; and they who keep not their first estate shall not have glory in the same kingdom with those who keep their first estate; and they who keep their second estate shall have glory added upon their heads for ever and ever.

27. And the Lord said: Whom shall I send?

27b. And one answered like unto the Son of Man: Here am I, send me. And another answered and said: Here am I, send me. And the Lord said: I will send the first.

28. And the second was angry, and kept not his first estate; and, at that day, many followed after him.
Abraham 3:24-28.

God's revelation to Moses regarding Satan's offer to be the Savior and his rebellion:

1. And I, the Lord God, spake unto Moses, saying: That Satan, whom thou hast commanded in the name of mine Only Begotten, is the same which was from the beginning, and he came before me, saying—Behold, here am I, send me, I will be thy son, and I will redeem all mankind, that one soul shall not be lost, and surely I will do it; wherefore give me thine honor.

2. But, behold, my Beloved Son, which was my Beloved and Chosen from the beginning, said unto me—Father, thy will be done, and the glory be thine forever.

3. Wherefore, because that Satan rebelled against me, and sought to destroy the agency of man, which I, the Lord God, had given him, and also, that I should give unto him mine own power; by the power of mine Only Begotten, I caused that he should be cast down;

4. And he became Satan, yea, even the devil, the father of all lies, to deceive and to blind men, and to lead them captive at his will, even as many as would not hearken unto my voice.
Moses 4:1-4.

---

[3]*Ibid.*, pp. 348-349.
[4]*Ibid.*, p. 349.

The foregoing account given in Abraham explains briefly the gospel plan as presented by the Father to His spirit-children and the rewards for keeping the first and second estates (verses 24-26). Then the Son of Man and "another" person both volunteered to be the Savior of the world (verse 27). When the Father selected Christ to be the Savior, the "second" one revolted and he and many others did not keep their first estate (verse 28).

The acount in Moses gives the added information that the "second" one who volunteered to be the Savior was Satan. He proposed a plan, one in which man would lose his free agency, a vital principle of life which had been practiced throughout the indefinite past. Lucifer also wanted an immediate assurance of a quick rise to Godhood and the receiving of all the honor and glory which would rightfully belong to the Eternal Father. Verse two, however, makes it clear that the "Beloved Son" accepted the plan proposed by the Father, signifying His acceptance with the humble remark, "thy will be done, and the glory be thine forever."

WAR IN HEAVEN

The readers should refer again to Abraham 3:28 and Moses 4:3-4, just quoted. Herein are given the *Pearl of Great Price's* accounts of what has come to be known as the "War in Heaven," and in the latter verse is given an explanation of the assignment that Satan received. Other Latter-day Saint scriptures, including the *Bible,* confirm the teachings of the *Pearl of Great Price* and give the following additional information regarding this momentous event:

And there was war in heaven: Michael and his angels fought against the dragon; and the dragon fought and his angels, and prevailed not; neither was their place found any more in heaven. And the great dragon was cast out, that old serpent, called the Devil, and Satan, which deceiveth the whole world: he was cast out into the earth, and his angels were cast out with him.

And I heard a loud voice saying in heaven, Now is come salvation, and strength, and the kingdom of our God, and the power of his Christ: for the accuser of our brethren is cast down, which accused them before our God day and night. And they overcame him by the blood of the Lamb, and by the word of their testimony; and they loved not their lives unto the death.

Therefore rejoice, ye heavens, and ye that dwell in them. Woe to the inhabiters of the earth and of the sea! for the devil is come down unto you, having great wrath, because he knoweth that he hath but a short time.[5]

Isaiah, the great Hebrew prophet, lamented the tragic fall of Lucifer and expressed his feelings as follows:

How art thou fallen from heaven, O Lucifer, son of the morning! how art thou cut down to the ground! . . . For thou hast said in thine heart, I will ascend into heaven, I will exalt my throne above the stars of God: I will sit also upon the mount of the congregation, in the sides of the north: I will ascend above the heights of the clouds; I will be like the most High. Yet thou shalt be brought down to hell, to the sides of the pit.[6]

In modern revelation the Lord declared:

The devil . . . rebelled against me, saying, Give me thine honor, which is my power; and also a third part of the hosts of heaven turned he away from me because of their agency; and they were thrust down, and thus came the devil and his angels.[7]

The Prophet Joseph Smith and Sidney Rigdon beheld the following in a vision:

And this we saw also, and bear record, that an angel of God who was in authority in the presence of God, who rebelled against the Only Begotten Son whom the Father loved and who was in the bosom of the Father, was thrust down from the presence of God and the Son, and was called Perdition, for the heavens wept over him—he was Lucifer, a son of the morning.

And we beheld, and lo, he is fallen! is fallen, even a son of the morning! . . . We beheld Satan, that old serpent, even the devil, who rebelled against God, and sought to take the kingdom of our God and his Christ.[8]

SUMMARY STATEMENT

Thus God the Eternal Father proposed the plan of salvation, the same plan which had been used on other worlds. Jehovah, Michael, Gabriel and other faithful men and women championed this plan. All of the spirit-children of our Eternal Parents had their free agency to choose the Father's plan or the one proposed by Lucifer. To quote the Prophet Joseph Smith in regard to those who accepted the latter: "So the devil rose up in rebellion against God, and was cast down, with all who put up their heads for him."[9] On the other hand, all the spirits

[5]Revelation 12:7-12.
[6]Isaiah 14:12-15.
[7]*Doctrine and Covenants* 29:36-37.
[8]*Ibid.*, 76:25-28.
[9]Smith, *op. cit.*, p. 357.

who accepted Jesus as their Savior have been or shall be permitted to come to this earth and take mortal bodies.

SPIRIT WORLD AND FOREORDINATION

The ancient prophets, Enoch and Abraham, both were privileged to see in vision the spirit world. There they beheld the sons and daughters of God the Eternal Father and the Eternal Mother, and those sons and daughters were at that time spirit beings. In Enoch's vision we read: "And he beheld the spirits that God had created; and he beheld also things which were not visible to the natural eye."[10] The significant point in the foregoing statement is that what Enoch saw attests the truths revealed to Father Abraham. The latter prophet was permitted to view the spirit world at the time that the Grand Council was held in which Jesus Christ was chosen by the Father and foreordained to be the Savior of the world.

Abraham's vision of the spirit world:

22. Now the Lord had shown unto me, Abraham, the intelligences that were organized before the world was; and among all these there were many of the noble and great ones;
23. And God saw these souls that they were good, and he stood in the midst of them, and he said: These I will make my rulers; for he stood among those that were spirits, and he saw that they were good; and he said unto me; Abraham, thou art one of them; thou wast chosen before thou wast born.

Abraham 3:22-23.

As pointed out in an earlier chapter, God revealed to Father Abraham that His spirit-children differed one from another in talents, abilities, faithfulness and righteousness.[11] Many of them, because of their obedience to the Gospel of Jesus Christ, i.e., to the eternal laws of truth, in the spirit world prior to the creating of this earth, had attained great heights in knowledge, wisdom, and Godliness. These are the ones that the foregoing scripture claims that the Father selected to be His "rulers"—in other words, God foreordained them at the time of the Grand Council in heaven to be the prophets, apostles, and other great religious leaders who were commissioned to establish His kingdom on the earth and carry forward the gospel plan through the various dispensations.[12] For example, Michael, the Archangel, was appointed to be the "first man"—the father of the human family, and Eve—an equally

---

[10]Moses 6:36.
[11]Abraham 3:17-19, 21.
[12]1 Nephi 11:13-21; Mosiah 3:8; 2 Nephi 3:6, 15.

intelligent and faithful female spirit—was selected to be Adam's helpmate and to become the mother of all human flesh.[13] The Prophet Joseph Smith described the foreordination of Adam, Noah, and Christ as follows: "Adam was made to open the way of the world, and for dressing the garden. Noah was born to save seed of everything, when the earth was washed of its wickedness by the flood! and the Son of God came into the world to redeem it from the fall."[14] The Son of Man declared in modern revelation the following:

> And the Lord appeared unto them, and they rose up and blessed Adam, and called him Michael, the Prince, the Archangel. And the Lord administered comfort unto Adam, and said unto him: I have set thee to be at the head, a multitude of nations shall come of thee, and thou art a prince over them forever.[15]

The foreordination of Jeremiah to be a prophet was recorded by the ancient prophet himself. To quote:

> Then the word of the Lord came unto me, saying, Before I formed thee in the belly I knew thee; and before thou camest forth out of the womb I sanctified thee, and I ordained thee a prophet unto the nations.[16]

Joseph Smith was one of the "noble and great ones" that stood in the council of the Gods before mortals were placed on this earth, and he was foreordained to be the prophet to open the last dispensation of the gospel—the Dispensation of the Fullness of Times. Thirty-five hundred years before the Prophet's birth, Joseph who was sold into Egyptian bondage gave evidence of Joseph Smith's foreordination by predicting his name and describing the work he would perform.[17] And the greatest of all the individuals who was foreordained to perform a great mission on this earth was Jesus Christ. In the First Epistle of Peter we read:

> Forasmuch as ye know that ye were not redeemed with corruptible things, as silver and gold, from your vain conversation received by tradition from your fathers; but with the precious blood of Christ, as of a lamb without blemish and without spot: *Who verily was foreordained before the foundation of the world,* but was manifest in these last times for you.[18]

Joseph Smith had the following to say regarding foreordination:

---

[13]*Doctrine and Covenants* 27:11; 78:16; 88:112-115; 128:20; Smith, *op. cit., pp.* 157-158, 167-169.
[14]*Ibid.,* p. 12.
[15]*Doctrine and Covenants* 107:54-55.
[16]Jeremiah 1:4-5.
[17]2 Nephi 3:1-25.
[18]1 Peter 1:18-20.

Every man who has a calling to minister to the inhabitants of the world was ordained to that very purpose in the Grand Council of heaven before this world was.[19]

Thus the teachings of the *Pearl of Great Price,* wherein God told Abraham that "the noble and great ones" among His spirit-children were chosen (foreordained) at the Grand Council in heaven to be the "rulers" (church leaders) when they came into mortality, were verified by the revelations from the Lord to the various prophets from age to age.

---

[19]Smith, *op. cit.,* p. 365.

Chapter 13

CREATION OF THE EARTH

Introductory Statement

There are three accounts of the creation of the earth given in the scriptures. They are found in the first and second chapters of Genesis, the second and third chapters of Moses, and the fourth and fifth chapters of Abraham. Since this book deals primarily with the teachings of the *Pearl of Great Price* and two of the accounts of the creation are in that scripture, those two will be printed in parallel columns in this book. However, this chapter will be devoted to a study of the three accounts; therefore, the readers should refer to Genesis in making the comparisons.

Abraham's account is probably the oldest of the three. It was written approximately 2,000 B. C. The story of the creation in Genesis is credited to Moses; thus this report would have been written several hundred years after Abraham's time. The creation story in the Book of Moses is a revelation given to Moses by the Lord and then re-revealed to the Prophet Joseph Smith in December, 1830. Since two of the accounts—the ones found in Moses and Genesis—are credited to Moses, one would expect them to agree with each other more than with the creation story told by Father Abraham.

Abraham's account of the creation represents a vision that he was privileged to behold of the Grand Council of the Gods at the time that they were making their plans to create the heavens and the earth; therefore, his account represents the Gods' "blueprint" or plans regarding the steps and the work that They would follow in creating the world. Such statements as the following appear here and there throughout Abraham's account: "And the Gods said: Let us prepare the waters to bring forth abundantly the moving creatures that have life; ... And the Gods said: We will bless them, and cause them to be fruitful and multiply" (Abraham 4:20, 22); "And the Gods said: We will do everything that we have said, and organize them; and behold, they shall be very obedient" (*ibid.*, 31); "And thus were their decisions at the time that they counseled among themselves to form the heavens and the earth" (*ibid.*, 5:3). Such statements as these prove beyond a shadow of a doubt that Abraham's account represents the Gods' "blueprint" or plans regarding the creating of the heavens and the earth.

The principal portion of Moses' account, on the other hand, is the story of the actual work of creating the heavens and the earth; in other words, the putting into effect of the plans that the Gods had made, as recorded in the Book of Abraham. The purpose of printing the two accounts side by side is that the plans of the Gods might be studied; and in conjunction therewith, how those plans were put into effect could be observed.

ACCOUNTS OF THE CREATION

The creation story as recorded by Father Abraham:

The First Day:

1. And then the Lord said: Let us go down. And they went down at the beginning, and they, that is the Gods, organized and formed the heavens and the earth.

2. And the earth, after it was formed, was empty and desolate, because they had not formed anything but the earth; and darkness reigned upon the face of the deep, and the Spirit of the Gods was brooding upon the face of the waters.

3. And they (the Gods) said: Let there be light; and there was light.

4. And they (the Gods) comprehended the light, for it was bright; and they divided the light, or caused it to be divided, from the darkness.

5. And the Gods called the light Day, and the darkness they called Night. And it came to pass that from the evening until morning they called night; and from the morning until the evening they called day; and this was the first, or the beginning, of that which they called day and night.

Abraham 4:1-5.

Story of creating the world as revealed to Moses and re-revealed to Joseph Smith in December, 1830:

The First Day:

1. And it came to pass that the Lord spake unto Moses, saying: Behold, I reveal unto you concerning this heaven, and this earth; write the words which I speak. I am the Beginning and the End, the Almighty God; by mine Only Begotten I created these things; yea, in the beginning I created the heaven, and the earth upon which thou standest.

2. And the earth was without form, and void; and I caused darkness to come up upon the face of the deep; and my Spirit moved upon the face of the water; for I am God.

3. And I, God, said: Let there be light; and there was light.

4. And I, God, saw the light; and that light was good. And I, God, divided the light from the darkness.

5. And I, God, called the light Day; and the darkness, I called Night; and this I did by the word of my power, and it was done as I spake; and the evening and the morning were the first day. Moses 2:1-5.

Abraham's report of the creation begins with the use of the term "Gods" as the creators and uses the plural throughout the entire story instead of the singular form "God," as is found in the other two accounts. The Prophet Joseph Smith and modern revelation confirm the doctrine of the plurality of the Gods.[1] The first verse in Moses' description makes the contribution of explaining by what power the earth was created. To quote: "By mine Only Begotten I created these things," which means by the power of the Priesthood. (See chapters 20 and 21 on Priesthood.) The report in the Book of Moses differs from the other two accounts in that it is written in the first person. The work accomplished during the first day is practically identical in all three creation stories.

The Second Day:

6. And the Gods also said: Let there be an expanse in the midst of the waters, and it shall divide the waters from the waters.

7. And the Gods ordered the expanse, so that it divided the waters which were under the expanse from the waters which were above the expanse; and it was so, even as they ordered.

8. And the Gods called the expanse, Heaven. And it came to pass that it was from evening until morning that they called night; and it came to pass that it was from morning until evening that they called day; and this was the second time that they called night and day.   Abraham 4:6-8.

The Second Day:

6. And again, I, God, said: Let there be a firmament in the midst of the water, and it was so, even as I spake; and I said: Let it divide the waters from the waters; and it was done;

7. And I God, made the firmament and divided the waters, yea, the great waters under the firmament from the waters which were above the firmament, and it was so even as I spake.

8. And I, God, called the firmament Heaven; and the evening and the morning were the second day. Moses 2:6-8.

The principal difference in the story recorded in the Book of Abraham concerning the second day and that delineated in Moses and Genesis is that in the former account the word "expanse" is used and in the latter two the term is "firmament."

The Third Day:

9. And the Gods ordered, saying: Let the waters under the heaven be gathered together unto one place, and let the earth come up dry; and it was so as they ordered;

10. And the Gods pronounced the dry land, earth; and the gathering together of the waters, pronounced they, great waters; and the Gods saw that they were obeyed.

The Third Day:

9. And I, God, said: Let the waters under the heaven be gathered together unto one place, and it was so; and I, God, said: Let there be dry land; and it was so.

10. And I, God, called the dry land Earth; and the gathering together of the waters, called I the Sea; and I, God, saw that all things which I had made were good.

---

[1]*Doctrine and Covenants* 76:58; 131:28; 132:17-20, 37; Joseph Fielding Smith, *Teachings of the Prophet Joseph Smith*, pp. 138, 311-312, 346-349, 368-373.

11. And the Gods said: Let us prepare the earth to bring forth grass; the herb yielding seed; the fruit tree yielding fruit, after his kind, whose seed in itself yieldeth its own likeness upon the earth; and it was so, even as they ordered.

12. And the Gods organized the earth to bring forth grass from its own seed, and the herb to bring forth herb from its own seed, yielding seed after his kind; and the earth to bring forth the tree from its own seed, yielding fruit, whose seed could only bring forth the same in itself, after his kind; and the Gods saw that they were obeyed.

13. And it came to pass that they numbered the days; from the evening until the morning they called night; and it came to pass, from the morning until the evening they called day; and it was the third time.

Abraham 4:9-13.

11. And I, God, said: Let the earth bring forth grass, the herb yielding seed, the fruit tree yielding fruit, after his kind, and the tree yielding fruit, whose seed should be in itself upon the earth, and it was so even as I spake.

12. And the earth brought forth grass, every herb yielding seed after his kind, and the tree yielding fruit, whose seed should be in itself, after his kind; and I, God saw that all things which I had made were good;

13. And the evening and the morning were the third day. Moses 2:9-13.

In Moses' narration it seems that shortly after God spoke the act was accomplished, which is indicative of the fact that the account is telling the story of the actual process of creating the world. In Abraham's story "the Gods saw that they were obeyed" and in the other account, "I, God, saw that all things which I had made were good." It is to be noted that in all three accounts the law established by God was that every form of life should produce its own kind—in other words, like produces like.

The Fourth Day:

14. And the Gods organized the lights in the expanse of the heaven, and caused them to divide the day from the night; and organized them to be for signs and for seasons, and for days and for years;

15. And organized them to be for lights in the expanse of the heaven to give light upon the earth; and it was so.

16. And the Gods organized the two great lights, the greater light to rule the day, and the lesser light to rule the night; with the lesser light they set the stars also;

17. And the Gods set them in the expanse of the heavens, to give light upon the earth, and to rule over the day and over the night, and to cause to divide the light from the darkness.

18. And the Gods watched those things which they had ordered until they obeyed.

The Fourth Day:

14. And I, God, said: Let there be lights in the firmament of the heaven, to divide the day from the night, and let them be for signs, and for seasons, and for days, and for years;

15. And let them be for lights in the firmament of the heaven to give light upon the earth; and it was so.

16. And I, God, made two great lights; the greater light to rule the day, and the lesser light to rule the night, and the greater light was the sun, and the lesser light was the moon; and the stars also were made even according to my word.

17. And I, God, set them in the firmament of the heaven to give light upon the earth; and it was so.

18. And the sun to rule over the day, and the moon to rule over the night, and to divide the light from the

19. And it came to pass that it was from evening until morning that it was night; and it came to pass that it was from morning until evening that it was day; and it was the fourth time.

Abraham 4:14-19.

darkness; and I, God, saw that all things which I had made were good;

19. And the evening and the morning were the fourth day.

Moses 2:14-19.

The Fifth Day:

20. And the Gods said: Let us prepare the waters to bring forth abundantly the moving creatures that have life; and the fowl, that they may fly above the earth in the open expanse of heaven.

21. And the Gods prepared the waters that they might bring forth great whales, and every living creature that moveth, which the waters were to bring forth abundantly after their kind; and every winged fowl after their kind. And the Gods saw that they would be obeyed, and that their plan was good.

22. And the Gods said: We will bless them, and cause them to be fruitful and multiply, and fill the waters in the seas or great waters; and cause the fowl to multiply in the earth.

23. And it came to pass that it was from evening until morning that they called night; and it came to pass that it was from morning until evening that they called day; and it was the fifth time. Abraham 4:20-23.

The Fifth Day:

20. And I, God, said: Let the waters bring forth abundantly the moving creature that hath life, and fowl which may fly above the earth in the open firmament of heaven.

21. And I, God, created great whales, and every living creature that moveth, which the waters brought forth abundantly, after their kind, and every winged fowl after his kind; and I, God, saw that all things which I had created were good.

22. And I, God, blessed them, saying: Be fruitful, and multiply, and fill the waters in the sea; and let fowl multiply in the earth;

23. And the evening and the morning were the fifth day.   Moses 2:20-23.

The principal difference in the creative stories on the fifth day is that in Abraham's account the plan is being formulated and would be put into effect later, thus indicating that the whole mortal creative process as being described was not completed at this point, but that the Gods were merely making their plans which would later be put into effect.

The Sixth Day:

24. And the Gods prepared the earth to bring forth the living creature after his kind, cattle and creeping things, and beasts of the earth after their kind; and it was so, as they had said.

25. And the Gods organized the earth to bring forth the beasts after their kind, and cattle after their kind, and every thing that creepeth upon the earth after its kind; and the Gods saw they would obey.

31. And the Gods said: We will do everything that we have said, and organize them; and behold, they shall be

The Sixth Day:

24. And I, God, said: Let the earth bring forth the living creature after his kind, cattle, and creeping things, and beasts of the earth after their kind, and it was so;

25. And I, God, made the beasts of the earth after their kind, and cattle after their kind, and everything which creepeth upon the earth after his kind; and I, God, saw that all these things were good.

31. And I, God, saw everything that I had made, and, behold, all things which I had made were very good; and

very obedient. And it came to pass that it was from evening until morning they called night; and it came to pass that it was from morning until evening that they called day; and they numbered the sixth time.   Abraham 4:24-25, 31.

the evening and the morning were the sixth day.   Moses 2:24-25, 31.

Note that the same difference exists in the creative stories of the sixth day to that which was mentioned in regards to the fifth day; for example, "And the Gods said: We will do everything that we have said;" thus Abraham gives an account of their plans.

Verses twenty-six to thirty tell the story of the creation of man, who was organized on the sixth day. That portion of the account of the creation was omitted from this chapter in order that it might be used later in the chapter on "The Dignity and Eternal Nature of Man."

The Seventh Day:

1. And thus we will finish the heavens and the earth, and all the hosts of them.

2. And the Gods said among themselves: On the seventh time we will end our work, which we have counseled; and we will rest on the seventh time from all our work which we have counseled.

3. And the Gods concluded upon the seventh time, because that on the seventh time they would rest from all their works which they (the Gods) counseled among themselves to form; and sanctified it. And thus were their decisions at the time that they counseled among themselves to form the heavens and the earth.   Abraham 5:1-3.

The Seventh Day:

1. Thus the heaven and the earth were finished, and all the host of them.

2. And on the seventh day I, God, ended my work, and all things which I had made; and I rested on the seventh day from all my work, and all things which I had made were finished, and I, God, saw that they were good;

3. And I, God, blessed the seventh day, and sanctified it; because that in it I had rested from all my work which I, God, had created and made.   Moses 3:1-3.

Abraham's account definitely points out that the Gods planned to rest from all their labors on the "seventh time" (day); and the narratives in Moses and Genesis attest that God or the Gods did rest on the seventh day and sanctified it; thus we have the origin of the Sabbath Day.

Chapter 14

SPIRITUAL AND TEMPORAL CREATIONS

INTRODUCTORY STATEMENT

In the last chapter the story of the creation of the world as given in the books of Abraham, Moses, and Genesis was discussed. A comparison was made of the three accounts through the seven days or creative periods. This chapter will continue the discussion of the creation narratives as presented in the foregoing three scriptures, placing special emphasis on the spiritual and temporal creations.

Suddenly, in the midst of the discussion of the physical creation of the world, the Book of Moses interpolates a statement regarding the creation of the spirits of plants and animals, as well as of men and women, prior to the time of their mortal creation. Abraham 5:4-5 and Genesis 2:4-5 contain short statements which seem to fit in well with the more definite declaration of a spiritual creation of all things as found in Moses. However, Abraham 5:5 also points out the fact that the mortal creation was going to be accomplished "according to all that which they [the Gods] had said [or planned] concerning" the life which would inhabit this earth; thus even this portion of Abraham's account can still be referred to as the Gods' "blueprint" of the creation.

SPIRITUAL CREATION

Abraham's account:

4. And the Gods came down and formed these the generations of the heavens and of the earth, when they were formed in the day that the Gods formed the earth and the heavens,

5. According to all that which they had said concerning every plant of the field before it was in the earth, and

Moses' account of the spiritual creation:

4. And now, behold, I say unto you, that these are the generations of the heaven and of the earth, when they were created, in the day that I, the Lord God, made the heaven and the earth;

5. And every plant of the field before it was in the earth, and every herb of the field before it grew. For I, the Lord

every herb of the field before it grew; for the Gods had not caused it to rain upon the earth when they counseled to do them, and had not formed a man to till the ground.   Abraham 5:4-5.

God, created all things, of which I have spoken, spiritually, before they were naturally upon the face of the earth. For I, the Lord God, had not caused it to rain upon the face of the earth. And I, the Lord God, had created all the children of men; and not yet a man to till the ground; for in heaven created I them; and there was not yet flesh upon the earth, neither in the water, neither in the air.   Moses 3:4-5.

One of the most vital and enlightening contributions to an understanding of the creation story is Moses' account of all things being created spiritually before they received their mortal tabernacles. The spiritual creation, therefore, was preparatory for the placing of life upon the earth.

In modern revelation the Lord confirms the facts given in the *Pearl of Great Price* regarding a spiritual creation of all things preceding the temporal or mortal creation. To quote the words of the Lord:

For by the power of my Spirit created I them; yea, all things both spiritual and temporal—first spiritual, secondly temporal, which is the beginning of my work; and again, first temporal, and secondly spiritual, which is the last of my work—speaking unto you that you may naturally understand; but unto myself my works have no end, neither beginning; but it is given unto you that ye may understand, because ye have asked it of me and are agreed.

Wherefore, verily I say unto you that all things unto me are spiritual, and not at any time have I given unto you a law which was temporal; neither any man, nor the children of men; neither Adam, your father, whom I created.[1]

SECOND ACCOUNT OF TEMPORAL OR MORTAL CREATION

Abraham's account of the temporal creation:

6. But there went up a mist from the earth, and watered the whole face of the ground.

20. And out of the ground God formed every beast of the field, and every fowl of the air, and brought them unto Adam to see what he would call them; and whatsoever Adam called every living creature, that should be the name thereof.

21. And Adam gave names to all

Moses' account of the temporal creation:

6. But I, the Lord God, spake, and there went up a mist from the earth, and watered the whole face of the ground.

9. And out of the ground made I, the Lord God, to grow every tree, naturally, that is pleasant to the sight of man; and man could behold it. And it became also a living soul. For it was spiritual in the day that I created it; for it remaineth in the sphere in which I, God, created it, yea, even all things

[1]*Doctrine and Covenants* 29:31-34.

cattle, to the fowl of the air, to every beast of the field; and for Adam, there was found an help meet for him.

Abraham 5:6,20-21.

which I prepared for the use of man; and man saw that it was good for food.

19. And out of the ground I, the Lord God, formed every beast of the field, and every fowl of the air; and commanded that they should come unto Adam, to see what he would call them; and they were also living souls; for I, God, breathed into them the breath of life, and commanded that whatsoever Adam called every living creature, that should be the name thereof.

20. And Adam gave names to all cattle, and to the fowl of the air, and to every beast of the field; but as for Adam, there was not found an help meet for him.   Moses 3:6, 9, 19-20.

These scriptures are Abraham's and Moses' accounts of the temporal or mortal creation of plants and animals. It should be noted, however, that the latter story is Moses' second delineation of a temporal or physical creation.

SELF-EXISTENT AND ETERNAL MATTER

Reference will now be made again to the first verse of each of the three creation stories. The Book of Genesis begins with the following statement: "In the beginning God created the heaven and the earth." In Moses the Lord states: "I created the heaven, and the earth upon which thou standest." At the time the Gospel of Jesus Christ was restored to the Prophet Joseph Smith, the common concept held by Christian denominations was that the world was made out of nothing. The first verse in Abraham's account of the creation throws much light on the subject and gives the true picture of what occurred. To quote: ". . . and they, that is the Gods, *organized and formed the heavens and the earth.*" Thus the meaning of create is to organize. The Gods organized the heavens and the earth out of self-existent matter. At no time has something been made out of nothing. Regarding this important subject, the Prophet Joseph Smith gave to the world the following explanation:

You ask the learned doctors why they say the world was made out of nothing; and they will answer, "Doesn't the Bible say He created the world?" And they infer, from the word create, that it must have been made out of nothing. Now, the word create came from the word *baurau,* which does not mean to create out of nothing; it means to organize; the same as man would organize materials and build a ship. Hence we infer that God had materials to organize the world out of chaos—chaotic matter, which is element, and in which dwells all glory. Element had an existence from the time He had. The pure principles of element are principles which can never be destroyed; they may be organized and re-organized, but not destroyed. They had no beginning, and can have no end.[2]

Since the time that Joseph Smith made the foregoing statement, it has become common knowledge that matter and energy cannot be created nor destroyed. Their forms may be changed, but they cannot be put out of existence. Prominent theologians, philosophers and scientists throughout the past one hundred years have confirmed the teachings of Joseph the Prophet; thus, as the Lord told the Prophet, "The elements are eternal."[3] The following quotations attest the truthfulness of these facts:

The view of the Prophet on this subject of creation is abundantly sustained by men of learning subsequent to his time. The Rev. Baden Powell, of Oxford University, for instance, writing for Kitto's *Cyclopaedia of Biblical Literature*, says: "The meaning of this word (create) has been commonly associated with the idea of 'making out of nothing.' But when we come to inquire more precisely into the subject, we can of course satisfy ourselves as to the meaning only from an examination of the original phrase." The learned professor then proceeds to say that three distinct Hebrew verbs are in different places employed with reference to the same divine act, and may be translated, respectively, "create," "make," "form or fashion." "Now," continues the Professor, "though each of these has its shade of distinction, yet the best critics understand them as so nearly synonymous that, at least in regard to the idea of making out of nothing, little or no foundation for that doctrine can be obtained from the first of these words." And, of course, if no foundation for the doctrine can be obtained from the first of these words—viz., the verb translated "create," then the chances are still less for there being any foundation for the doctrine of creation from nothing in the verb translated, "made," "formed," or "fashioned."

Professor Powell further says: "The idea of 'creation,' as meaning absolutely 'making out of nothing,' or calling into existence that which did not exist before, in the strictest sense of the term, is not a doctrine of scripture; but it has been held by many on the grounds of natural theology, as enhancing the ideas we form of the divine power, and more especially since the contrary must imply the belief in the eternity and self existence of matter. . . . "

The philosophers with equal emphasis sustain the contention of the Prophet. Herbert Spencer, in his *First Principles*, (1860), said: "There was once universally current, a notion that things could vanish into absolute nothing, or arise out of absolute nothing. . . . The current

---

[2]Joseph Fielding Smith, *Teachings of the Prophet Joseph Smith*, pp. 350-352.
[3]*Doctrine and Covenants* 93:35.

theology, in its teachings respecting the beginning and end of the world, is clearly pervaded by it. . . . The gradual accumulation of experiences, has tended slowly to reverse this conviction; until now, the doctrine that matter is indestructible has become a commonplace. All the apparent proofs that something can come of nothing, a wider knowledge has one by one cancelled. . . . "

Fiske follows Spencer, of course, and in his *Cosmic Philosophy* sums up the matter in these words. "It is now unconceivable that a particle of matter should either come into existence, or lapse into-non-existence."[4]

During the early part of this century, the concept of the conservation of matter and the conservation of energy, i.e., that neither matter nor energy can be created nor destroyed, was taught universally throughout the schools of our land. But as a result of the wonderful experiments and studies made by such brilliant scientists as Madame Curie, Dr. Steinmetz, Dr. Rutherford, Dr. Soddy, and others, an enlarged understanding of matter and energy was given to the world. These scientists discovered that matter could be transferred into energy and energy into matter; and yet they maintain that the sum total of matter and energy in the universe remains constant. Although matter and energy may be transferred into one another, yet no new matter is brought into existence out of nothing and the same holds true in regard to energy. The atomic bomb, in which a very small amount of matter was transferred into energy, is the outstanding example of the culmination of the scientists' efforts to transfer matter into energy.

God not only created the heavens and the earth out of matter which had always been in existence, but He also organized or created His spiritual creations out of eternal spirit matter. In the words of the Prophet: *"There is no such thing as immaterial matter. All spirit is matter, but it is more fine or pure, and can only be discerned by purer eyes."*[5]

SPIRIT AND MORTAL BEINGS

When the Gods organized the plants, animals, and human beings on this earth, They patterned their physical bodies after their spirit bodies. The Prophet Joseph Smith explained that the physical bodies of men, beasts, creeping things, and fowls of the air resembled their spirit bodies. To quote his words:

. . . that which is spiritual being in the likeness of that which is

---

[4]B. H. Roberts, cited in footnotes in Smith, *op. cit.*, pp. 350-351.
[5]*Doctrine and Covenants* 131:7.

temporal; and that which is temporal in the likeness of that which is spiritual; the spirit of man in the likeness of his person, as also the spirit of the beast, and every other creature which God has created.[6]

Since mortal beings are patterned after spirit beings, they look so much alike that if we were to see both of them standing side by side we could not tell them apart by looking at them. For example, when the brother of Jared saw in vision the Savior as a spirit personage over 2,000 years before His birth into mortality, the ancient Jaredite Prophet thought that he was looking at a man composed of "flesh and blood;"[7] therefore, it was necessary for the Redeemer of mankind to explain to the brother of Jared as follows:

Behold, I am he who was prepared from the foundation of the world to redeem my people. Behold, I am Jesus Christ. . . . Behold this body, which ye now behold, is the body of my spirit; and man have I created after the body of my spirit; and even as I appear unto thee to be in the spirit, will I appear unto my people in the flesh.[8]

In modern revelation, the Lord made known the fact that a spirit personage who had never had a mortal body and the spirit of a person who had once lived in this world but had passed on into the spirit world and also a personage who had resurrected his physical body all three looked alike. As previously mentioned, all of these personages in appearance are like mortals. Since they look so much alike and by merely seeing them we would probably be unable to tell them apart, God revealed to the Prophet "the three grand keys by which good or bad angels or spirits may be distinguished." He told Joseph that if a spirit appeared unto him, claiming that he had a message from God, that the Prophet should offer to shake hands with him. If he was a spirit of a righteous man from the spirit world he would refuse to shake hands but would deliver his message. In this way Joseph would know that this messenger was from the Lord. If a resurrected being appeared unto him and was asked to shake hands, this personage would extend his hand and the Prophet would be able to feel it because it is composed of flesh and bones. To continue the explanation by quoting directly from the revelation:

If it be the devil as an angel of light, when you ask him to shake hands he will offer you his hand, and you will not feel anything; you may therefore detect him.

---

[6] Ibid., 77:2.
[7] Ether 3:8.
[8] Ibid., 3:14, 16.

These are three grand keys whereby you may know whether any administration is from God.[9]

Conclusions

Thus through the *Pearl of Great Price,* through revelation in the latter days, and through the teachings of the Prophet Joseph Smith, we have learned that all things were created spiritually before they were created temporally and that all matter that exists today has always existed. Matter can have its formed changed, and yet matter and energy cannot be brought into existence out of nothing, nor can they be destroyed or lapse into complete nothingness. The Gods organized both spiritual and temporal matter when They brought about the creation of the heavens and the earth; but They did not bring spiritual matter into existence out of nothing nor did They produce one atom of temporal matter which had not previously existed in one form or another. Also, we have learned that all temporal or mortal things have their spiritual likenesses, the temporal being organized in the likeness of the spiritual.

---

[9]*Doctrine and Covenants* 129:1-9

Chapter 15

VISIONS OF GOD'S CREATIONS

ANCIENT PROPHETS VIEW GOD'S CREATIONS

Both Father Abraham and Moses the Lawgiver, two of the great prophets of antiquity, were privileged by the Lord to look off into space and view the countless worlds which He had created. In this chapter we shall consider their marvelous visions.

ABRAHAM'S VISION AND ASTROLOGY

One evening after Father Abraham had left Ur of the Chaldees and before he arrived in Egypt, the Lord appeared to him and showed him a multitude of heavenly bodies which He had created (Abr. 3:11-12). They talked together, "face to face, as one man talketh with another," and the Lord explained to the ancient Patriarch the times, seasons, and laws which governed those heavenly bodies.

It was the natural thing for Abraham to be outside during the nighttime observing the stars and contemplating the majesty of the heavens, because he had migrated from a land whose people during ancient times possessed an extensive understanding of the solar system. The pagan religion of those ancient Orientals—which religion could also be regarded as a pseudo-science—was known as astrology or astralism. Since the stars and the other heavenly bodies were its focal center, astrology could be regarded as the ancient forerunner of astronomy.

Astrology had its home in ancient Babylonia, where it was cultivated by the original Sumerians and bequeathed as a science and a religion to the Babylonians of Abraham's day. Those ancient pagan worshipers of the heavens named the most common stars and constellations. With their scientific enquiry and mathematical genius, they "made the calculations of the positions of the heavenly bodies at any given date and hour a fairly simple matter."[1] The signs of the zodiac were formulated by them; and, in accordance with their religious beliefs, the astral worshipers were said to be born either under their lucky or unlucky star. Thus astrology—that ancient Babylonian brand of paganism—was a religion pregnant with magic and fatalism.

Of all the heavenly bodies, the sun became the most important object of worship. In the words of S. Angus:

> Though the *Chaldaei* paid most attention to the host of stars, they could not but recognize the premier place of the Sun among the seven planets and the stars. The Sun, as the source of heat and light, became the chief deity of the heaven, and Sun-worship was the ultimate result of astralism.[2]

Father Abraham testifies that at the time of his residence in Ur, in the land of the Babylonians, even his own father and relatives had become pagans and worshiped at the shrines of astrology. To quote his words:

> My fathers having turned from their righteousness, and from the holy commandments which the Lord their God had given unto them, unto the worshiping of the gods of the heaven, utterly refused to hearken to my voice.[3]

Father Abraham, however, held fast to the gospel doctrines as taught by the antediluvian patriarchs and worshiped the true and living God. But since he had been reared in the Chaldean environment where the practice of astral lore necessitated the diligent contemplation of the shining heavenly bodies, which never have failed to inspire awe and awaken a religious sentiment of some kind in the hearts of human beings, he had a deep appreciation for God's numerous creations. The beauty of the Eastern night, the long and silent contemplation, Abraham's desire to commune with the true and living God, and his intense religious purpose were all conducive to bringing about the following vision:

[1] S. Angus, *The Mystery Religions and Christianity*, p. 165.
[2] *Ibid.*, p. 168.
[3] Abraham 1:5.

ABRAHAM'S VISION OF THE HEAVENLY BODIES

Abraham's vision of God and the heavenly bodies which the Lord had created:

1. And I, Abraham, had the Urim and Thummim, which the Lord my God had given unto me, in Ur of the Chaldees;

2. And I saw the stars, that they were very great, and that one of them was nearest unto the throne of God; and there were many great ones which were near unto it;

3. And the Lord said unto me: These are the governing ones; and the name of the great one is Kolob, because it is near unto me, for I am the Lord thy God: I have set this one to govern all those which belong to the same order as that upon which thou standest.

4. And the Lord said unto me, by the Urim and Thummim, that Kolob was after the manner of the Lord, according to its times and seasons in the revolutions thereof; that one revolution was a day unto the Lord, after his manner of reckoning, it being one thousand years according to the time appointed unto that whereon thou standest. This is the reckoning of the Lord's time, according to the reckoning of Kolob.

5. And the Lord said unto me: The planet which is the lesser light, lesser than that which is to rule the day, even the night, is above or greater than that upon which thou standest in point of reckoning, for it moveth in order more slow; this is in order because it standeth above the earth upon which thou standest, therefore the reckoning of its time is not so many as to its number of days, and of months, and of years.

6. And the Lord said unto me: Now, Abraham, these two facts exist, behold thine eyes see it; it is given unto thee to know the times of reckoning, and the set time, yea, the set time of the earth upon which thou standest, and the set time of the greater light which is set to rule the day, and the set time of the lesser light which is set to rule the night.

7. Now the set time of the lesser light is a longer time as to its reckoning than the reckoning of the time of the earth upon which thou standest.

8. And where these two facts exist, there shall be another fact above them, that is, there shall be another planet whose reckoning of time shall be longer still;

9. And thus there shall be the reckoning of the time of one planet above another, until thou come nigh unto Kolob, which Kolob is after the reckoning of the Lord's time; which Kolob is set nigh unto the throne of God, to govern all those planets which belong to the same order as that upon which thou standest.

10. And it is given unto thee to know the set time of all the stars that are set to give light, until thou come near unto the throne of God.

11. Thus I, Abraham, talked with the Lord, face to face, as one man talketh with another; and he told me of the works which his hands had made;

12. And he said unto me: My son, my son (and his hand was stretched out), behold I will show you all these. And he put his hand upon mine eyes, and I saw those things which his hands had made, which were many; and they multiplied before mine eyes, and I could not see the end thereof.

13. And he said unto me: This is Shinehah, which is the sun. And he said unto me: Kokob, which is star. And he said unto me: Olea, which is the moon. And he said unto me: Kokaubeam, which signifies stars, or all the great lights, which were in the firmament of heaven.

15. And the Lord said unto me: Abraham, I show these things unto thee before ye go into Egypt, that ye may declare all these words.

16. If two things exist, and there be one above the other, there shall be greater things above them; therefore Kolob is the greatest of all the Kokaubeam that thou hast seen, because it is nearest unto me.

17. Now, if there be two things, one above the other, and the moon be above the earth, then it may be that a planet or a star may exist above it; and there is nothing that the Lord thy God shall take in his heart to do but what he will do it.

Abraham 3:1-13, 15-17.

URIM AND THUMMIM

The foregoing quotation from the *Pearl of Great Price* (verses 1 and 4) states that God gave Father Abraham the Urim and Thummim before he left Ur of the Chaldees and that they were used for the purpose of receiving revelations from the Lord. The *Bible* proclaims the fact that many of the ancient Hebrew prophets possessed similar instruments, if not the same ones that the Lord had given to Abraham.[4] It seems that the Urim and Thummim were handed down from prophet to prophet. The possession and use of these constituted men "Seers" in ancient times; that is, through them they received revelations from God, and, on certain occasions, through these mediums they translated strange languages.[5]

Not only did the Hebrew prophets possess the Urim and Thummim, but the prophets who lived in ancient America also had a set of them which they referred to as "Interpreters." However, the author does not know whether there were two sets in existence in ancient days at the same time or only one set, as the records do not indicate that two prophets who lived at the same time both possessed the Urim and Thummim.

The particular instruments used by the Prophet Joseph Smith in translating the *Book of Mormon* and the Book of Abraham were first given by the Lord to an ancient Jaredite prophet, called in the Book of Ether the "brother of Jared." In that record we read:

And behold, these two stones will I [the Lord] give unto thee, and ye shall seal them up also with the things which ye shall write. For behold, the language which ye shall write I have confounded; wherefore I will cause in my own due time that these stones shall magnify to the eyes of men these things which ye shall write.[6]

The *Book of Mormon* record declares that many centuries after the time of the brother of Jared's receiving from the Lord the Urim and Thummim that the Nephite prophets had in their possession the same curious instruments. These holy men of God handed them down from prophet to prophet; and finally Moroni, the last of the Nephite prophets and record keepers, hid them with the writings of his people. Fourteen hundred years later he delivered them, along with the "gold

---

[4]Exodus 28:15, 28-30; Leviticus 8:6-8; Numbers 28:21; Deuteronomy 33:8; 1 Samuel 28:6; Ezra 2:62-63; Nehemiah 7:65.
[5]Ether 4:5; Mosiah 8:11-19; 28:20.
[6]Ether 3:23-24.

plates," into the hands of the Prophet Joseph Smith. In modern revelation the Lord confirms these facts.[7]

Joseph the Prophet described the Urim and Thummim as "a curious instrument, which the ancients called 'Urim and Thummim,' which consists of two transparent stones set in the rim of a bow fastened to a breastplate."[8] Joseph not only had in his possession these instruments but he also had a "seer stone." Martin Harris, one of the three witnesses to the *Book of Mormon*, said " . . . that the seer stone differed from the Urim and Thummim that was obtained with the plates, which were clear stones set in two rims, very much resembling spectacles, only they were larger."[9]

ABRAHAM'S KNOWLEDGE OF THE HEAVENLY BODIES AND MODERN ASTRONOMY

It is our purpose in this topic to make a brief comparison of Father Abraham's vision of the heavenly bodies and comparable knowledge obtained by astronomers at the present time. When we consider that Abraham's vision was recorded nearly 4,000 years ago, the facts presented therein cause us to marvel. Although his account is brief and a little of the terminology differs somewhat from the terms used today, nevertheless many of the ideas presented in the *Pearl of Great Price* are sustained by the knowledge obtained by modern astronomers.

The science of astronomy, like the majority of the other sciences, has made wonderful advancements during the past few hundred years. Probably no time in history have mortal beings penetrated so deeply into the vastness of the universe as have the scientists during our day. Aided by powerful telescopes, the astronomers have penetrated billions and billions of miles outward into the universe, and have tabulated and named numerous galaxies of heavenly bodies—approximately one hundred millions of them. Each of these galaxies is composed of from two to five hundred billions of stars. Thus these modern scientists have verified through their discoveries the words of the Lord to the ancient prophets as recorded in the *Pearl of Great Price*. For example, in that holy scripture the God of heaven and earth made the following declaration:

---

[7] *Doctrine and Covenants* 17:1.
[8] Joseph Smith, "The Wentworth Letter," cited in Preston Nibley, *The Witnesses of the Book of Mormon*, p. 22.
[9] Martin Harris to Edward Stevenson, cited in *ibid.*, p. 131.

Worlds without number have I created. . . . For behold, there are many worlds that have passed away by the word of my power and there are many that now stand, and innumerable are they unto man; but all these are numbered unto me, for they are mine and I know them.[10]

We shall now turn our attention to an examination of Father Abraham's marvelous vision. In the foregoing scripture (Abr. 3:2-4, 9), the ancient Patriarch describes a massive body of matter which the Lord called Kolob. God showed him in vision many stars which were "very great, and that one of them was nearest unto the throne of God; and there were many great ones which were near unto it; and the Lord said unto me [Abraham]: These are the governing ones; and the name of the great one is Kolob because it is near unto me, for I am the Lord thy God." Then the Lord explained to the Father of the Faithful that He had set Kolob "to govern all those which belong to the *same order* as that upon which thou standest."

Modern astronomy holds the viewpoint that larger bodies of matter govern smaller bodies of matter through the law known as gravitation. Certainly that concept is in harmony with the words of the Lord to Abraham. However, astronomers have not, in our age, discovered one separate and distinctive body of matter which serves as the center of our galaxy and which seems to govern all the stars in said galaxy. In other words, they have not located a star which could be definitely designated as being Kolob. Instead of one large star serving as the center of this galaxy, astronomers maintain that there are numerous large stars located rather close together and that they are all nearly equal in mass. That idea seems to fit well with Abraham's statement that there were "many great ones which were near unto it [Kolob]," although astronomers have not designated one of these stars as being the governor of the others.

In verse 4 the Lord described to Abraham the revolutions of Kolob. The word revolutions is used correctly, according to modern terminology, when the description is referring to seasons. Then Abraham records the fact that "one revolution was a day unto the Lord, after His manner of reckoning, it being one thousand years according to the time appointed unto" this earth. The word *revolution* in that particular phrase, according to our terminology, should be interpreted as meaning

[10]Moses 1:33a, 35b.

rotation,[11] because it is the rotation of the earth upon its axis that determines day and night.

The Lord pointed out to Abraham that Kolob was immense in size. The fact that it took one thousand years of our time for it to make one complete turn on its axis—in other words, for one days' time to elapse—also is indicative of its enormity. Modern astronomers have discovered many stars which are gigantic in size. These they call "super-giant stars." One of the largest of them is named *Betelgeuse.* It has a diameter of approximately four hundred sixty millions of miles. Another super-giant star, also enormous in size, is named *Antares.* This immense body of matter is located in the *Scorpia* constellation. It has a diameter of approximately three hundred millions of miles. Another giant star, being a little larger than *Antares,* is named *Myra,* and another is called *Arcturus.* The latter one has a diameter of thirty-six millions of miles. Any of these massive bodies of matter could easily be accepted as being comparable in size to the great star Kolob which God showed to Father Abraham.

In verse 5 the Lord describes the motions of the moon (which satellite He named Olea in verse 13), comparing its motion to the rotation of the earth in determining the reckoning of time. He told Abraham that the moon rotates more slowly on its axis than does the earth, and, therefore, a day on that satellite is much longer than a day on the earth. The discoveries of modern astronomers have attested this revealed fact. Although the moon is much smaller than the earth, being only 2,163 miles in diameter compared to 7,900 miles, yet it takes 27 1/3 days (sidereal time—pertaining to the stars) for it to rotate once on its axis; therefore, a day on the moon is as long a period of time as 27 1/3 sidereal days upon the earth. It also takes 29½ synodic days (pertaining to the sun) for the moon to revolve once around the earth; and so the same side or face of the moon is turned towards the earth at all times.

According to the teachings of astronomy, the revolutions of the moon are faster than those of the earth. Since the moon revolves around the earth and the earth revolves around the sun, in addition to the moon following its own orbit around the earth—which it completes once every 27 1/3 days—it is

---

[11]Rotation is the turning about an axis within the body; revolution is the turning about an axis which is outside the body.

also accompanying the earth in its orbit around the sun; there-fore, the moon has two voluntary motions compared to the earth's one, which results in its moving more rapidly.

The Lord pointed out to Abraham (verses 6 to 10) that to each heavenly body He gave a law which governed the motion of that particular body of matter. Also, since each body of matter has its own separate movements, its rate of motion differs from the rate of motion of other bodies of matter. In modern revelation the Lord told the Prophet Joseph Smith certain truths which sustain the facts given to Father Abraham. To quote:

> All kingdoms have a law given; and there are many kingdoms; for there is no space in which there is no kingdom; and there is no kingdom in which there is no space, either a greater or a lesser kingdom. And unto every kingdom is given a law; and to every law there are certain bounds also and conditions. . . .
>
> And again, verily I say unto you, He [God] hath given a law unto all things, by which they move in their times and their seasons; and their courses are fixed, even the courses of the heavens and the earth, which comprehend the earth and all the planets. And they give light to each other in their times and in their seasons, in their minutes, in their hours, in their days, in their weeks, in their months, in their years—all these are one year with God but not with men.
>
> The earth rolls upon her wings, and the sun giveth his light by day, and the moon giveth her light by night, and the stars also give their light, as they roll upon their wings in their glory, in the midst of the power of God.[12]

Again, it can be said that modern astronomy verifies the facts revealed to Father Abraham and to Joseph Smith regarding the laws which govern heavenly bodies. The speed of each body of matter which exists throughout the entire universe has been determined by the law which was established and set into operation for the control of that particular body of matter. After the Divine Omnipotent God put the laws into operation, each body of matter traveled at its own definite given speed year after year and age after age.[13]

It has already been pointed out that the earth rotates on its axis many times faster than does the moon. The fact could be mentioned that Jupiter rotates on its axis as much faster than the earth as the earth does faster than the moon. For example, Jupiter has a diameter of 88,000 miles and its rota-

---

[12]*Doctrine and Covenants* 88:36-38, 42-45.
[13]In perfect agreement with the Laws of Planetary Motion as enunciated by Sir Isaac Newton.

tion period is 9 hours 50 minutes and 30 seconds. This planet is hundreds of times as large as the earth and yet it takes a third as much time for a day to transpire on it as it does upon the earth. Saturn, another of the planets in this solar system, has a diameter of 72,000 miles and a rotation length of time of 10 hours and 2 minutes. The sun has a diameter of approximately 865,000 miles and its rotation period, or length of day, is 25.14 days measured by our time at the sun's equator or 35 days near the poles. Thus the speed at which each of the heavenly bodies is traveling differs from the speed of each other. To further illustrate this point, we shall direct our attention to the speed of revolutions of some of these bodies of matter. For example, the earth is revolving at the rate of 18½ miles per second in its course around the sun in contrast to Pluto's speed of 1½ miles per second. Thus we see that to every kingdom God has given its own individual law which law regulates the speed at which that kingdom moves throughout space as long as that Divine Being wills that it should do so.

In verse 12 Abraham describes the eternal and innumerable amount of heavenly bodies that exist throughout the universe. To quote: "I saw those things which His [God's] hands had made, which were many; and they multiplied before mine eyes, and I could not see the end thereof." That statement suggests that there is no end to matter nor to space. As far as Abraham was able through vision to penetrate the immensity of space, he beheld body after body of matter, or in other words, star after star. The fact that matter and space have no limit is also confirmed by modern astronomers.

There was a time a few hundred years ago when all the stars that were known were those that could be seen with the naked eye. Then came the invention of the telescope. By the use of that instrument numerous heavenly bodies were discovered which had not been known to man heretofore. Later stronger telescopes were invented and many new galaxies of stars came within view and these were studied by the astronomers. Following this, time and time again telescopes have been improved and numerous new galaxies have been discovered. At the present time there are a hundred million of them known to man. Each of them is composed of two to five hundred billions of stars. Certainly the astronomers are of the firm conviction that if they could continue to invent more powerful telescopes that galaxy after galaxy of stars beyond the bounds of what are known today would be brought under observation. In other words, as Father Abraham saw in his vision, so are modern astronomers seeing and knowing today—that there is no end to the vast multitude of heavenly bodies, as there is no end to time nor to space.

MOSES' VISION OF GOD'S CREATIONS

Moses' vision of God, the earth, and the numerous worlds:

7. And now, behold, this one thing I show unto thee, Moses, my son; for thou art in the world, and now I show it unto thee.

8. And it came to pass that Moses looked, and beheld the world upon which he was created; and Moses beheld the world and the ends thereof, and all the children of men which are, and which were created; of the same he greatly marveled and wondered.

27. And it came to pass, as the voice was still speaking, Moses cast his eyes and beheld the earth, yea, even all of it; and there was not a particle of it which he did not behold, discerning it by the Spirit of God.

28. And he beheld also the inhabitants thereof, and there was not a soul which he beheld not; and he discerned them by the Spirit of God; and their numbers were great, even numberless as the sand upon the sea shore.

29. And he beheld many lands; and each land was called earth, and there were inhabitants on the face thereof.

30. And it came to pass that Moses called upon God, saying: Tell me, I pray thee, why these things are so, and by what thou madest them?

31. And behold, the glory of the Lord was upon Moses, so that Moses stood in the presence of God, and talked with him face to face. And the Lord God said unto Moses: For mine own purpose have I made these things. Here is wisdom and it remaineth in me.

32. And by the word of my power, have I created them, which is mine Only Begotten Son, who is full of grace and truth.

33. And worlds without number have I created; and I also created them for mine own purpose; and by the Son I created them, which is mine Only Begotten.

34. And the first man of all men have I called Adam, which is many.

35. But only an account of this earth, and the inhabitants thereof, give I unto you. For behold, there are many worlds that have passed away by the word of my power. And there are many that now stand, and innumerable are they unto man; but all things are numbered unto me, for they are mine and I know them.

36. And it came to pass that Moses spake unto the Lord, saying: Be merciful unto thy servant, O God, and tell me concerning this earth, and the inhabitants thereof, and also the heavens, and then thy servant will be content.

37. And the Lord God spake unto Moses, saying: The heavens, they are many, and they cannot be numbered unto man; but they are numbered unto me, for they are mine.

38. And as one earth shall pass away, and the heavens thereof, even so shall another come; and there is no end to my works, neither to my words.

39. For behold, this is my work and my glory—to bring to pass the immortality and eternal life of man.

40. And now, Moses, my son, I will speak unto thee concerning this earth upon which thou standest; and thou shalt write the things which I shall speak.

42. (These words were spoken unto Moses in the mount, the name of which shall not be known among the children of men. And now they are spoken unto you. Show them not unto any except them that believe. Even so. Amen.)

Moses 1:7-8, 27-40, 42.

In the foregoing vision Moses was privileged by the Lord to behold all the countries of the earth and the countless peoples who inhabited them (verses 7-8, 27-29). The fact should be emphasized that it was "by the Spirit of God" that he was able to see all these things. Modern revelation confirms this truth.[14] To illustrate we quote from the *Doctrine and Covenants* the following regarding Joseph Smith and Sidney Rigdon:

> By the power of the Spirit our eyes were opened and our understandings were enlightened, so as to see and understand the things of God— even those things which were from the beginning before the world was, which were ordained of the Father, through his Only Begotten Son, who was in the bosom of the Father, even from the beginning. . . . The Lord touched the eyes of our understandings and they were opened, and the glory of the Lord shone round about. And we beheld the glory of the Son, on the right hand of the Father, and received of his fulness. And saw the holy angels, and them who are sanctified before his throne, worshiping God, and the Lamb, who worship him forever and ever.[15]

Moses asked the Lord to tell him how He created the world and for what purpose (verses 30-33, 39). God's answer on how He did His work will be discussed in the chapter on Priesthood; and the purpose was to prepare a mortal home for His children in order that He might *"bring to pass the immortality and eternal life of man."* This scripture will be discussed in connection with the chapter on the "Atonement and Mission of Jesus Christ," and, therefore, needs only be mentioned at this point.

Since Moses' vision of God's creation is centered primarily on this earth, the meaning of verse 34 is that Adam is the first man of all the men of our race who were created for this earth and not necessarily the first man that God had created for any of His worlds. The word of the Lord to Enoch confirms this view, as we shall see in the following quotation. In speaking of the wickedness that should prevail throughout the world at the time of Noah, the Lord told Enoch that "all the creations which I have made . . . and among all the workmanship of mine hands there has not been so great wickedness as among thy brethren;"[16] thus, according to His own statement, the Lord had peopled other worlds before He placed Adam and Eve on this earth.

The Lord God also told Moses that He had created so

---

[14]*Doctrine and Covenants* 67:10-13; 76:28; 110:1-2.
[15]*Ibid.,* 76:12-14, 19.
[16]Moses 7:36.

many worlds that to man they were innumerable. As some of these worlds passed away, others were brought into existence. Also, according to the marvelous revelations recorded in the *Pearl of Great Price,* God's creations, His works, and His words are all eternal. Both Enoch and Abraham attest this great fact; therefore, these ancient holy prophets confirm Moses' vision.[17]

---

[17]Abraham 3:12.

Chapter 16

DIGNITY AND ETERNAL NATURE OF MAN

God's Masterpiece

Of all of God's creations, MAN is His masterpiece—and we are using the term "man" in its genetic sense, meaning men and women or mortal beings. One of the ancient Hebrew writers of the Psalms, according to the *American Standard Version* of the *Bible,* declared: "What is man, that thou art mindful of him? . . . For thou hast made him but little lower than God."[1] Not only did the Hebrew prophets understand that man was but a little lower than God, but Father Adam, Enoch, Abraham, and the other ancient prophets whose religious concepts are recorded in the *Pearl of Great Price* had a thorough understanding of the dignity and eternal nature of man. In this chapter the teachings of these great men of God regarding this important subject will be presented.

Man an Eternal Being

God tells Abraham that man is an eternal being:

18. Howbeit that he [God] made the greater star; as, also, if there be two spirits, and one shall be more intelligent than the other, yet these two spirits, notwithstanding one is more intelligent than the other, have no beginning; they existed before, they shall have no end, they shall exist after, for they are gnolaum, or eternal. Abraham 3:18.

The setting of the foregoing scripture was the great vision which Father Abraham had of the heavenly bodies, followed by a vision of God's sons and daughters in the spirit world at the time of the Grand Council and an explanation from the Lord regarding what the ancient Patriarch was seeing.

The foregoing scripture (quoted from the *Pearl of Great Price*), which definitely points out the fact that individual differences existed in the spirit world among God's spirit-children just as we know that they do here in mortality, is one

---

[1] *American Standard Version, Bible,* Psalms 8:4a, 5a.

99

of the greatest truths ever proclaimed by the Lord to any of
His holy prophets. In fact, an eternal law of life is the law of
individual differences. Also, the foregoing scripture states
clearly the significant fact that notwithstanding one spirit was
more intelligent than the other, they had no beginning; *"they
existed before, they shall have no end, they shall exist after,
for they are gnolaum, or eternal."*

VERIFIED BY MODERN REVELATION

Modern revelation not only verifies the teachings of the
Pearl of Great Price regarding the eternal nature of man, but
it also helps to clarify the meaning of "they existed before."
The Lord declared the following to Joseph Smith:

> *Man was also in the beginning with God. Intelligence, or the light
> of truth, was not created or made, neither indeed can be.*[2]

Later the Prophet made the following statement which
attests God's revelation to him:

> *Intelligence is eternal and exists upon a self-existent principle. It is
> spirit from age to age, and there is no creation about it.*[3]

Therefore, that which existed prior to the spirit personages
of men and women was their intelligence, life, mind, "light
of truth," or whatever name one desires to give to the
center of the personality of man.[4] This is what the Lord declared to Joseph Smith, as well as to the ancient Prophet
Abraham, to be uncreatable, eternally existent, and indesruc-
tible. Also, as previously discussed, men are spirit beings and
their spirits are composed of spirit matter or elements. The
Lord also revealed in the latter days the following:

> For man is spirit. The elements are eternal, and spirit and element,
> inseparably connected, receive a fulness of joy.[5]

Thus it is made clear in the foregoing revelations from the
Lord that both the intelligence or life that is in us and the spirit
matter that we are composed of are eternal. They had no
beginning and they, therefore, can have no end, for everything
which had a beginning must of necessity have an end. Regard-

---

[2]*Doctrine and Covenants* 93:29.
[3]Joseph Fielding Smith, *Teachings of the Prophet Joseph Smith*, p. 354.
[4]*Doctrine and Covenants* 93:23-24, 29-33, 36; B. H. Roberts, *Seventy's Course in Theology*,
   (Second Year, 1908) pp. 7-32; footnotes in Smith, *op. cit.*, pp. 342-360; Milton R. Hunter,
   The Gospel Through the Ages, pp. 124-128.
[5]*Doctrine and Covenants* 93:33.

ing this very important subject, Joseph Smith, the Prophet, made the following firm declaration:

I have another subject to dwell upon, which is calculated to exalt man. . . . It is associated with the subject of the resurrection of the dead— namely, the soul—the mind of man—the immortal spirit. Where did it come from? All learned men and doctors of divinity say that God created it in the beginning; but it is not so; the very idea lessens man in my estimation. I do not believe the doctrine; I know better. Hear it, all ye ends of the world; for God has told me so; and if you don't believe me, it will not make the truth without effect. . . .

We say that God Himself is a self-existent being. Who told you so? Who told you that man did not exist in like manner upon the same principles? Man does exist upon the same principles. . . .

The mind or the intelligence which man possesses is co-equal [co-eternal] with God Himself. I know that my testimony is true; hence when I talk to these mourners, what have they lost? Their relatives and friends are only separated from their bodies for a short season; their spirits which existed with God have left the tabernacle of clay only for a little moment, as it were, and they now exist in a place where they converse together the same as we do on the earth.

I am dwelling on the immortality of the spirit of man. Is it logical to say that the intelligence of spirits is immortal, and yet that it had a beginning? The intelligence of spirits had no beginning, neither will it have an end. There never was a time when there were not spirits; for they are co-equal [co-eternal] with our Father in heaven.[6]

Elder B. H. Roberts came to the following conclusion regarding this doctrine taught by the Prophet Joseph:

It appears to be very clear that the Prophet had in mind the *intelligence*, when he said "the soul—the mind of man—the immortal spirit," was not created or made, and he did not have reference to the spirit as a begotten child of God. It was the doctrine of the Prophet, and is of the Church, that the spirits of men are begotten sons and daughters of God.[7]

Man's Spiritual Eyes

Since, as was pointed out in the chapter "Spiritual and Temporal Creations," man's spirit body is "in the likeness of that which is temporal; and that which is temporal in the likeness of that which is spiritual; the spirit of man in the likeness of his person,"[8] our spirits possess eyes, ears, and the other organs. Thus when righteous men and women have the privilege of looking into the unseen world or, while they are in

[6]Smith, *op. cit.*, pp. 352-353.
[7]Footnote on *ibid.*, p. 353; Hunter, *op. cit.*, pp. 96-103.
[8]*Doctrine and Covenants* 77:2b.

mortality, behold a vision of God, they do so through their spiritual eyes. This doctrine is made clear by Moses after he had beheld a vision of God.

Moses' statement regarding spiritual eyes:

9. And the presence of God withdrew from Moses, that his glory was not upon Moses; and Moses was left unto himself. And as he was left unto himself, he fell unto the earth.

10. And it came to pass that it was for the space of many hours before Moses did again receive his natural strength like unto man; and he said unto himself: Now, for this cause I know that man is nothing, which thing I never had supposed.

11. But now mine own eyes have beheld God; but not my natural, but my spiritual eyes, for my natural eyes could not have beheld; for I should have withered and died in his presence; but his glory was upon me; and I beheld his face, for I was transfigured before him.

Moses 1:9-11.

In a revelation received by the Prophet Joseph Smith, the Lord confirmed the truthfulness of the statement made by Moses. To quote the words of the Lord:

And again, verily I say unto you that it is your privilege, and a promise I give unto you that have been ordained unto this ministry, that inasmuch as you strip yourselves from jealousies and fears, and humble yourselves before me, for ye are not sufficiently humble, the veil shall be rent and you shall see me and know that I am—not with the carnal neither natural mind, but with the spiritual.

For no man has seen God at any time in the flesh, except quickened by the Spirit of God. Neither can any natural man abide the presence of God, neither after the carnal mind.[9]

CREATION OF MAN AND HIS DOMINION

Abraham's account of the Gods' plans for the temporal creation of man, and his dominion:

26. And the Gods took counsel among themselves and said: Let us go down and form man in our image, after our likeness; and we will give them dominion over the fish of the sea, and over the fowl of the air, and over the cattle, and over all the earth, and over every creeping thing that creepeth upon the earth.

27. So the Gods went down to organize man in their own image, in the image of the Gods to form they him, male and female to form they them.

28. And the Gods said: We will bless them. And the Gods said: We will cause them to be fruitful, and multiply, and replenish the earth, and subdue it, and to have dominion over the fish of

Moses' account of the temporal or mortal creation of man, and his dominion:

26. And I, God, said unto mine Only Begotten, which was with me from the beginning: Let us make man in our image, after our likeness; and it was so. And I, God, said: Let them have dominion over the fishes of the sea, and over the fowl of the air, and over the cattle, and over all the earth, and over every creeping thing that creepeth upon the earth.

27. And I, God, created man in mine own image, in the image of mine Only Begotten created I him; male and female created I them.

28. And I, God, blessed them, and said unto them: Be fruitful, and multiply, and replenish the earth, and subdue it, and have dominion over the fish of

[9]*Ibid.*, 67:10-12.

the sea, and over the fowl of the air, and over every living thing that moveth upon the earth.

29. And the Gods said: Behold, we will give them every herb bearing seed that shall come upon the face of all the earth, and every tree which shall have fruit upon it; yea, the fruit of the tree yielding seed to them we will give it; it shall be for their meat.

30. And to every beast of the earth, and to every fowl of the air, and to every thing that creepeth upon the earth, behold, we will give them life, and also we will give to them every green herb for meat, and all these things shall be thus organized.

31. And the Gods said: We will do everything that we have said, and organize them; and behold, they shall be very obedient. And it came to pass that it was from evening until morning they called night; and it came to pass that it was from morning until evening that they called day; and they numbered the sixth time.

Abraham 4:26-31.

the sea, and over the fowl of the air, and over every living thing that moveth upon the earth.

29. And I, God, said unto man: Behold, I have given you every herb bearing seed, which is upon the face of all the earth, and every tree in the which shall be the fruit of a tree yielding seed; to you it shall be for meat.

30. And to every beast of the earth, and to every fowl of the air, and to everything that creepeth upon the earth, wherein I grant life, there shall be given every clean herb for meat; and it was so, even as I spake.

31. And I, God, saw everything that I had made, and behold, all things which I had made were very good; and the evening and the morning were the sixth day.   Moses 2:26-31.

Abraham's account is the story of the Gods making plans for the temporal creation of man—male and female—and declaring the dominion that should be theirs after they were placed in mortality. The story in Moses is the actual delineation of the temporal or mortal creation of men and women and their receiving from God an extensive dominion to be enjoyed and properly used here in mortality.

The fact was mentioned, but not discussed, in the chapter on the "Spiritual and Temporal Creations" that the first creation of man was the organizing of his spiritual body. Since this entire chapter is devoted to a study of man, it is appropriate to discuss more fully at this point the doctrine of man's spiritual creation, followed by his temporal or mortal creation. In Moses 3:5 is found the following significant statement:

For I, the Lord God, created all things, of which I have spoken, spiritually, before they were naturally upon the face of the earth. . . . And I, the Lord God, had created all the children of men; and not yet a man to till the ground; for in heaven created I them.

While this process was being carried forward, the Gods were looking ahead and planning the mortal probation where the Eternal Father's children eventually would live and be assigned dominion over all the creatures and elements of the earth.

Abraham's account (4:26-27) states that the Gods organized man in Their own image and after Their likeness, both male and female. They were created first as spirit beings in the image of their Heavenly Parents and later as mortals in a similar likeness. Thus the males were created in the image and likeness of God the Eternal Father while the females were formed in the image and likeness of God their Eternal Mother. In other words, all the men and women who have ever lived on this earth or who ever shall live here are literally sons and daughters of Heavenly Parents.[10] They were begotten and born in the spirit world and grew to maturity in that realm prior to their assignment to come into mortality.[11] To quote the teachings of Joseph F. Smith, John R. Winder and Anthon H. Lund, at the time that they were serving as the First Presidency of the Church:

> Man, as a spirit, was begotten and born of Heavenly Parents, and reared to maturity in the eternal mansions of the Father prior to coming upon the earth in a temporal body to undergo an experience in mortality.[12]

The account in Moses (verses 26 and 27) states: "I, God, said unto mine Only Begotten, which was with me from the beginning: Let us make man in our image, after our likeness." Since Jesus Christ was the oldest son of our Eternal Parents in the spirit world,[13] all the human family were patterned after their oldest brother, and He and they in the image and likeness of their Parents.

Being the offspring of the Gods, mortals inherit intelligence, reasoning powers, memory, and other mental faculties which endow them with power to have dominion over all living things and an extensive dominion over the elements.[14] Men's possibilities are so extensive that it is even possible for them to attain the state that God the Father, the Eternal Mother, and Jesus Christ have attained, and some of them

---

[10]Numbers 27:16; 16:22; Hosea 1:10; Isaiah 63:16; 64:8; Jeremiah 3:19; 1 Chronicles 29:10; Psalms 89:26; 82:16; Deuteronomy 14:1; 32:5; Ecclesiastes 12:7; John 20:17; Hebrews 12:9; Romans 8:16-17; Matthew 6:4, 8, 9; 7:11; 18:10, 14, 19; Mark 11:25; 1 Corinthians 1:3; Galatians 1:3.
[11]Brigham Young, *Journal of Discourses*, vol. 11, p. 122.
[12]Joseph F. Smith, *Improvement Era*, vol. 13, p. 80.
[13]Romans 8:29; *Doctrine and Covenants* 93:21.
[14]Psalms 8:1-9.

will reach that high position of exaltation.[15] In fact, according
to the word of the Lord, Abraham, Isaac, and Jacob have already "entered into their exaltation, according to the promises,
and sit upon thrones, and are not angels, but are Gods."[16]
Probably a number of the other holy prophets of old have attained Godhood. Thus the wonderful gospel doctrine regarding the dignity and majesty of man and his future possibilities
is made known to members of the true Church through the
sacred scriptures and the Holy Ghost.

MORTAL CREATION OF MAN

*Abraham's account of the mortal crea-
tion of man:*

7. And the Gods formed man from
the dust of the ground, and took his
spirit (that is, the man's spirit), and
put it into him; and breathed into his
nostrils the breath of life, and man became a living soul.   Abraham 5:7.

*Moses' account of the mortal creation
of man:*

7. And I, the Lord God, formed man
from the dust of the ground, and
breathed into his nostrils the breath of
life; and man became a living soul, the
first flesh upon the earth, the first man
also; nevertheless, all things were before created; but spiritually were they
created and made according to my
word.   Moses 3:7.

Mortals created in the image of God:

8. Now this prophecy Adam spake,
as he was moved upon by the Holy
Ghost, . . . saying: In the day that God
created man, in the likeness of God
made he him.

9. In the image of his own body,
male and female, created he them, and
blessed them, and called their name
Adam, in the day when they were created and became living souls in the
land upon the footstool of God.
                              Moses 6:8-9.

God's statement to Moses:

6. And I have a work for thee,
Moses, my son; and thou art in the
similitude of mine Only Begotten; . . .

16. . . . God said unto me: Thou
art after the similitude of mine Only
Begotten.   Moses 1:6a, 16b.

The preceding scriptures (Abraham 5:7; Moses 3:7)
make it clear that man's mortal body is composed of the elements of the earth and in that mortal body God placed man's
spirit and thereby "man became a living soul." This scripture is attested by modern revelation. To quote: "And the
spirit and the body are the soul of man."[17]

Also, the foregoing scriptures (Moses 6:8-9; 1:6a, 16b) indicate that the mortal bodies of men and women, like their
spirits, were created in the image of God and in the similitude

[15]*Doctrine and Covenants* 132:15-21, 37; 76:58; 121:28, 32; Moses 6:66-67; Joseph Fielding
  Smith, *op. cit.*, pp. 344-348; Hunter, *op. cit.*, 104-123.
[16]*Doctrine and Covenants* 132:37.
[17]*Ibid.*, 88:15.

of the Only Begotten. At the time these statements were made, the Savior was a spirit-personage; therefore, man's mortal body was created in the image of Christ's spirit body.

Conclusions

To summarize, it has been pointed out in this chapter that MAN is God's masterpiece. His intelligence and his spirit are both composed of self-existent, eternal matter. Since man's spirit is literally the offspring of Divine Parents, he is endowed with all the attributes that the Eternal Father and the Eternal Mother possess. The Gods, however, being infinite, possess those attributes in a highly developed, magnified form while mortals are endowed with such attributes as love, kindliness, pity, charity, honesty, justice, virtue, and all other godly attributes in an immature and finite portion. However, as God the Father and the Eternal Mother are, so may their sons and daughters become; and so it is possible for mortals someday to attain the status of Godhood. This can be done only as a result of rendering obedience to all the principles and ordinances of the Gospel of Jesus Christ. Herein lies the "Dignity and Eternal Nature of Man."

Chapter 17

EDEN AND THE TWO GREAT COMMANDMENTS

LOCATION OF GARDEN OF EDEN

In three of the holy scriptures (Genesis, Abraham, and Moses), the story is told of God's planting a beautiful garden in a country known as Eden and placing Father Adam and Mother Eve, the first man and woman, in that garden to "dress it and keep it."

There is no uniform belief among Christian scholars and members of various churches as to the geographical location of the Garden of Eden. The majority of people outside of the Church of Jesus Christ of Latter-day Saints, however, claim that it was located somewhere in the Mesopotamia Valley or in western Persia. The reason for this viewpoint is that the *Bible* mentions four rivers, one named the Euphrates, another which "goes toward the east of Assyria," and another that "compasseth the whole land of Ethiopia."[1] Since there are such rivers today as the Euphrates, the Tigris going east of Assyria, and the Nile which runs from Ethiopia northward to the Mediterranean Sea, the conclusion has been reached that the names that are attached today to those geographic places must be the same names that were attached to the same spots in the days of Father Adam; and, therefore, Eden must have been located in western Asia. Those arriving at the foregoing conclusions fail to take into consideration the fact that during various ages in history a certain name may be attached to several different geographical spots. As people migrate from one country to another, they carry with them names of places and objects which were dear to them. For example, when the Pilgrims came to America, they brought with them the name "Plymouth."

[1]Genesis 2:10-14; Moses 3:10-14.

A careful reading of the account in Genesis and also of the one in the Book of Moses makes it clear that one "river went out of Eden" and it had "four heads."[2] In other words, four rivers flowed together, making one. It is very evident that since the river that ran through Ethiopia (Nile) and the Euphrates River are hundreds of miles apart, they could never have been joined together. Therefore, the geography of the western part of Persia or the Mesopotamia Valley fails to fit the description given in the scriptures.

Where then in the world are there four rivers that flow together, making one? The Mississippi River and its tributaries fit well with the description given in Genesis and in the Book of Moses. Among the principal rivers that flow together in the upper Mississippi Valley are the Mississippi, Missouri, Ohio, and Illinois.

As a result of modern revelation, Latter-day Saints believe that the Garden of Eden was located in America, in the present state of Missouri.[3] In the *Scrapbook of Mormon Literature,* the following statement is made: "In 1832 Joseph Smith made the startling declaration that the Garden of Eden had its existence on the American continent, even in Jackson County, Missouri."[4] President Brigham Young declared:

In the beginning, after this earth was prepared for man, the Lord commenced His work upon what is now called the American continent, where the Garden of Eden was made. In the days of Noah, in the days of the floating ark, He took the people to another part of the earth; the earth was divided, and there He set up His kingdom.[5]

In March, 1832, the Lord made His first mention in latter days of "Adam-ondi-Ahman."[6] Six years later (July, 1838), He pointed out to the Prophet that Adam-ondi-Ahman was "the land where Adam dwelt."[7] The previous month the Prophet and some of the other church leaders were looking around for a place to establish a Latter-day Saint settlement. They selected a beautiful site which they named Spring Hill, Missouri.[8] Even

[2]Genesis 2:10; Moses 3:10.
[3]James E. Talmage, *The Articles of Faith*, p. 74.
[4]*Scrapbook of Mormon Literature*, vol. 1, pp. 101-104.
[5]*Discourses of Brigham Young*, p. 157; Brigham Young, in *Millennial Star*, vol. 22, p. 766.
[6]*Doctrine and Covenants* 78:15.
[7]*Ibid.*, 117:8-9.
[8]Joseph Smith, *History of the Church*, vol. 3, pp. 39-40; B. H. Roberts, in *The Contributor*, vol. 7, pp. 314-315.

before this time (March 28, 1835) God told the Prophet Joseph Smith that three years prior to Adam's death the Ancient of Days called all of his righteous posterity together "into the valley of Adam-ondi-Ahman, and there bestowed upon them his last blessing."[9] Regarding this event, the Prophet had the following vision:

> I saw Adam in the valley of Adam-ondi-Ahman. He called together his children and blessed them with a patriarchal blessing. The Lord appeared in their midst, and he, Adam, blessed them all, and foretold what should befall them to the last generation.[10]

On May 19, 1838, the Prophet Joseph Smith recorded the following in his journal regarding the place where Adam and Eve lived:

> In the afternoon I went up the river about half a mile to Wight's Ferry, accompanied by President Rigdon, and my clerk, George W. Robinson, for the purpose of selecting and laying claim to a city plat near said ferry in Daviess County, . . . which the brethren called "Spring Hill," but by the mouth of the Lord it was named Adam-ondi-Ahman, because, said He, it is the place where Adam shall come to visit his people, or the Ancient of Days shall sit, as spoken of by Daniel the Prophet.[11]

It is reasonable to believe that Adam and Eve would not migrate far after the expulsion; and the accounts given in Genesis and the Book of Moses confirm that belief. We read in the *Pearl of Great Price* that after they had had children and grandchildren "Adam and Eve, his wife, called upon the name of the Lord, and they heard the voice of the Lord from the way towards the Garden of Eden, speaking unto them, and they saw Him not; for they were shut out from His presence."[12] Furthermore, after Cain killed Abel, the account in Moses states: "Cain was shut out from the presence of the Lord, and with his wife and many of his brethren dwelt in the land of Nod, *on the east of Eden*."[13] The record in Genesis states: "Cain went out from the presence of the Lord and dwelt in the land of Nod, *on the east of Eden*."[14]

From the foregoing evidence, it is certain that the Garden of Eden was located in America, in what today is known as the state of Missouri and probably the adjacent region.

---

[9]*Doctrine and Covenants* 107:53.
[10]Joseph Fielding Smith, *Teachings of the Prophet Joseph Smith*, p. 158.
[11]Joseph Smith, *op. cit.*, vol. 3, p. 35; *Doctrine and Covenants* 116:1, 27:11; Daniel 7.
[12]Moses 5:4.
[13]*Ibid.*, 5:41.
[14]Genesis 4:16.

GARDEN OF EDEN

Abraham's acount of the Garden of Eden:

8. And the Gods planted a garden, eastward in Eden, and there they put the man, whose spirit they had put into the body which they had formed.

9. And out of the ground made the Gods to grow every tree that is pleasant to the sight and good for food; the tree of life, also, in the midst of the garden, and the tree of knowledge of good and evil.

10. There was a river running out of Eden, to water the garden, and from thence it was parted and became into four heads.

11. And the Gods took the man and put him in the Garden of Eden, to dress it and to keep it.

Abraham 5:8-11.

Moses' account of the Garden of Eden:

8. And I, the Lord God, planted a garden eastward in Eden, and there I put the man whom I had formed.

9. And out of the ground made I, the Lord God, to grow every tree, naturally, that is pleasant to the sight of man; and man could behold it. And it became also a living soul. For it was spiritual in the day that I created it; for it remaineth in the sphere in which I, God, created it, yea, even all things which I prepared for the use of man; and man saw that it was good for food. And I, the Lord God, planted the tree of life also in the midst of the garden, and also the tree of knowledge of good and evil.

10. And I, the Lord God, caused a river to go out of Eden to water the garden; and from thence it was parted, and became into four heads.

11. And I, the Lord God, called the name of the first Pison, and it compasseth the whole land of Havilah, where I, the Lord God, created much gold;

12. And the gold of that land was good, and there was bdellium and the onyx stone.

13. And the name of the second river was called Gihon; the same that compasseth the whole land of Ethiopia.

14. And the name of the third river was Hiddekel; that which goeth toward the east of Assyria. And the fourth river was the Euphrates.

15. And I, the Lord God, took the man, and put him into the Garden of Eden, to dress it, and to keep it.

Moses 3:8-15.

In Abraham's account it is evident that the Gods had created a physical body for Adam and placed his spirit in it before Adam was placed in the Garden of Eden. Since this occurred prior to the time that Adam partook of the forbidden fruit, the change had not yet come over his body to make him mortal. Elder Joseph Fielding Smith described Adam's body as follows:

There was no blood in his body, but he had a spiritual body until it was changed by the fall. A spiritual body is one which is not quickened by blood, but by spirit. Before the fall Adam had a physical, tangible body of flesh and bones, but it was not quickened by blood.[15]

---

[15]Joseph Fielding Smith, *Church History and Modern Revelation*, second series, p. 5.

In addition to all the other fruit-bearing trees of the Garden, there were two trees of special importance—"the tree of life, . . . and the tree of knowledge of good and evil." The account of the Garden of Eden in Genesis is very nearly like the one in the Book of Moses, the principal difference being the statement made in Moses that all the things which God had prepared for the use of man as food were spiritual at this time.

FIRST GREAT COMMANDMENT

The principal purpose that God had in placing Adam and Eve (and also the plants and animals) on the earth was that they might reproduce themselves and provide mortal bodies for the spirits which had been organized for this world. By being privileged to come to this earth, the sons and daughters of God could enjoy the experiences of mortality and walk by faith instead of by sight. When Father Adam and Eve were placed in the Garden of Eden, they were given the following commandment:

Abraham's account of the first great commandment:	*Moses' account of the first great commandment:*
27. So the Gods went down to organize man in their own image, in the image of the Gods to form they him, male and female to form they them.	27. And I, God, created man in mine own image, in the image of mine Only Begotten created I him; male and female created I them.
28. And the Gods said: We will bless them. And the Gods said: We will cause them to be fruitful, and multiply, and replenish the earth, and subdue it, and to have dominion over the fish of the sea, and over the fowl of the air, and over every living thing that moveth upon the earth. Abraham 4:27-28.	28. And I, God, blessed them, and said unto them: Be fruitful, and multiply, and replenish the earth, and subdue it, and have dominion over the fish of the sea, and over the fowl of the air, and over every living thing that moveth upon the earth. Moses 2:27-28.

God's commandment to men and women not only required them to bear children, but to work; and they were also to become acquainted with and control the laws and forces of nature and have dominion over all the plant and animal life in the entire world. Thus it was the Lord's will that the elements and forces of nature be understood by mortals and be brought under their subjection. Since God was the creator who stood in supreme control over the universe, differing from the angels in that He had the power of procreation, He, therefore, endowed mortal men and women with the power of procreation and gave unto them an extensive dominion within their realm similar to the powers and dominion that He exercised within His realm. Thus mortals were provided with sufficient intelligence and opportunity to advance toward Godhood.

The principal purpose of multiplying and replenishing the earth was to make it possible for all of God's spirit-children to have the opportunity to receive mortal bodies "that the earth might answer the end of its creation."[16] And the purpose of mortals subduing the earth and having dominion over the elements, animals, and plants was to provide men and women —the sons and daughters of God—with numerous experiences in order that they might through obedience to all gospel truths prepare themselves to come back into the presence of the Father and His Only Begotten Son. When He proclaimed the plan of salvation to His children at the Grand Council in heaven, the Eternal Father said: "they who keep their first estate shall be added upon; . . . and they who keep their second estate shall have glory added upon their heads for ever and ever."[17]

SECOND GREAT COMMANDMENT

Abraham's acount of the second great commandment:

12. And the Gods commanded the man, saying: Of every tree of the garden thou mayest freely eat,

13. But of the tree of knowledge of good and evil, thou shalt not eat of it; for in the time that thou eatest thereof, thou shalt surely die. Now I, Abraham, saw that it was after the Lord's time, which was after the time of Kolob; for as yet the Gods had not appointed unto Adam his reckoning. Abraham 5:12-13.

Moses' account of the second great commandment:

16. And I, the Lord God, commanded the man, saying: Of every tree of the garden thou mayest freely eat,

17. But of the tree of the knowledge of good and evil, thou shalt not eat of it, nevertheless, thou mayest choose for thyself, for it is given unto thee; but, remember that I forbid it, for in the day thou eatest thereof thou shalt surely die.   Moses 3:16-17.

The Lord made it clear to Adam that he could eat freely of all the fruits of the Garden except of the fruit "of the tree of knowledge of good and evil . . . for in the day thou eatest thereof thou shalt surely die." Therefore, as long as Adam did not partake of the forbidden fruit, he could have remained in Eden indefinitely and not become a mortal being. In the words of Father Lehi:

If Adam had not transgressed he would not have fallen, but he would have remained in the garden of Eden. And all things which were

---

[16]*Doctrine and Covenants* 49:15-16.
[17]Abraham 3:26.

created must have remained in the same state in which they were after they were created; and they must have remained forever, and had no end.[18]

Eating of the fruit, however, would make his body mortal and he then would be subject to earthly conditions. Both of the foregoing accounts point out that our first parents would die in the day[19] that they partook of the forbidden fruit; and the account in Abraham states that the day referred to was according to the measurement of time on Kolob which we have already learned was 1,000 years according to the reckoning of time on this earth. The Lord had reference to a spiritual death of Adam and Eve, and that prediction was fulfilled shortly after they partook of the forbidden fruit, which fact will soon be pointed out. Also, He meant the mortal death, that took place with Father Adam 930 years after he was cast out of the Garden of Eden, which was 70 years before the close of a day on Kolob.

In giving the second great commandment, God not only made it possible for Adam and Eve to become mortal beings, but He pointed out to them how that condition could be brought about—by partaking of the "forbidden fruit."

---

[18] 2 Nephi 2:22.
[19] Abraham's account uses the word "time" to mean day. This was done throughout his account of the six days (time) of creation and the seventh day (time) of rest.

Chapter 18

THE FALL

THE TWO GREAT COMMANDMENTS AND FREE AGENCY

It was pointed out in the last chapter that when God placed Adam and Eve in the Garden of Eden He gave them two great commandments, namely: first, "to be fruitful, and multiply, and replenish the earth;" second, not to partake of the fruit "of the tree of knowledge of good and evil," commonly referred to as "the forbidden fruit."[1] It was impossible for the first parents of the human race to obey both of God's commandments. If the first and most important one was observed, the second one of necessity must be broken. In other words, Adam and Eve could not bear children until they became mortal beings. Then why did God give them what seem to be two conflicting commandments? The most important reason was that they might have a choice to make and thereby exercise their free agency.[2] This truth was pointed out by the Lord to Father Adam and later to Enoch as is attested in the two following scriptures quoted from the *Pearl of Great Price:*

God's declaration to Adam:

56. And it is given unto them to know good from evil; wherefore they are agents unto themselves, and I have given unto you another law and commandment. Moses 6:56.

God's declaration to Enoch:

32. The Lord said unto Enoch: Behold these thy brethren; they are the workmanship of mine own hands, and I gave unto them their knowledge, in the day I created them; and in the Garden of Eden, gave I unto man his agency. Moses 7:32.

Agency is the eternal principle upon which personal growth is based and the principle which was the basic cause of the war in heaven and the fall of one-third of God's spirit-children. Lucifer attempted to do away with the agency of man but the Eternal Father would not permit him to do so;

---

[1]Abraham 4:28; 5:12-13; Moses 2:28; 3:16-17. The story of the creation of Eve has not been presented yet in either of the accounts, but it is understood that the two commandments applied to her as well as to Adam.
[2]James E. Talmage, *The Articles of Faith*, pp. 54-74.

therefore, the Lord insisted that Adam and Eve have their free agency in the Garden of Eden and each of their posterity was to be free to choose eternal life or spiritual death according to his desires.

FREE AGENCY AND MORAL RESPONSIBILITY

In modern revelation the Lord made known to the Prophet Joseph Smith the reason for giving Adam and Eve and all their posterity their free agency. He declared, "Behold, I gave unto him [man] that he should be an agent unto himself; and I gave unto him commandment;"[3] and the Lord pointed out His reason as follows:

> . . . that every man may act in doctrine and principle pertaining to futurity, according to the moral agency which I have given unto him, that every man may be accountable for his own sins in the day of judgment.[4]

And again the Lord declared:

> All truth is independent in that sphere in which God has placed it, to act for itself, as all intelligence also; otherwise there is no existence. Behold, here is the agency of man, and here is the condemnation of man; because that which was in the beginning is plainly manifest unto them, and they receive not the light. And every man whose spirit receiveth not the light is under condemnation.[5]

Whenever the Gospel of Jesus Christ has been on the earth, the holy prophets have proclaimed the doctrine of the agency of man and have permitted the people to choose whom they would serve. For example, Joshua, the prophet of God who succeeded Moses in the leadership of Israel, declared unto the people: "And if it seem evil unto you to serve the Lord, choose you this day whom ye will serve; . . . but as for me and my house, we will serve the Lord."[6] None of the ancient prophets have given a clearer explanation of the free agency of man than did Father Lehi to his children. In the words of the ancient prophet:

> Adam fell that men might be; and men are that they might have joy. And the Messiah cometh in the fullness of times, that he may redeem the children of men from the fall. And because they are redeemed from the fall they have become free forever, knowing good from evil; to

---

[3]*Doctrine and Covenants* 29:35.
[4]*Ibid.*, 101:78.
[5]*Ibid.*, 93:30-32; 37:4.
[6]Joshua 24:15; Alma 30:7-9.

act themselves and not to be acted upon, save it be by the punishment of the law at the great and last day, according to the commandments which God hath given. Wherefore, men are free according to the flesh; and all things are given them which are expedient unto them. And they are free to choose liberty and eternal life, through the great mediation of all men, or to choose captivity and death, according to the captivity and power of the devil; for he seeketh that all men might be miserable like unto himself.[7]

Other *Book of Mormon* prophets, such as Nephi, Jacob, Alma, and Samuel the Lamanite, continuously reminded the people of their agency and moral responsibility.[8] For example, the first of these prophets explained to the Nephites as follows: "Remember that you are free to act for yourselves—to choose the way of everlasting death or the way of eternal life."[9] And Samuel the Lamanite, the last named prophet in the foregoing group, warned the people in the city of Zarahemla in the following words:

He has given unto you that you might know good from evil, and he has given unto you that you might choose life or death; and ye can do good and be restored to that which is good, or have that which is good restored to you; or you can do evil and have that which is evil restored unto you.[10]

For the foregoing reasons, God gave unto Adam and Eve their free agency when He placed them in the Garden of Eden and throughout the entire history of the world He has not interfered with the agency of man.

CREATION OF WOMAN

Abraham's account of the creation of Eve:

14. And the Gods said: Let us make an help meet for the man, for it is not good that the man should be alone, therefore we will form an help meet for him.

15. And the Gods caused a deep sleep to fall upon Adam; and he slept, and they took one of his ribs, and closed up the flesh in the stead thereof;

16. And of the rib which the Gods had taken from man, formed they a woman, and brought her unto the man.

17. And Adam said: This was bone of my bones, and flesh of my flesh; now

Account in Moses of the creation of Eve:

18. And I, the Lord God, said unto mine Only Begotten, that it was not good that the man should be alone; wherefore, I will make an help meet for him.

20. . . . but as for Adam, there was not found an help meet for him.

21. And I, the Lord God, caused a deep sleep to fall upon Adam; and he slept, and I took one of his ribs and closed up the flesh in the stead thereof;

22. And the rib which I, the Lord God, had taken from man, made I a woman, and brought her unto the man.

[7]2 Nephi 2:25-29.
[8]*Ibid.*, 26:10; Alma 13:3.
[9]2 Nephi 10:23.
[10]Helaman 41:31.

she shall be called Woman, because she was taken out of man;

18. Therefore shall a man leave his father and his mother, and shall cleave unto his wife, and they shall be one flesh.

19. And they were both naked, the man and his wife, and were not ashamed.

21. . . . and for Adam, there was found an help meet for him.

Abraham 5:14-19, 21b.

23. And Adam said: This I know now is bone of my bones, and flesh of my flesh; she shall be called Woman, because she was taken out of man.

24. Therefore shall a man leave his father and his mother, and shall cleave unto his wife; and they shall be one flesh.

25. And they were both naked, the man and his wife, and were not ashamed.   Moses 3:18, 20b-25.

In the foregoing accounts, the story is told of the creation of Eve; but the principal meaning or symbolism in that story will not be presented yet. Later when the doctrine of celestial marriage is discussed the meaning of this scripture will be explained. It is sufficient at this point to present the accounts of the creation of woman merely to bring Mother Eve into the picture.

However, before leaving these scriptures we should observe that in each of them the statement is made that Adam and Eve "were both naked, the man and his wife, and were not ashamed." That statement is definite evidence that they were not ye mortal beings and experiencing the physical emotions of mortal men and women.

THE FALL

The account in the Book of Moses of the partaking of the forbidden fruit and of Adam's and Eve's becoming mortal beings:[11]

5. And now the serpent was more subtle than any beast of the field which I, the Lord God, had made.

6. And Satan put it into the heart of the serpent, (for he had drawn away many after him,) and he sought also to beguile Eve, for he knew not the mind of God, wherefore he sought to destroy the world.

7. And he said unto the woman: Yea, hath God said—Ye shall not eat of every tree of the garden? (And he spake by the mouth of the serpent.)

8. And the woman said unto the serpent: We may eat of the fruit of the trees of the garden;

9. But of the fruit of the tree which thou beholdest in the midst of the garden, God hath said—Ye shall not eat

also gave unto her husband with her, and he did eat.

13. And the eyes of them both were opened, and they knew that they had been naked. And they sewed fig-leaves together and made themselves aprons.

14. And they heard the voice of the Lord God, as they were walking in the garden, in the cool of the day; and Adam and his wife went to hide themselves from the presence of the Lord God amongst the trees of the garden.

15. And I, the Lord God, called unto Adam, and said unto him: Where goest thou?

16. And he said: I heard thy voice in the garden, and I was afraid, because I beheld that I was naked, and I hid myself.

[11]Abraham's account of Adam and Eve ends with the story of the creation of Eve.

of it, neither shall ye touch it, lest ye die.

10. And the serpent said unto the woman: Ye shall not surely die;

11. For God doth know that in the day ye eat thereof, then your eyes shall be opened, and ye shall be as gods, knowing good and evil.

12. And when the woman saw that the tree was good for food, and that it became pleasant to the eyes, and a tree to be desired to make her wise, she took of the fruit thereof, and did eat, and

17. And I, the Lord God, said unto Adam: Who told thee thou wast naked? Hast thou eaten of the tree whereof I commanded thee that thou shouldst not eat, if so thou shouldst surely die?

18. And the man said: The woman thou gavest me, and commandest that she should remain with me, she gave me of the fruit of the tree and I did eat.

19. And I, the Lord God, said unto the woman: What is this thing which thou hast done? And the woman said: The serpent beguiled me, and I did eat.

Moses 4:5-19.

The fact was pointed out in an earlier chapter that Lucifer and his angels had been cast down to earth as spirit-beings and given the following assignment: "I [the Lord] caused that he should be cast down; and he became Satan, yea, even the devil, the father of all lies, to deceive and to blind men, and to lead them captive at his will, even as many as would not hearken unto my voice."[12] Thus we find Lucifer in the Garden of Eden exerting his efforts to persuade Mother Eve to partake of the forbidden fruit and thereby become a mortal. It was not only God's will that the earth become filled with His sons and daughters, but it was also in harmony with the devil's desires. Satan had done all the damage to the plan of salvation and to God's spirit-children that he could in the spirit world before he was cast out; and now if he continued to destroy God's sons and daughters, it was necessary for them to become mortals and dwell upon the earth. For these reasons Lucifer was anxious for Adam and Eve to partake of the forbidden fruit.

In verses 13, 18 and 19, there is evidence that Adam and Eve had now become mortal. After they had partaken of the forbidden fruit "they knew that they had been naked," and in verses 18 and 19, Adam and Eve both attempted to shift the blame to somebody else which indicates that they were now quite mortal.

CONDITIONS OF MORTALITY

The account in the Book of Moses:

20. And I, the Lord God, said unto the serpent: Because thou hast done this thou shalt be cursed above all cattle, and above every beast of the field; upon thy belly shalt thou go, and dust shalt thou eat all the days of thy life;

26. And Adam called his wife's name Eve, because she was the mother of all living; for thus have I, the Lord God, called the first of all women, which are many.

27. Unto Adam, and also unto his wife, did I, the Lord God, make coats of skins, and clothed them.

[12]Moses 4:3-4.

21. And I will put enmity between thee and the woman, between thy seed and her seed; and he shall bruise thy head, and thou shalt bruise his heel.

22. Unto the woman, I, the Lord God, said: I will greatly multiply thy sorrow and thy conception. In sorrow thou shalt bring forth children, and thy desire shall be to thy husband, and he shall rule over thee.

23. And unto Adam, I, the Lord God, said: Because thou hast hearkened unto the voice of thy wife, and hast eaten of the fruit of the tree of which I commanded thee, saying— Thou shalt not eat of it, cursed shall be the ground for thy sake; in sorrow shalt thou eat of it all the days of thy life.

24. Thorns also, and thistles shall it bring forth to thee, and thou shalt eat the herb of the field.

25. By the sweat of thy face shalt thou eat bread, until thou shalt return unto the ground—for thou shalt surely die—for out of it wast thou taken: for dust thou wast, and unto dust shalt thou return.

28. And I, the Lord God, said unto mine Only, Begotten: Behold, the man is become as one of us to know good and evil; and now lest he put forth his hand and partake also of the tree of life, and eat and live forever,

29. Therefore I, the Lord God, will send him forth from the Garden of Eden, to till the ground from whence he was taken;

30. For as I, the Lord God, liveth, even so my words cannot return void, for as they go forth out of my mouth thy must be fulfilled.

31. So I drove out the man, and I placed at the east of the Garden of Eden, cherubim and a flaming sword, which turned every way to keep the way of the tree of life.

32. (And these are the words which I spake unto my servant Moses, and they are true even as I will; and I have spoken them unto you. See thou show them unto no man, until I command you, except to them that believe. Amen.) Moses 4:20-32.

The foregoing scripture gives an account of the curses that God placed on the serpent, on Eve, on Adam and on the earth; or, in other words, God explained to them the conditions that would confront them in mortality. Pains and suffering are part of the law or natural conditions connected with bearing children. Mortal or telestial earths produce thorns and thistles and mortal beings must earn their living through hard work by "the sweat of their faces."

Adam and Eve were cast from the Garden of Eden in order that they might not partake of "the tree of life, and eat and live forever." This means that if they partook of the "tree of life" which bore a "celestial fruit"[13] they would pass from mortality into immortality, i.e., they would die the mortal death, before they had time to obey the first great commandment of bearing children and thereby populating the earth.

SPIRITUAL AND TEMPORAL DEATHS

Before partaking of the forbidden fruit, Adam and Eve had intimate association with heavenly beings, because they were still immortals and living sinless lives. However, when

[13]Talmage, *op. cit.*, p. 68. See also Talmage's entire chapter on "Transgression and the Fall," *The Articles of Faith*, pp. 54-75.

they were placed in the Garden of Eden and given their physical bodies, a veil was drawn over their minds. They could no
longer remember their pre-mortal experiences, nor could they
recollect the plan of salvation with its various gospel principles
and ordinances. In this condition they partook of the forbidden fruit and thereafter were cast out of the Garden of Eden
and also from the presence of God. In the *Book of Mormon*
the doctrine is taught that the coming into mortality—or the
banishment from the presence of God with its accompanying
forgetfulness of the gospel plan—constituted the first death or
a spiritual death. Alma explained that our first parents were
cut off both temporally and spiritually from God's presence
and were free to follow their own inclinations. Since men's
spirits could never cease existing "and the fall had brought
upon mankind a spiritual death as well as a temporal; that is,
they were cast off from the presence of the Lord; it was expedient that mankind should be reclaimed from this spiritual
death."[14] In other words, it was imperative that Adam and
Eve receive the gospel again. In modern revelation, the Lord
confirmed to the Prophet Joseph Smith the doctrine taught by
Alma. To quote:

Wherefore, I, the Lord God, caused that he should be cast out from
the Garden of Eden, from my presence, because of his transgression,
wherein he became spiritually dead, which is the first death, even that
same death which is the last death, which is spiritual, which shall be pronounced upon the wicked when I shall say: Depart, ye cursed.[15]

Thus the fall caused Adam and Eve to become mortal
beings, made it possible for them to beget children, brought
upon them a spiritual death, and made them and their posterity
subject to a temporal death. Regarding the latter, the Lord
declared: "Thou shalt return unto the ground—for thou shalt
surely die—for out of it wast thou taken: for dust thou wast,
and unto dust thou shalt return."[16]

---

[14]Alma 42:6-14; 12:22-24; Helaman 14:16.
[15]*Doctrine and Covenants* 29:41.
[16]Moses 4:25.

Chapter 19

ATONEMENT AND MISSION OF JESUS CHRIST

ATONEMENT OF JESUS CHRIST

The atonement means literally *at-one-ment,* "denoting reconciliation, or the bringing into agreement of those who have been estranged." Since the fall brought upon Adam and Eve and all of their posterity an estrangement from God, it was necessary for a means to be improvised through which a reconciliation could be brought about. This reconciliation or atonement was to be accomplished through the work of a Savior—a Redeemer—who was endowed with sufficient power: first, to offer Himself as an infinite and eternal sacrifice for the sins of the world that through the saving graces of that sacrifice all men and women would eventually rise from the grave and receive immortality; and, second, to reveal to mortals the gospel truths and plan of salvation, or, in other words, to offer them eternal life. This latter phase of the atonement puts the burden of living in harmony with every gospel principle and ordinance upon the shoulders of each mortal being; therefore, complete atonement can never be attained by those who reject the Gospel of Jesus Christ. In the words of the ancient Prophet Amulek: "Therefore the wicked remain as though there had been no redemption made, except it be the loosing of the bands of death."[1]

As was pointed out in the last chapter, when Adam and Eve received their mortal bodies and partook of the forbidden fruit and became mortal beings, they died a spiritual death, i.e., they were cut off from the presence of God and had a veil drawn over their minds so they could not remember their premortal experiences nor the gospel plan. Thereupon Jesus Christ, the One who had been chosen and foreordained to be the Savior and Redeemer of the world, immediately began revealing the gospel plan of salvation to the first parents of the human race. Since that day that phase of the atonement has been carried forward.

[1]Alma 11:41.

Also, neither Adam nor Eve nor any of their posterity except Jesus Christ had the power within himself or herself to rise from the grave and come back into the presence of God. Thus, as previously suggested, in formulating the great plan of salvation for His children, the Eternal Father provided a Savior endowed with the power to lay down His life and pick it up again. The words of the Master of life and salvation on this subject are as follows:

Therefore doth my Father love me, because I lay down my life that I may take it again. No man taketh it from me, but I lay it down of myself. I have power to lay it down, and I have power to take it again. This commandment have I received of my Father.[2]

On another occasion Jesus testified of Himself as follows:

For as the Father hath life in himself, so hath he given to the Son to have life in himself; and hath given him authority to execute judgment also, because he is the Son of man.[3]

The Savior not only had power to raise His own body from the grave, but through His sacrifice He put into operation the process of universal resurrection. Thus all men throughout the entire world and throughout all ages of history will be brought forth from the grave. In the words of Paul, the ancient apostle:

For as in Adam all die, even so in Christ shall all be made alive. . . . In a moment, in the twinkling of an eye, at the last trump: for the trumpet shall sound, and the dead shall be raised incorruptible, and we shall be changed. For this corruptible must put on incorruption, and this mortal must put on immortality.[4]

IMMORTALITY AND ETERNAL LIFE

As previously mentioned but not discussed, the Lord proclaimed the following to Moses: *"For behold, this is my work and my glory—to bring to pass the immortality and eternal life of man."*[5] No other place in the standard works of the Church is there recorded a statement defining the activities of the Father and the Son and declaring what will add to their glory which measures up to the foregoing quotation from the

---

[2]John 10:17-18.
[3]*Ibid.*, 5:26-27.
[4]I Corinthians 15:22, 52-53.
[5]Moses 1:39.

Pearl of Great Price. In the effort to discuss and unfold the meaning of this great declaration made by God Himself, some of the teachings of the Prophet Joseph Smith and also statements made by the Savior and other holy prophets as recorded in the other three volumes of holy scripture will be quoted.

It is the work of God the Eternal Father and His Only Begotten Son to create worlds and place spirit beings in mortal tabernacles on those worlds and then to give to them the Gospel of Jesus Christ—which is the plan of salvation—in order that as many as will render obedience to the gospel plan will eventually come into the presence of the Father and the Son and receive eternal life in celestial glory. The greater the number of individuals who become glorified like God, even as God is, the greater becomes the glory of our Eternal Father and His Only Begotten Son. In the words of the Prophet Joseph Smith:

> Here, then, is eternal life—to know the only wise and true God; and you have got to learn how to be Gods yourselves, and to be kings and priests to God, the same as all Gods have done before you, namely, by going from one small degree to another, and from a small capacity to a great one; from grace to grace, from exaltation to exaltation, until you attain to the resurrection of the dead, and are able to dwell in everlasting burnings, and to sit in glory, as do those who sit enthroned in everlasting power. . . .

> These are the first principles of consolation. How consoling to the mourners when they are called to part with the husband, wife, father, mother, child, or dear relative, to know that, although the earthly tabernacle is laid down and dissolved, they shall rise again to dwell in everlasting burnings in immortal glory, not to sorrow, suffer, or die any more; but they shall be heirs of God and joint heirs with Jesus Christ. What is it? To inherit the same power, the same glory and the same exaltation, until you arrive at the station of a God, and ascend the throne of eternal power, the same as those who have gone before. What did Jesus do? Why; I do the things I saw my Father do when worlds came rolling into existence. My Father worked out his kingdom with fear and trembling, and I must do the same; and when I get my kingdom, I shall present it to my Father, so that he may obtain kingdom upon kingdom, and it will exalt him in glory. He will then take a higher exaltation, and I will take his place, and thereby become exalted myself. So that Jesus treads in the tracks of his Father, and inherits what God did before; and *God is thus glorified and exalted in the salvation and exaltation of all his children.*[6]

The meaning of immortality is to rise from the grave and live on forever.[7] Thus immortality is the gift of God, through Jesus Christ, to the entire human family, constituting one of

[6]Joseph Fielding Smith, *Teachings of the Prophet Joseph Smith,* pp. 346-348.
[7]*Doctrine and Covenants* 29:42-45; 75:5; 81:6.

the phases of the atonement. As was previously mentioned, every man, woman, and child will come forth in the resurrection to die no more, regardless of how righteous or how wicked they have been while in mortality. The grace of Jesus Christ is His free gift to all mankind in bringing them forth from the grave. The meaning of immortality was explained quite thoroughly by Amulek, the ancient Nephite prophet. To quote:

> Now there is a death which is called a temporal death: and the death of Christ shall loose the bands of this temporal death, that all shall be raised from this temporal death. The spirit and the body shall be reunited again in its perfect form; both limb and joint shall be restored to its proper frame, even as we now are at this time; . . .

> Now this restoration shall come to all, both old and young, both bond and free, both male and female, both the wicked and the righteous; and even there shall not so much as a hair of their heads be lost; but every thing shall be restored to its perfect frame. . . .

> Now, behold, I have spoken unto you concerning the death of the mortal body, and also concerning the resurrection of the mortal body. I say unto you that *this mortal body is raised to an immortal body, that is from death, even from the first death unto life, that they can die no more; their spirits uniting with their bodies, never to be divided; thus the whole becoming spiritual and immortal, that they can no more see corruption.*[8]

In the same sermon Amulek explained the meaning of eternal life, or the second phase of the atonement. He said: *"And he* [Jesus Christ] *shall come into the world to redeem his people; and he shall take upon him the transgressions of those who believe on his name; and these are they that shall have eternal life, and salvation cometh to none else."*[9] The Lord explained both immortality and eternal life to the Prophet Joseph Smith and definitely made it clear that they were entirely different things. To quote the words of the Lord:

> And thus did I, the Lord God, appoint unto man the days of his probation—*that by his natural death he might be raised in immortality unto eternal life,* even as many as would believe; and they that believe not unto *eternal damnation;* for they cannot be redeemed from their spiritual fall, because they repent not.[10]

Thus we see that eternal life is a special blessing to a relatively few people because of their obedience to the Gospel of Jesus Christ. The Lord declared to the people of His Church in the latter days the following: "If you keep my command-

---

[8]Alma 11:42-45.
[9]*Ibid.,* 11:40; *Helaman* 14:12-19; *Doctrine and Covenants* 19:16-19.
[10]*Doctrine and Covenants* 29:43-44.

ments and endure to the end you shall have eternal life, which is the greatest of all the gifts of God."[11] "He that hath eternal life is rich."[12]

Eternal life is the kind of life possessed by the Heavenly Father and His Only Begotten Son; therefore, those mortals who attain it shall dwell in the presence of those Divine Beings. They shall rise to the powers of Godhood and become even as God is. Exaltation and eternal life are one and the same thing. Those who receive it shall have the power of eternal increase; in other words, the power to beget spirit-children and create worlds to place those children upon. Eternal life can be gained only by and through obedience to all the principles and ordinances of the Gospel of Jesus Christ. Thus the Lord declared to Enoch (as recorded in the *Pearl of Great Price*) that He had given mortals the gospel in order that they might "enjoy the words of eternal life in this world and eternal life in the world to come, even immortal glory."[13] One of the eternal decrees that came from the lips of the Savior in the latter days is as follows:

Strait is the gate and narrow is the way that leadeth unto exaltation and continuation of the lives. . . . If ye receive me in the world, then shall ye know me, and shall receive your exaltation; that where I am ye shall be also. This is eternal lives--to know the only wise and true God, and Jesus Christ, whom he hath sent. I am he. Receive ye, therefore, my law.[14]

Thus, to summarize, immortality means to be resurrected and continue to live forever. Eternal life, on the other hand, is the condition of life that those who live righteous lives and render obedience to all the words that have come from the mouth of God will enjoy throughout the ages in the kingdom of God. In fact, it means exaltation. He who attains eternal life in its fullest sense becomes a God; therefore, he receives the blessings of complete atonement.

Adam's Knowledge Regarding Jesus Christ

After Adam and Eve had been driven from the Garden of Eden and had died the spiritual death, Jesus Christ began to reveal to them "the words of eternal life," or, in other words,

[11]*Ibid.*, 14:7; 6:13.
[12]*Ibid.*, 11:7.
[13]*Moses* 6:58.
[14]*Doctrine and Covenants* 132:22-24; John 17:3; 2 Nephi 9:15, 18; Mosiah 2:41.

the Gospel of Jesus Christ. Alma explained the interest that God had in Adam and Eve in the following words:

[God] saw that it was expedient that men should know concerning the things whereof he had appointed unto them; therefore, he sent angels to converse with them, who caused men to behold of his glory. And they began from that time forth to call on his name; therefore, God conversed with men, and made known unto them the plan of redemption, which had been prepared from the foundation of the world; and this he made known unto them according to their faith and repentance and their holy works.[15]

The scripture which contains the most complete account of Father Adam receiving through revelation the Gospel of Jesus Christ—the same gospel with the same principles and ordinances that we have today—is the *Pearl of Great Price*. The gospel was given to Adam and Eve gradually, just as we learn the principles of eternal truth one by one. According to the account given in the Book of Moses, Adam and Eve had sons and daughters and grandsons and granddaughters before they received the following revelation:

Adam receives the law of sacrifice and revelation regarding the atonement of Jesus Christ:

4. And Adam and Eve, his wife, called upon the name of the Lord, and they heard the voice of the Lord from the way toward the Garden of Eden, speaking unto them, and they saw him not; for they were shut out from his presence.

5. And he gave unto them commandments, that they should worship the Lord their God, and should offer the firstlings of their flocks, for an offering unto the Lord. And Adam was obedient unto the commandments of the Lord.

6. And after many days an angel of the Lord appeared unto Adam, saying: Why dost thou offer sacrifices unto the Lord? And Adam said unto him: I know not, save the Lord commanded me.

7. And then the angel spake, saying: This thing is a similitude of the sacrifice of the Only Begotten of the Father, which is full of grace and truth.

8. Wherefore, thou shalt do all that thou doest in the name of the Son, and thou shalt repent and call upon God in the name of the Son forevermore.

9. And in that day the Holy Ghost fell upon Adam, which beareth record of the Father and the Son, saying: I am the Only Begotten of the Father from the beginning, henceforth and forever, that as thou hast fallen thou mayest be redeemed, and all mankind, even as many as will.

10. And in that day Adam blessed God and was filled, and began to prophesy concerning all the families of the earth, saying: Blessed be the name of God, for because of my transgression my eyes are opened, and in this life I shall have joy, and again in the flesh I shall see God.

11. And Eve, his wife, heard all these things and was glad, saying: Were it not for our transgression we never should have had seed, and never should have known good and evil, and the joy of our redemption, and the eternal life which God giveth unto all the obedient.

12. And Adam and Eve blessed the name of God, and they made all things known unto their sons and their daughters. Moses 5:4-12.

[15]Alma 12:28-34; *Doctrine and Covenants* 29:42-45.

In the foregoing revelations, Adam and Eve received knowledge regarding the following principles and doctrines of the Gospel of Jesus Christ: sacrifice as a similitude of the Only Begotten Son; atonement of Jesus Christ; prayer to be offered to the Father in the name of the Son; worship of God continuously; and redemption and resurrection of mankind. Mother Eve's statement regarding eternal life shows that they had a clear and true concept of that important gospel doctrine. She also understood that the partaking of the forbidden fruit made it possible for mortals to know the difference between good and evil in this world and above all she expressed her gratitude for the opportunity to become the mother of children, which opportunity would not have been afforded her if she had not become a mortal. Lehi confirms Eve's statement wherein he declared: "Adam fell that men might be; and men are, that they might have joy."[16]

---

[16] 2 Nephi 2:25.

Chapter 20

THE HOLY PRIESTHOOD

MEANING OF PRIESTHOOD

Priesthood is the power of God. It is the power by which He created the heavens and the earth. Since the Eternal Father understands all of the eternal laws of nature He has the power to regulate and use those laws according to His divine will and purposes; therefore, the power by which He creates and controls the heavenly bodies is Priesthood.

At the Grand Council in heaven when God the Eternal Father was planning this mortal earth with His spirit-children and was explaining to them the conditions that they would meet in mortality, He selected Jesus Christ to be the Savior of the world and foreordained Him to that great calling. The Only Begotten Son was to be the Mediator between God and mortal beings through and by Whom all gospel truths were to be revealed to the inhabitants of the earth throughout its entire telestial and terrestrial probations. Therefore, in regards to its operation on this earth, the Eternal Father honored the Savior by naming the gospel after Him, namely: "the Gospel of Jesus Christ." God also bestowed upon His Only Begotten Son the keys of authority to perform all the ordinances of the gospel and to declare all the divine truths which emanate from the throne of the Most High. Again He honored His Son by naming the Priesthood *"the Holy Priesthood, after the Order of the Son of God."*[1] Thus Jesus Christ was foreordained to be the first great High Priest of the sons and daughters of God who should inhabit this earth. His calling was to minister the gospel ordinances and principles and to hold the keys of the Holy Priesthood under the immediate direction of the Eternal

[1]*Doctrine and Covenants* 107:3.

Father. Joseph Smith described the workings of the Priesthood as follows:

[The Holy Priesthood after the Order of the Son of God or Melchizedek Priesthood holds] the keys of the Kingdom of God in all ages of the world to the latest posterity on the earth; and is the channel through which all knowledge, doctrine, the plan of salvation and every important matter is revealed from heaven. . . . It is the channel through which the Almighty commenced revealing his glory at the beginning of the creation of this earth, and through which He has continued to reveal Himself to the children of men to the present time, and through which He will make known His purposes to the end of time.[2]

Priesthood is the authority by which all the gospel ordinances are performed and are made vaild and binding not only in this world but also in the world to come. Only those contracts, ordinances, and blessings which are sealed upon us by the power of the Priesthood will be recognized throughout the eternities by God the Father and His Only Begotten Son. Priesthood is the authority by which all the great prophets in the various dispensations have organized and operated the true Church of Jesus Christ. At no time in history has the true Church been on the earth unless the Priesthood was here. The Lord revealed the following pertinent doctrine to the Prophet Joseph Smith:

And this greater priesthood administereth the gospel and holdeth the keys of the mysteries of the kingdom, even the key of the knowledge of God. Therefore, in the ordinances thereof, the power of godliness is manifest. And without the ordinances thereof, and the authority of the priesthood, the power of godliness is not manifest unto men in the flesh.[3]

Elder Joseph Fielding Smith explained the meaning of Priesthood in the following words:

[Priesthood] is the authority of God delegated to man, by which he is given power to officiate in all the ordinances of the gospel, speak in the name of the Lord, perform all duties pertaining to the building up of the kingdom of God on the earth, and obtain knowledge of revelation.[4]

Thus the Prophet Joseph Smith defined Priesthood as being the *"power of God delegated to man to act in his stead here on earth."*

[2] Joseph Fielding Smith, *Teachings of the Prophet Joseph Smith*, pp. 166-167.
[3] *Doctrine and Covenants* 84:19-21.
[4] Joseph Fielding Smith, *The Way to Perfection*, p. 70.

CREATION THROUGH PRIESTHOOD

God revealed to Moses that He created the earth by the power of the Priesthood:

31. And behold, the glory of the Lord was upon Moses, so that Moses stood in the presence of God, and talked with him face to face. And the Lord God said unto Moses: For mine own purpose have I made these things. Here is wisdom and it remaineth in me.

32. And by the word of my power, have I created them, which is mine Only Begotten Son, who is full of grace and truth.

33. And worlds without number have I created; and I also created them for mine own purpose; and by the Son I created them, which is mine Only Begotten.

35. But only an account of this earth, and the inhabitants thereof, give I unto you. For behold, there are many worlds that have passed away by the word of my power. And there are many that now stand, and innumerable are they unto man; but all things are numbered unto me, for they are mine and I know them.   Moses 1:31-33, 35.

1. And it came to pass that the Lord spake unto Moses, saying: Behold, I reveal unto you concerning this heaven, and this earth; write the words which I speak. I am the Beginning and the End, the Almighty God; by mine Only Begotten I created these things; yea, in the beginning I created the heaven, and the earth upon which thou standest.

5. And I, God, called the light Day; and the darkness, I called Night; and this I did by the word of my power, and it was done as I spake. . . .
          Moses 2:1, 5a.

In verse 32 the Lord said, "And by the word of my power, have I created them, which is mine Only Begotten Son;" and in the following verse He said, "by the Son I created them." He made a similar statement in Moses 2:1; and in verses 35 and 5 He stated that He had created many worlds "by the word of my power." The meaning of these statements is that God created the world through the power[5] of the Priesthood which, as previously pointed out, was named "the Holy Priesthood after the Order of the Son of God."

CREATION THROUGH PRIESTHOOD CONFIRMED
BY MODERN REVELATION

The Lord revealed to the Prophet Joseph Smith the part that Christ played as a creator in conjunction with the Eternal Father and this revelation makes it clear that "the word of my power" (verses 35, 5) means Jesus Christ. Thus through the knowledge, power, and intelligence of the Gods, in other words, through the Holy Priesthood, the heavens and the earth were organized. Following is the word of the Lord regarding by what power the earth was created:

And John saw and bore record of the fulness of my glory. . . . And he bore record, saying: I saw his [Jesus Christ's] glory, that he was in

[5]For a more complete statement regarding the "power of the Priesthood" see Chapter 11, pages 62-63.

the beginning, before the world was; therefore, in the beginning the Word was, for he [Jesus] was the Word, even the messenger of salvation—the light and the Redeemer of the world; the Spirit of truth, who came into the world, because the world was made by him, and in him was the life of men and the light of men. The worlds were made by him; men were made by him; all things were made by him, and through him, and of him.

And I, John, bear record that I beheld his glory, as the glory of the Only Begotten of the Father, full of grace and truth, even the Spirit of truth.[6]

In the same revelation the following famous statement was made to the Prophet Joseph: "The glory of God is intelligence, or, in other words, light and truth." Thus the light and knowledge of all of the eternal truths that the Father and the Son possess constitutes their intelligence; and their use of that divine knowledge in organizing matter into worlds for the habitation of mortals gives to the Creator glory.

ADAM AND THE PRIESTHOOD

God declared that Adam held the Priesthood:

67. And thou art after the order of him who was without beginning of days or end of years, from all eternity to all eternity.   Moses 6:67.

Abraham's statement:

31. But the records of the fathers, even the patriarchs, concerning the right of Priesthood, the Lord my God preserved in mine own hands: . . .

3. It [the Priesthood] was conferred upon me from the fathers; it came down from the fathers, from the beginning of time, yea, even from the beginning, or before the foundations of the earth to the present time, even the right of the firstborn, on the first man, who is Adam, our first father, through the fathers, unto me.   Abraham 1:31a, 3.

Verse 67 means that Adam received "the Holy Priesthood after the Order of the Son of God," and that order of the Priesthood "was without beginning of days or end of years." Although he was speaking of Melchizedek instead of Father Adam, the Prophet Joseph Smith made it very clear in his translation of the *Bible* that the foregoing explanation is correct. To quote:

For this Melchizedek was ordained a priest after the order of the Son of God, which *order was without father, without mother, without descent, having neither beginning of days nor end of life.* And all those who are ordained unto this priesthood are made like unto the Son of God, abiding a priest continually.[7]

[6]*Doctrine and Covenants* 93:6-11, 1-23; John 1:1-15.
[7]Joseph Smith, *Inspired Version, Bible*, Hebrews 7:3

Also, in the *Book of Mormon* the same facts are plainly taught. In that sacred scripture, the following is recorded:

This High Priesthood being after the order of his Son, which order was from the foundation of the world: or in other words, being without beginning of days or end of years, being prepared from eternity to all eternity, according to his foreknowledge of all things. Now they were ordained after this manner: Being called with a holy calling, and ordained with a holy ordinance, and taking upon them the High Priesthood of the holy order, which calling, and ordinance, and High Priesthood, is without beginning or end: Thus they become High Priests forever, after the order of the Son, the Only Begotten of the Father.[8]

Thus the other holy scriptures not only sustain but amplify and explain the teachings of the *Pearl of Great Price*.

ADAM'S AND NOAH'S PRIESTHOOD

Following the Grand Council in heaven at which Lucifer and his hosts revolted against the gospel plan of salvation and the Messiahship of Jesus, Adam—who was known as Michael the Archangel—led the righteous ones in heaven in sustaining the eternal gospel plan and Jesus as the Christ. Because of his righteousness, obedience, intelligence and valor in the cause of truth, the Father appointed Michael to a position of power and leadership, that of being the father of the human family. He was foreordained in the spirit world to this great calling and made the second great High Priest, the one next in authority to Jesus Christ.[9] Adam at that time stood among the council of the Gods and was one of the creators of this earth, working in conjunction with the Father and the Son.

Then when Adam was placed upon the earth and became a mortal being, he was re-ordained to the Priesthood and given the great calling and position to which he had been foreordained. At that time, Father Adam not only received the Priesthood, but he also received the keys of the Priesthood. These he received directly from Jesus Christ, and in turn bestowed them upon his posterity. The Savior appointed Adam to hold the keys of the Priesthood throughout all gospel dispensations until the Son of Man should come to reign.[10] Therefore, wherever the Priesthood has been taken from the earth as a result of apostasy, the keys have been brought back

---

[8]Alma 13:7-9.
[9]Smith, *Teachings of the Prophet Joseph Smith*, pp. 157, 158, 168-169.
[10]*Ibid.*, pp. 167-168; *Doctrine and Covenants* 88: 112-115; 128:21.

from heaven by Adam's authority.[11] When angels are sent as messengers to restore the ordinances of the gospel and the Priesthood, "these angels also are under the direction of Michael or Adam, who acts under the direction of the Lord."[12]

The Prophet Joseph Smith made the following statement regarding Adam's position and keys of authority:

> The Priesthood was first given to Adam; he obtained the First Presidency, and held the keys of it from generation to generation. He obtained it in the Creation, before the world was formed. . . . He had dominion given him over every living creature. He is Michael the Archangel, spoken of in the scriptures. Then to Noah, who is Gabriel; he stands next in authority to Adam in the Priesthood; he was called of God to this office, and was the father of all living in his day, and to him was given the dominion. These men held keys first on earth and then in heaven.[13]

Modern revelation attests the teachings of the *Pearl of Great Price* regarding Adam's holding the Priesthood as did the patriarchs who succeeded him. In speaking of the Patriarchal Order of the Priesthood, the Lord revealed the following to the Prophet Joseph Smith:

> The order of this priesthood was confirmed to be handed down from father to son, . . . This order was instituted in the days of Adam, and came down by lineage in the following manner: From Adam to Seth, who was ordained by Adam at the age of sixty-nine years, . . . Enos was ordained at the age of one hundred and thirty-four years and four months, by the hand of Adam. God called upon Cainan in the wilderness in the fortieth year of his age; and he met Adam in journeying to the place Shedolamak. He was eighty-seven years old when he received his ordination. Mahalaleel was four hundred and ninety-six years and seven days old when he was ordained by the hand of Adam, who also blessed him. Jared was two hundred years old when he was ordained under the hand of Adam, who also blessed him. Enoch was twenty-five years old when he was ordained under the hand of Adam. . . . Methuselah was one hundred years old when he was ordained under the hand of Adam. Lamech was thirty-two years old when he was ordained under the hand of Seth. Noah was ten years old when he was ordained under the hand of Methuselah.[14]

ADAM'S PROPHECY AND NOAH'S ORDINATION

Adam's prophecy:

7. Now this same Priesthood, which was in the beginning, shall be in the end of the world also.

8. Now this prophecy Adam spake, as he was moved upon by the Holy Ghost, . . .   Moses 6:7-8a.

Noah's ordination:

19. And the Lord ordained Noah after his own order, and commanded him that he should go forth and declare his Gospel unto the children of men, even as it was given unto Enoch.   Moses 8:19.

[11]Smith, *op. cit.,* p. 157.
[12]*Ibid.,* p. 168.
[13]*Ibid.,* p. 157.
[14]*Doctrine and Covenants* 107:40-57.

Adam's prophecy was fulfilled when the Holy Priesthood and the Gospel of Jesus Christ were restored to the Prophet Joseph Smith over a hundred years ago.

Modern revelation not only declares that Noah, or Gabriel, was ordained to the Priesthood, as was recorded in the *Pearl of Great Price,* but that he held important keys and stands next in authority to Adam as the third great High Priest over the inhabitants of this earth.

Conclusions

Thus we have learned in this chapter that the most vital thing in regard to the accomplishment of the will and the mind of the Lord in the heavens and the earth is Priesthood. Through that power all of God's mighty works have been performed and will continue to be consummated throughout the ages. In fact, through that power worlds are created, all of the gospel ordinances are made binding, and mortal beings are brought back into the presence of God and given eternal life. Therefore, it was necessary for the Lord to give to the first man on earth the keys of the Holy Priesthood after the Order of the Son of God and also to continue to give similar keys to the prophet-leaders of each gospel dispensation; otherwise it would not be possible for the work of the Lord to be performed among the children of men and all of His purposes be fulfilled.

Chapter 21

DIVINE AUTHORITY

ABRAHAM AND THE PRIESTHOOD

This chapter is a continuation of the discussion of the Holy Priesthood, drawing much of the material from the items presented in the *Pearl of Great Price.*

Abraham's desire to receive the Priesthood and its fulfillment:

1. In the land of the Chaldeans, at the residence of my father, I, Abraham, saw that it was needful for me to obtain another place of residence;

2. And, finding there was greater happiness and peace and rest for me, I sought for the blessings of the fathers, and the right whereunto I should be ordained to administer the same; having been myself a follower of righteousness, desiring also to be one who possessed great knowledge, and to be a greater follower of righteousness, and to possess a greater knowledge, and to be a father of many nations, a prince of peace, and desiring to receive instructions, and to keep the commandments of God, I became a rightful heir, a High Priest, holding the right belonging to the fathers.

3. And it was conferred upon me from the fathers; it came down from the fathers, from the beginning of time, yea, even from the beginning, or before the foundations of the earth to the present time, even the right of the firstborn, on the first man, who is Adam, our first father, through the fathers, unto me.

4. I sought for mine appointment unto the Priesthood according to the appointment of God unto the fathers concerning the seed.

16. And his voice was unto me: Abraham, Abraham, behold, my name is Jehovah, . . .

18. Behold, I will lead thee by my hand, and I will take thee, to put upon thee my name, even the Priesthood of thy father, and my power shall be over thee.

19. As it was with Noah so shall it be with thee; but through thy ministry my name shall be known in the earth forever, for I am thy God.

Abraham 1:1-4, 16a, 18-19.

6. But I, Abraham, and Lot, my brother's son, prayed unto the Lord, and the Lord appeared unto me, and said unto me: Arise, and take Lot with thee; for I have purposed to take thee away out of Haran, and to make of thee a minister to bear my name in a strange land which I will give unto thy seed after thee for an everlasting possession, when they hearken to my voice.

9. And I will make of thee a great nation, and I will bless thee above measure, and make thy name great among all nations, and thou shalt be a blessing unto thy seed after thee, that in their hands they shall bear this ministry and Priesthood unto all nations;

10. And I will bless them through thy name; for as many as receive this Gospel shall be called after thy name, and shall be accounted thy seed, and shall rise up and bless thee, as their father;

11. And I will bless them that bless thee, and curse them that curse thee; and in thee (that is, in thy Priesthood) and in thy seed (that is, thy Priesthood), for I give unto thee a promise that this right shall continue in thee, and in thy seed after thee (that is to say, the literal seed, or the seed of the body) shall all the families of the earth be blessed, even with the blessings of the Gospel, which are the blessings of salvation, even of life eternal.

Abraham 2:6, 9-11.

135

Our interest at this point in the foregoing quotation from the Book of Abraham is to study the material as it relates to the Priesthood; and Abraham's other righteous desires will be presented in a later chapter.

In verses 2 and 3 of the foregoing scripture, Abraham said, "I became a rightful heir, a High Priest, holding the right belonging to the fathers . . . even the right of the firstborn." Modern revelation makes it clear that by this statement Abraham meant that he was the oldest son in the family, had lived a righteous life, and was thereby entitled to the High Priesthood and to be ordained a patriarch.[1] In verses 18 and 19 God promised Abraham the same divine powers that Noah had held, and that Abraham's posterity would be a nation of Priesthood bearers (verses 9-11). Through the Priesthood and the gospel, which he and his posterity would possess, the entire world would be blessed. The latter promise was fulfilled through the mission of the Savior. It should be recalled that it was through the literal seed of Abraham that Jesus came into mortality; and every family and every person in the entire world has been blessed through the Priesthood after the order of the Son of God and through the plan of salvation which Christ has promulgated from age to age. It was only through the power of the Priesthood that the Redeemer was able to break the bonds of death and bring about universal resurrection, thereby giving to mortals immortality. It is also through the Priesthood that any man or woman will ever be able to receive exaltation in the celestial glory, i.e., eternal life. Thus we learn of the great significance and meaning of the covenant of Priesthood that the Lord made with Father Abraham.

ABRAHAM'S RECEIVING THE PRIESTHOOD FROM MELCHIZEDEK

According to modern revelation, God's promises to Abraham have been and will continue to be fulfilled in every detail. The Lord revealed the fact to Joseph Smith that the ancient Hebrew Patriarch received the Priesthood from the great High Priest Melchizedek, king of Salem (Jerusalem). In that revelation, Abraham's line of Priesthood is traced back to Michael, the Ancient of Days, as follows:

Abraham received the Priesthood from Melchizedek, who received it through the lineage of his fathers, even till Noah; and from Noah till

[1] *Doctrine and Covenants* 107:40.

Enoch, through the lineage of their fathers; and from Enoch to Abel, who was slain by the conspiracy of his brother, who received the Priesthood by the commandments of God, by the hand of his father Adam, who was the first man.[2]

One of the most significant and comprehensive descriptions of the Holy Priesthood after the Order of the Son of God found in any of the scriptures is recorded in the *Inspired Version* of the *Bible,* as prepared by the Prophet Joseph Smith through the inspiration of the Lord. This description of the Priesthood is presented in connection with the ordaining of Abraham to the Priesthood and for that reason it will be quoted here:

And Melchizedek, king of Salem, brought forth bread and wine; and he break bread and blest it; and he blest the wine, he being the priest of the most high God. And he gave to Abram, and he blessed him, and said, Blessed Abram, thou art a man of the most high God, possessor of heaven and of earth; and blessed is the name of the most high God, which hath delivered thine enemies into thine hand.

And Abram gave him tithes of all he had taken. . . . Wherefore, Abram paid unto him tithes of all that he had, of all the riches which he possessed, which God had given him more than that which he had need. . . .

And Melchizedek lifted up his voice and blessed Abram.

Now Melchizedek was a man of faith, who wrought righteousness; and when a child he feared God, and stopped the mouths of lions, and quenched the violence of fire. And thus, having been approved of God, he was ordained an high priest after the order of the covenant which God had made with Enoch, it being after the order of the Son of God; which order came, not by man, nor the will of man; neither by father nor mother; neither by beginning of days nor end of years; but of God; and it was delivered unto men by the calling of his own voice, according to his own will, unto as many as believed on his name.

For God having sworn unto Enoch and unto his seed with an oath by himself; that every one being ordained after this order and calling should have power, by faith, to break mountains, to divide the seas, to dry up waters, to turn them out of their course; to put at defiance the armies of nations, to divide the earth, to break every band, to stand in the presence of God; to do all things according to his will, according to his command, subdue principalities and powers; and this by the will of the Son of God which was from before the foundation of the world.

And men having this faith, coming up unto this order of God, were translated and taken up into heaven. And now, Melchizedek was a priest of this order; therefore he obtained peace in Salem, and was called the Prince of peace. And his people wrought righteousness, and obtained heaven. . . . And this Melchizedek, having thus established righteousness, was called the king of heaven by his people, or, in other words, the King

[2]*Ibid.,* 84:14-16.

of peace. And he lifted up his voice, and he blessed Abram, being the high priest, and the keeper of the storehouse of God; him whom God had appointed to receive tithes for the poor.[3]

MOSES AND THE PRIESTHOOD

Through the power of the Priesthood Moses caused Satan to depart:

19. And now, when Moses had said these words, Satan cried with a loud voice, and rent upon the earth, and commanded, saying: I am the Only Begotten, worship me.

20. And it came to pass that Moses began to fear exceedingly; and as he began to fear, he saw the bitterness of hell. Nevertheless, calling upon God, he received strength, and he commanded, saying: Depart from me Satan, for this one God only will I worship, which is the God of glory.

21. And now Satan began to tremble, and the earth shook; and Moses received strength, and called upon God, saying: In the name of the Only Begotten, depart hence, Satan.

22. And it came to pass that Satan cried with a loud voice, with weeping, and wailing, and gnashing of teeth; and he departed hence, even from the presence of Moses, that he beheld him not.

23. And now of this thing Moses bore record; but because of wickedness it is not had among the children of men.   Moses 1:19-23.

God's declaration to Moses of the powers of the Priesthood that Moses possessed:

24. And it came to pass that when Satan had departed from the presence of Moses, that Moses lifted up his eyes unto heaven, being filled with the Holy Ghost, which beareth record of the Father and the Son;

25. And calling upon the name of God, he beheld his glory again, for it was upon him; and he heard a voice, saying: Blessed art thou, Moses, for I, the Almighty, have chosen thee, and thou shalt be made stronger than many waters; for they shall obey thy command as if thou wert God.

26. And lo, I am with thee, even unto the end of thy days; for thou shalt deliver my people from bondage, even Israel my chosen.   Moses 1:24-26.

When Moses said (verse 20-21) "Depart from me, Satan, . . . in the name of the Only Begotten, depart hence, Satan," Lucifer, "with weeping, and wailing, and gnashing of teeth" (verse 22), departed. He did so because Moses had given the command through the power of the Holy Priesthood which he held, the name of the "Only Begotten" being the key-word in exercising that power. Even devils must obey when an authorized servant of God commands them to depart in the name of the Son of God. Also, the sick are healed and other mighty works performed through the same power and through the same name. For example, shortly after the death of the Savior, Peter and John, two of the Lord's aspostles, passed through the temple gates at Jerusalem where "a certain man lame from his mother's womb . . . asked alms of them." Peter replied:

[3]Joseph Smith, *Inspired Version, Bible,* Genesis 14:17-20, 39, 25-34, 36-38; Alma 13:1-19.

"Silver and gold have I none; but such as I have give I thee: *In the name of Jesus Christ of Nazareth rise up and walk.*"[4] Thereupon the lame man was immediately healed. The following day Peter and John were brought before the rulers of the Jews to account for the healing that had been performed. We shall now let the scripture continue the story:

> And when they [the Jewish rulers] had set them [Peter and John] in the midst, they asked, By what power, or by what name, have ye done this?
>
> Then Peter, filled with the Holy Ghost, said unto them, Ye rulers of the people, and elders of Israel, If we this day be examined of the good deed done to the impotent man, by what means he is made whole; be it known unto you all, and to all the people of Israel, that *by the name of Jesus Christ of Nazareth,* whom ye crucified, whom God raised from the dead, *even by him doth this man stand here before you whole.*[5]

When God said unto Moses that "thou shalt be made stronger than many waters; for they shall obey thy command as if thou wert God" (verse 25), the Lord was describing the powers of the Priesthood which had been given to Moses. The *Bible* sustains the teachings of the *Pearl of Great Price* by giving accounts of the fulfillment of the words of the Lord to Moses. In fact, the Holy Book shows that on many occasions Moses used the Priesthood to perform miracles. For example: through the Priesthood he parted the waters of the Red Sea; he brought water forth from a rock; he caused the plagues to come upon the Egyptians; and, most important of all, as previously discussed, "he saw God face to face, and talked with him."

MOSES' PRIESTHOOD AND MODERN REVELATION

The *Doctrine and Covenants* states that Moses received the Holy Priesthood "under the hand of his father-in-law, Jethro."[6] In speaking to the members of the Church of Jesus Christ of Latter-day Saints in 1832, the Lord said:

> And the sons of Moses and of Aaron shall be filled with the glory of the Lord, upon Mount Zion in the Lord's house, whose sons are ye; and also many whom I have called and sent forth to build up my church. For whoso is faithful unto the obtaining these two priesthoods of which I have spoken, and the magnifying their calling, are sanctified by the Spirit unto the renewing of their bodies. They become the sons of Moses

[4]Acts 3:6-16.
[5]*Ibid.*, 4:7-10; James 5:14.
[6]*Doctrine and Covenants* 84:6.

and of Aaron and the seed of Abraham, and the church and kingdom, and the elect of God. And also all they who receive this priesthood receive me, saith the Lord; . . . and he that receiveth me receiveth my Father; and he that receiveth my Father receiveth my Father's kingdom; therefore all that my Father hath shall be given unto him. And this is according to the oath and covenant which belongeth to the priesthood.[7]

Moses not only held the Priesthood, but he also held important keys of the Priesthood. These he brought back to Joseph Smith and Oliver Cowdery in the Kirtland temple on April 3, 1836. Regarding this event, the Prophet wrote:

After this vision closed, the heavens were again opened unto us; and Moses appeared before us, and committed unto us the keys of the gathering of Israel from the four parts of the earth, and the leading of the ten tribes from the land of the north.[8]

DENIED THE PRIESTHOOD

The descendants of Cain and Ham could not hold the Priesthood:

21. Now this king of Egypt was a descendant from the loins of Ham, and was a partaker of the blood of the Canaanites by birth.

22. From this descent sprang all the Egyptians, and thus the blood of the Canaanites was preserved in the land.

23. The land of Egypt being first discovered by a woman, who was the daughter of Ham, and the daughter of Egyptus, which in the Chaldean signifies Egypt, which signifies that which is forbidden.

24. When this woman discovered the land it was under water, who afterward settled her sons in it; and thus, from Ham, sprang that race which preserved the curse in the land.

25. Now the first government of Egypt was established by Pharaoh, the eldest son of Egyptus, the daughter of Ham, and it was after the manner of the government of Ham, which was patriarchal.

26. Pharaoh, being a righteous man, established his kingdom and judged his people wisely and justly all his days, seeking earnestly to imitate that order established by the fathers in the first generations, in the days of the first patriarchal reign, even in the reign of Adam, and also of Noah, his father, who blessed him with the blessings of the earth, and with the blessings of wisdom, but cursed him as pertaining to the Priesthood.

27. Now, Pharaoh being of that lineage by which he could not have the right of Priesthood, notwithstanding the Pharaohs would fain claim it from Noah, through Ham, therefore my father was led away by their idolatry.

Abraham 1:21-27.

Since the Lord appeared unto Cain and conversed with him many times before Cain killed Abel, Cain must have held the Priesthood.[9] God said unto Cain, "For from this time forth thou shalt be the father of his [Satan's] lies; thou shalt be called Perdition;"[10] and the Lord cursed Cain with severe

---

[7]*Ibid.*, 84:32-39.
[8]*Ibid.*, 110:11.
[9]Joseph Fielding Smith, *The Way to Perfection*, p. 98.
[10]Moses 5:24.

cursings. One of these cursings was a mark placed upon Cain, which mark would be carried by his posterity throughout all generations. According to the teachings of the *Pearl of Great Price,* this mark was a black skin. That scripture states:

And Enoch also beheld the residue of the people which were the sons of Adam; and they were a mixture of all the seed of Adam save it were the seed of Cain, for the seed of Cain were black, and had not place among them.[11]

But the greatest curse of all that came upon Cain and his descendants was that they were "cursed as pertaining to the Priesthood," that is, the entire lineage "could not have the right of Priesthood" (verses 26-27).

From the foregoing scripture we learn that Ham, the son of Noah, preserved the curses of Cain in the land. Since Ham was a son of Noah, it is quite definite that he did not have a black skin and was not a descendant of Cain. But the scripture seems to indicate that the wife of Ham was a descendant of Cain and through her the curses were preserved (verses 21-25). Her name was Egyptus, "which signifies that which is forbidden." Also, her daughter was known by the name of Egyptus, and Pharaoh was her grandson. He and his descendants could not hold the Priesthood (verses 21, 25-27).

Joseph Smith identified the negroes as the descendants of Cain. In Nauvoo in 1842 a group of the brethren were discussing the question as to whether the negroes or the Indians had received the greater ill-treatment from the whites. The Prophet said: "The Indians have greater cause to complain of the treatment of the whites, than the negroes, or sons of Cain."[12] Therefore it is due to the teachings of the *Pearl of Great Price* and the Prophet Joseph Smith and the other early leaders of the Church that the negro today is barred from the Priesthood. Negroes may be baptized into the Church but they have not the right of the Priesthood. President Brigham Young, Wilford Woodruff, George A. Smith, and others of the early church leaders held out the hope that eventually the descendants of Cain who had lived righteous lives in mortality would receive the blessings of the Priesthood.[13] They made statements similar to the folowing:

---

[11]*Ibid.,* 7:22.
[12]Cited in *ibid.,* p. 111.
[13]For a more complete discussion of this subject see Joseph Fielding Smith, *The Way to Perfection,* pp. 97-111.

When all the rest of the children have received their blessings in the holy Priesthood, then that curse will be removed from the seed of Cain, and they will come up and possess the Priesthood.[14]

Brigham Young did not originate the doctrine that Negroes could not hold the Priesthood in this life but some day some of them may be granted that privilege, but he was taught it by the Prophet Joseph. The minutes of a meeting of the general authorities of the Church which was held on August 22, 1895, read as follows:

President George Q. Cannon remarked that the Prophet taught this doctrine: That the seed of Cain could not receive the Priesthood nor act in any of the offices of the Priesthood until the seed of Abel should come forward and take precedence over Cain's offspring.[15]

The Church of Jesus Christ of Latter-day Saints teaches, however, that God will reward every man, woman, and child—regardless of his or her color or the land in which he or she lives—for every good act that he or she performs. Since God is no respecter of persons, faithfulness will not go unrewarded in the least degree. The law of the Lord is as follows: *"There is a law, irrevocably decreed in heaven before the foundation of this world, upon which all blessings are predicated—and when we obtain any blessing from God, it is by obedience to that law upon which it is predicated."*[16]

---

[14]Brigham Young, *Journal of Discourses*, vol. 11, p. 272.
[15]Cited in Smith, *The Way to Perfection*, p. 111.
[16]*Doctrine and Covenants* 130:20-21.

Chapter 22

LAW OF CELESTIAL MARRIAGE

MARRIAGE ORDAINED OF GOD

Whenever the Gospel of Jesus Christ has been upon the earth in its fullness during the various dispensations, the law of celestial marriage has been practiced and has been the heart of all the gospel principles and doctrines. In the words of Elder Joseph Fielding Smith, "Marriage is the grandest, most glorious and most exalting principle connected with the gospel."[1] In fact, the crowning gospel ordinance requisite for Godhood is celestial marriage. Abraham, Isaac, Jacob, David, Solomon, Moses, and—according to the Lord—"also many others of my servants from the beginning of creation until this time," have known and practiced the law of celestial marriage.[2] Paul, the ancient Christian apostle, taught that "neither is the man without the woman, neither the woman without the man, in the Lord."[3] Over one hundred years ago God revealed His will and assurance to the Prophet Joseph Smith regarding the sanctity of marriage. To quote the words of the Lord:

Verily, I say unto you, that whoso forbiddeth to marry is not ordained of God, for marriage is ordained of God unto man. Wherefore, it is lawful that he should have one wife, and they twain shall be one flesh, and all this that the earth might answer the end of its creation; and that it might be filled with the measure of man, according to his creation before the world was made.[4]

Shortly thereafter the Lord revealed to the Prophet the law of celestial marriage, known in the Church of Jesus Christ today as temple marriage. This revelation is found in section 132 of the *Doctrine and Covenants*.

Marriage is not only a righteous institution, but obedience to this law is absolutely necessary in order to obtain the highest

---

[1]Joseph Fielding Smith, *The Way to Perfection*, p. 233.
[2]*Doctrine and Covenants* 132:37-40.
[3]1 Corinthians 11:11.
[4]*Doctrine and Covenants* 49:15-17.

exaltation in the kingdom of God—even eternal life. If men and women ever gain that high exaltation they must always remember that those who enter into this holy covenant of marriage do so in purity and continue to live worthily enough that they may be sealed by the "Holy Spirit of promise." The word of the Lord came to the Prophet Joseph Smith, declaring that it is impossible for men and women to attain the highest glory in the celestial kingdom except they obey the law of celestial marriage and keep all the other commandments. God declared: *"In the celestial glory there are three heavens or degrees: and in order to obtain the highest, a man must enter into this order of the Priesthood (meaning the new and everlasting covenant of marriage)."*[5] If men and women obey all the other laws of the gospel except that of celestial marriage, they "are appointed angels in heaven, which angels are ministering servants, to minister for those who are worthy of a far more, and an exceeding, and an eternal weight of glory." The revelation to the Prophet continues as follows:

For these angels did not abide my law; therefore, they cannot be enlarged, but remain separately and singly, without exaltation, in their saved condition, to all eternity; and from henceforth are not Gods, but are angels of God forever and ever. . . .

And again, verily I say unto you, if a man marry a wife by my word, which is my law, and by the new and everlasting covenant, and it is sealed unto them by the Holy Spirit of promise, by him who is anointed, unto whom I have appointed this power and the keys of the Priesthood [and if they commit no sin to break that seal]; . . . they shall pass by the angels, and the Gods, which are set there, to their exaltation and glory in all things, as hath been sealed upon their heads, which glory shall be a fulness and a continuation of the seeds forever and ever. *Then shall they be Gods. . . .*

Verily, verily, I say unto you, except ye abide my law ye cannot attain to this glory.[6]

Later the Prophet Joseph explained what the revelation meant by the statement, "which glory shall be a fulness and a continuation of the seeds forever and ever." He pointed out that the Gods were to be parents of spirit-children just as our Heavenly Father and Heavenly Mother were the parents of the people of this earth. Following are the words of the Prophet:

Except a man and his wife enter into an everlasting covenant and be married for eternity, while in this probation, by the power and author-

---
[5]*Ibid.,* 131:1-2.
[6]*Ibid.,* 132:16-21.

ity of the Holy Priesthood, they will cease to increase when they die; that is, they will not have any children after the resurrection. But those who are married by the power and authority of the Priesthood in this life, and continue without committing the sin against the Holy Ghost, will continue to increase and have children in the celestial glory.[7]

Thus we see that celestial marriage is the crowning gospel ordinance, and the home is the basic institution in society. It is in family life that men, women, and children learn to love most deeply, sacrifice most completely, divide with each other more often, and develop the greatest amount of charity. Thus if properly lived, the covenant of marriage becomes the means of the greatest happiness, satisfaction, and love in this life, and will result in the highest honor, dominion, power, and perfect love in the world to come. If men and women have obeyed this holy ordinance and all the other principles of the gospel while in mortality, the Lord has decreed "then shall they be Gods" following the resurrection and great judgment day; and all of His words must be fulfilled.

Adam and Eve and Celestial Marriage

The first law that God gave unto Adam and Eve when He placed them upon the earth was the law of celestial marriage. They practiced this law and so did their posterity, the ancient patriarchs. The *Pearl of Great Price* testifies to this fact in both the Abraham and Moses accounts. The Lord God mentioned the fact that "for Adam, there was not found an help meet for him."[8] Then, according to Abraham's statement, "the Gods said: Let us make an help meet for the man, for it is not good that the man should be alone, therefore we will form an help meet for him."[9] In the Book of Moses the declaration reads as follows: "And I, the Lord God, said unto mine Only Begotten, that it was not good that the man should be alone; wherefore, I will make an help meet for him."[10] Then, in each of the accounts, the story of the creation of Eve, which is symbolical of marriage, is presented.

---

[7]Joseph Fielding Smith, *Teachings of the Prophet Joseph Smith*, pp. 300-301.
[8]Moses 3:20b.
[9]Abraham 5:14.
[10]Moses 3:18.

Symbolism of marriage in the story of the creation of Eve:

18. And I, the Lord God, said unto mine Only Begotten, that it was not good that the man should be alone; wherefore, I will make an help meet for him.

21. And I, the Lord God, caused a deep sleep to fall upon Adam; and he slept, and I took one of his ribs and closed up the flesh in the stead thereof;

22. And the rib which I, the Lord God, had taken from man, made I a woman, and brought her unto the man.

23. And Adam said: This I know now is bone of my bones, and flesh of my flesh; she shall be called Woman, because she was taken out of man.

24. Therefore shall a man leave his father and his mother, and shall cleave unto his wife; and they shall be one flesh.   Moses 3:18- 21-24.

See also Abraham 5:14-19.

The Church looks upon the story of the creation of woman as symbolizing the unity of man and woman under the holy covenant of celestial marriage. The man was appointed by the Lord and foreordained to be the head of his household; hence the symbolism in the creating of Eve from Adam's rib and his statement that woman was bone of his bone and flesh of his flesh. It is God's plan and purpose that young men and young women should do their courting on a pure, spiritual plane and fall in love with each other. Then they should enter one of the temples of the Most High, and there in a beautiful ceremony which was ordained of God be pronounced husband and wife not only for life but for all eternity. And it is the will of the Lord that following the marriage ceremony the husband and wife should continue to love each other so devotedly, live for and sacrifice for each other so completely, think and act so much alike, and be in harmony with each other so perfectly— being true to each other in every respect through living clean moral lives and rendering complete obedience to the principles of the gospel—that they would become as one in thoughts, in purposes, and in all their activities. In this way the husband and wife would become one flesh. Divorce would be impossible if they lived completely in harmony with the eternal plan of God.

Jesus Christ informed the people of His day that in the very beginning God gave to Adam and Eve the law of celestial marriage. In the words of the Master:

He who made them at the beginning made them male and female, and said, "For this cause shall a man leave father and mother, and shall cleave to his wife: and they twain shall be one flesh." Wherefore they are no more twain but one flesh. What therefore God hath joined together, let no man put asunder.[11]

---

[11]Matthew 19:4-6; Genesis 2:24; Moses 2:27-28; 3:24; Abraham 5:14-19.

Thus, according to the explanation made by the Son of Man, men and women were sealed together in marriage through the power of the Holy Priesthood—("What therefore God hath joined together"), and in God's law there was no divorce—("let no man put asunder"). This has been the law of the Lord in every gospel dispensation, and whenever men and women have deviated from this law, they have followed man-made ordinances which contracts are binding only as long as they live in mortality.

However, there are certain situations that may arise after temple marriages have been performed which warrant the annulment of the marriage. For example, one of the contracting parties may commit adultery and thereby make himself unworthy of being sealed by "the Holy Spirit of promise," or it may be that one party deserts his mate. The President of the Church of Jesus Christ of Latter-day Saints holds "the keys of the kingdom of heaven" and the Lord has declared that "whatsoever he shalt bind on earth shall be bound in heaven: and whatsoever he shalt loose on earth shall be loosed in heaven."[12] Therefore, when conditions warrant, by the same power that temple marriages are performed, those marriages may be annulled.

CELESTIAL MARRIAGE AND LARGE FAMILIES

Abraham's teachings on God's commandment to rear children:	*Moses' teachings on God's commandment to rear children:*
27. So the Gods went down to organize man in their own image, in the image of the Gods to form they him, male and female to form they them.	27. And I, God, created man in mine own image, in the image of mine Only Begotten created I him; male and female created I them.
28. And the Gods said: We will bless them. And the Gods said: We will cause them to be fruitful, and multiply, and replenish the earth, and subdue it, . . . Abraham 4:27-28a.	28. And I, God, blessed them, and said unto them: Be fruitful, and multiply, and replenish the earth, and subdue it, . . . Moses 2:27-28a.

In the very beginning God gave to Adam and Eve as part of the law of celestial marriage the commandment to "be fruitful and multiply and replenish the earth." The Gospel of Jesus Christ teaches today that it is the duty of parents, when they are physically and mentally capable, to rear large families in order that the numerous spirits in the spirit world may have

---

[12]*Doctrine and Covenants* 132:40-49 ; Matthew 16:16-19.

opportunity to come to the earth and receive mortal bodies. In the words of Brigham Young:

There are multitudes of pure and holy spirits waiting to take tabernacles, now what is our duty? To prepare tabernacles for them; to take a course that will not tend to drive those spirits into the families of the wicked, where they will be trained in wickedness, debauchery, and every species of crime. It is the duty of every righteous man and woman to prepare tabernacles for all the spirits they can.[13]

Therefore, to rear large families is the eternal law of God, given to those who accept the Gospel of Jesus Christ.

OBEDIENCE TO THE LAW OF CELESTIAL MARRIAGE

Law of celestial marriage obeyed by Adam and his posterity:

2. And Adam knew his wife, and she bare unto him sons and daughters, and they began to multiply and to replenish the earth.

3. And from that time forth, the sons and daughters of Adam began to divide two and two in the land, and to till the land, and to tend flocks, and they also begat sons and daughters.

16. And Adam knew Eve his wife, and she conceived and bare Cain, . . .

17. And she again conceived and bare his brother Abel. . . .
Moses 5:2-3, 16-17.

2. And Adam knew his wife again, and she bare a son, and he called his name Seth. And Adam glorified the name of God; for he said: God hath appointed me another seed, instead of Abel, whom Cain slew.

3. And God revealed himself unto Seth, and he rebelled not, but offered an acceptable sacrifice, like unto his brother Abel. And to him also was born a son, and he called his name Enos.

4. And then began these men to call upon the name of the Lord, and the Lord blessed them;

10. And Adam lived one hundred and thirty years, and begat a son in his own likeness, after his own image, and called his name Seth.[14]

11. And the days of Adam, after he had begotten Seth, were eight hundred years, and he begat many sons and daughters;

12. And all the days that Adam lived were nine hundred and thirty years, and he died.   Moses 6:2-4, 10-12.

As Cain was the first child born to Adam and Eve mentioned in the *Bible,* many people think that he was their eldest child. The foregoing quotation from the Book of Moses gives to members of the Church of Jesus Christ the added knowledge that Adam and Eve had sons and daughters and grandsons and granddaughters before Cain was born. The majority of Adam's and Eve's children were righteous and they paired off two by two in accordance with the law of celestial marriage and begat many children. The ancient record testifies that our first parents also obeyed the celestial law of being fruitful for they "begat many sons and daughters" (verse 11).

---

[13]John A. Widtsoe, *Discourses of Brigham Young,* p. 305.
[14]*Doctrine and Covenants* 107:42-43.

GREAT PATRIARCHS—"SONS OF GOD"

Line of great patriarchs who were descendants of Adam through Seth:

13. Seth lived one hundred and five years, and begat Enos, and prophesied in all his days, and taught his son Enos in the ways of God; wherefore Enos prophesied also.

14. And Seth lived, after he begat Enos, eight hundred and seven years, and begat many sons and daughters.

16. All the days of Seth were nine hundred and twelve years, and he died.

17. And Enos lived ninety years, and begat Cainan. And Enos and the residue of the people of God came out from the land, which was called Shulon, and dwelt in a land of promise, which he called after his own son, whom he had named Cainan.

18. And Enos lived, after he begat Cainan, eight hundred and fifteen years, and begat many sons and daughters. And all the days of Enos were nine hundred and five years, and he died.

19. And Cainan lived seventy years, and begat Mahalaleel; and Cainan lived after he begat Mahalaleel eight hundred and forty years, and begat sons and daughters. And all the days of Cainan were nine hundred and ten years, and he died.

20. And Mahalaleel lived sixty-five years, and begat Jared; and Mahalaleel lived, after he begat Jared, eight hundred and thirty years, and begat sons and daughters. And all the days of Mahalaleel were eight hundred and ninety-five years, and he died.

21. And Jared lived one hundred and sixty-two years, and he begat Enoch; and Jared lived, after he begat Enoch, eight hundred years, and begat sons and daughters. And Jared taught Enoch in all the ways of God.

22. And this is the genealogy of the sons of Adam, who was the son of God, with whom God, himself, conversed.

23. And they were preachers of righteousness, and spake and prophesied, and called upon all men, everywhere, to repent; and faith was taught unto the children of men.

24. And it came to pass that all the days of Jared were nine hundred and sixty-two years, and he died.

25. And Enoch lived sixty-five years, and begat Methuselah.

Moses 6:13-14, 16-25.

1. And all the days of Enoch were four hundred and thirty years.

2. And it came to pass that Methuselah, the son of Enoch, was not taken, that the covenants of the Lord might be fulfilled, which he made to Enoch; for he truly covenanted with Enoch that Noah should be of the fruit of his loins.

3. And it came to pass that Methuselah prophesied that from his loins should spring all the kingdoms of the earth (through Noah), and he took glory unto himself.

4. And there came forth a great famine into the land, and the Lord cursed the earth with a sore curse, and many of the inhabitants thereof died.

5. And it came to pass that Methuselah lived one hundred and eighty-seven years, and begat Lamech;

6. And Methuselah lived, after he begat Lamech, seven hundred and eighty-two years, and begat sons and daughters;

7. And all the days of Methuselah were nine hundred and sixty-nine years, and he died.

8. And Lamech lived one hundred and eighty-two years, and begat a son.

9. And he called his name Noah, saying: This son shall comfort us concerning our work and toil of our hands, because of the ground which the Lord hath cursed.

10. And Lamech lived, after he begat Noah, five hundred and ninety-five years, and begat sons and daughters;

11. And all the days of Lamech were seven hundred and seventy-seven years, and he died.

12. And Noah was four hundred and fifty years old, and begat Japheth; and forty-two years afterward he begat Shem of her who was the mother of Japheth, and when he was five hundred years old he begat Ham. Moses 8:1-12.

All the foregoing patriarchs were godly men, walking in harmony with the principles and ordinances of the Gospel of

Jesus Christ.[15] Thus it is believed that they observed the law of celestial marriage. As previously pointed out, they received the Holy Priesthood and magnified their callings in that Priesthood. The foregoing scripture proclaims that they were preachers of righteousness and prophesied regarding future events; therefore, they were known as "the sons of God."

LAW OF CELESTIAL MARRIAGE DISREGARDED

"The sons of men" (non-church members) married the daughters of "the sons of God" (church members):

13. And Satan came among them, saying: I am also a son of God; and he commanded them, saying: Believe it not; and they believed it not, and they loved Satan more than God. And men began from that time forth to be carnal, sensual, and devilish.

15. And the children of men were numerous upon all the face of the land. And in those days Satan had great dominion among men, and raged in their hearts; and from thenceforth came wars and bloodshed; and a man's hand was against his own brother, in administering death, because of secret works, seeking for power.

Moses 5:13; 6:15.

13. And Noah and his sons hearkened unto the Lord, and gave heed, and they were called the sons of God.

14. And when these men began to multiply on the face of the earth, and daughters were born unto them, the sons of men saw that those daughters were fair, and they took them wives, even as they chose.

15. And the Lord said unto Noah: The daughters of thy sons have sold themselves; for behold mine anger is kindled against the sons of men, for they will not hearken to my voice.

Moses 8:13-15.

According to the *Pearl of Great Price,* in the days of the antediluvians, members of the true Church of Jesus Christ were known as the "sons of God" or "the children of God." The God referred to was Jesus Christ. Every man and woman who came into this world was actually and literally a son or a daughter of God the Eternal Father, being His spiritual offspring, but only those who affiliated themselves with the true Church in this life and kept the commandments of God were known as "the sons of God [Jesus Christ]." This concept was made clear and definite in connection with Father Adam. He had faith in God the Father and His Only Begotten Son, was baptized, and received the Holy Ghost, and thereby became a member of the Church of Jesus Christ, or, in other words, he became "a son of God [Jesus Christ];" and this was the pattern set unto which all mortals must conform in order to become the sons of the Savior. Regarding this momentous event, the following is recorded in the *Pearl of Great Price:*

[15]Wilford Woodruff, *Journal of Discourses,* vol. 16, pp. 263-264, October 8, 1873.

And he [Adam] heard a voice out of heaven, saying: Thou art baptized with fire, and with the Holy Ghost. This is the record of the Father and the Son, from henceforth and forever; and thou art after the order of him who was without beginning of days or end of years, from all eternity to all eternity. Behold, thou art one in me, *a son of God; and thus may all become my sons.*[16]

Thus the words of Jesus Christ to the Ancient of Days clarify the foregoing scriptures (Moses 5:13; 6:15; 8:14-15). A description is given in those scriptures of the apostasy of many of Adam's descendants from the true Church of Jesus Christ, designating those who did not belong to the true Church as "the children of men," or "the sons of men;" and, in contrast to them, designating those of Adam's posterity who accepted the true Gospel of Jesus Christ and were faithful to their callings as "the sons of God."

Further evidence sustaining the doctrine is found in other passages of the *Pearl of Great Price,* as well as in modern revelation.[17] For example, when Enoch was teaching the gospel to the people in his day, he declared: "Behold, our father Adam taught these things, and many have believed and become the sons of God."[18]

The fact is made clear that "Noah and his sons hearkened unto the Lord, and gave heed, and they were called the *sons of God.*" In Moses 8:13-15 it is pointed out that "the *sons of men*" "took them wives, even as they chose," from the daughters of "the sons of God," and it displeased God very much. In other words, daughters of church members married men who did not belong to the Church of Jesus Christ nor hold the Priesthood. In those cases the holy ordinance could not be performed according to God's law of celestial marriage. Those daughters of church members by marrying outside the Church lost the blessings of the Priesthood and their chances of attaining exaltation or eternal life in the presence of God. For these reasons the Eternal Father and His Only Begotten Son were greatly displeased.

---

[16]Moses 6:66-68.
[17]Modern revelations confirm the doctrine given by the Lord to Adam regarding how to become the son of Jesus Christ (God). *Doctrine and Covenants* 39:1-6; 11:30; 34-3; 42:52; 45:8; 76:58; 128:23.
[18]Moses 7:1.

Chapter 23

GOSPEL PLAN OF SALVATION

ADAM AND THE GOSPEL PLAN OF SALVATION

The fact has been pointed out that God the Eternal Father through His Only Begotten Son provided a plan whereby His sons and daughters could progress until they reached the exalted position of Godhood just as the Father had attained. This plan was based on eternal laws and is known as the *"Plan of Salvation"* or as the *"Gospel of Jesus Christ."* According to the plan, only those mortals who through the proper exercise of their agency accepted and obeyed the principles and ordinances of the Gospel of Jesus Christ would be permitted to come back into the presence of the Father and the Son and receive eternal life.

Many gospel doctrines which were revealed to Father Adam and the holy prophets who succeeded him have been discussed in this book up to this point. This chapter will present a number of quotations from the *Pearl of Great Price* which tell the story of the revealing to Father Adam of many other basic gospel principles and ordinances pertaining to the plan of salvation.

LAW OF WORK

Adam and Eve were given the commandment to work and were obedient to that commandment:

25. By the sweat of thy face shalt thou eat bread, until thou shalt return unto the ground—for thou shalt surely die—for out of it wast thou taken: for dust thou wast, and unto dust shalt thou return.

29. Therefore I, the Lord God, will send him forth from the Garden of Eden, to till the ground from whence he was taken.   Moses 4:25, 29.

1. And it came to pass that after I, the Lord God, had driven them out, that Adam began to till the earth, and to have dominion over all the beasts of the field, and to eat his bread by the sweat of his brow, as I the Lord had commanded him. And Eve, also, his wife, did labor with him.
                              Moses 5:1.

152

One of the eternal gospel principles and one that is basic in the development of men and women is the law of work, because it is only through work that human beings grow mentally and spiritually. God's commandment to the father of the human family—which commandment applied to all of Adam's descendants—was that all of them who were mentally and physically able were to work all the days of their lives, except on the Sabbath, until they should "return unto the ground." It is the law of God that each person work sufficiently to support himself or herself. The *Pearl of Great Price* declares that Adam and Eve were obedient to the commandment to work. In fact, the foregoing scripture states: "Adam began to till the earth . . . and to eat his bread by the sweat of his brow . . . and Eve, also, his wife, did labor with him."

LAW OF WORK REAFFIRMED IN LATTER DAYS

The law of work, which God gave to the first mortal man and his wife and proclaimed that it should be observed by all of the human family, was reaffirmed in modern revelation. During the days of the Prophet Joseph Smith, on several different occasions the Lord gave the commandment to church members for them to work. To quote the law of the Lord:

Thou shalt not be idle; for he that is idle shall not eat the bread nor wear the garments of the laborer.[1] . . . Thou shalt not idle away thy time, neither shalt thou bury thy talent that it may not be known.[2]

Behold, I say unto you that it is my will that you should go forth and not tarry, neither be idle but labor with your might. . . . Let every man be diligent in all things. And the idler shall not have place in the church, except he repent and mend his ways.[3]

Now, I, the Lord, am not well pleased with the inhabitants of Zion, for there are idlers among them; and their children are also growing up in wickedness; they also seek not earnestly the riches of eternity, but their eyes are full of greediness.[4]

LAW OF LOVE

The following scripture quoted from the *Pearl of Great Price* proclaims that in the beginning God gave unto Adam

---

[1] *Doctrine and Covenants* 42:42.
[2] *Ibid.,* 60:13.
[3] *Ibid.,* 75:3, 29.
[4] *Ibid.,* 68:31, 30; 88:69, 124.

and his posterity the great law of love—which commandment was to love the Lord their God and to love their fellow men:

God's statement to Enoch:

33. And unto thy brethren have I said, and also given commandment, that they should love one another, and that they should choose me, their Father; ...
Moses 7:33a.

When the Son of Man was living in His mortal probation, He once again emphasized the gospel doctrine of love and rated it as the most important of all commandments. The occasion was when a certain lawyer asked Jesus which was the greatest commandment in the law (scriptures). In reply the Master quoted from Deuteronomy and Leviticus[5] and gave as His conclusion that on those two commandments hung all the teachings of the scriptures. To quote the Savior's exact words:

Thou shalt love the Lord thy God with all thy heart, and with all thy soul, and with all thy mind. This is the first and great commandment. And the second is like unto it, Thou shalt love thy neighbor as thyself. On these two commandments hang all the law and the prophets.[6]

GOSPEL PLAN OF SALVATION

Gospel Plan of Salvation revealed to Father Adam:

50. But God hath made known unto our fathers that all men must repent.

51. And he called upon our father Adam by his own voice, saying: I am God; I made the world, and men before they were in the flesh.

52. And he also said unto him: If thou wilt turn unto me, and hearken unto my voice, and believe, and repent of all thy transgressions, and be baptized, even in water, in the name of mine Only Begotten Son, who is full of grace and truth, which is Jesus Christ, the only name which shall be given under heaven, whereby salvation shall come unto the children of men, ye shall receive the gift of the Holy Ghost, asking all things in his name, and whatsoever ye shall ask, it shall be given you.

53. And our father Adam spake unto the Lord, and said: Why is it that men must repent and be baptized in water? And the Lord said unto Adam: Behold I have forgiven thee thy transgression in the Garden of Eden.

54. Hence came the saying abroad among the people, That the Son of God hath atoned for original guilt, wherein the sins of the parents cannot be answered upon the heads of the children, for they are whole from the foundation of the world.

57. Wherefore teach it unto your children, that all men, everywhere, must repent, or they can in nowise inherit the kingdom of God, for no unclean thing can dwell there, or dwell in his presence; for, in the language of Adam, Man of Holiness is his name, and the name of his Only Begotten is the Son of Man, even Jesus Christ, a righteous Judge, who shall come in the meridian of time.

58. Therefore I give unto you a commandment, to teach these things freely unto your children, saying:

59. That by reason of transgression cometh the fall, which fall bringeth death, and inasmuch as ye were born into the world by water, and blood, and the spirit, which I have made, and so became of dust a living soul, even so ye must be born again into the kingdom

[5]Deuteronomy 6:5; Leviticus 19:18.
[6]Matthew 22:37-40; Mark 12:29-31.

of heaven, of water, and of the Spirit, and be cleansed by blood, even the blood of mine Only Begotten; that ye might be sanctified from all sin, and enjoy the words of eternal life in this world, and eternal life in the world to come, even immortal glory;

60. For by the water ye keep the commandment; by the Spirit ye are justified, and by the blood ye are sanctified;

61. Therefore it is given to abide in you; the record of heaven; the Comforter; the peaceable things of immortal glory; the truth of all things; that which quickeneth all things, which maketh alive all things; that which knoweth all things, and hath all power,

according to wisdom, mercy, truth, justice, and judgment.

62. And now, behold, I say unto you: This is the plan of salvation unto all men, through the blood of mine Only Begotten, who shall come in the meridian of time.

63. And behold, all things have their likeness, and all things are created and made to bear record of me, both things which are temporal, and things which are spiritual; things which are in the heavens above, and things which are on the earth, and things which are in the earth, and things which are under the earth, both above and beneath: all things bear record of me.

Moses 6:50-54, 57-63.

In Moses 6:50-54, 57-63 (quoted above), the Lord revealed to Father Adam the plan of salvation. He declared in verses 50 to 52 and in verse 57 that all men throughout the world must repent, have faith in Jesus Christ, be baptized, and confirmed in order that they might inherit the kingdom of God. If they obeyed these principles and ordinances of the gospel, they were promised the Holy Ghost which is a gift from God which provides a means by which "a man may place himself in touch with the whole universe and draw knowledge from it, including the beings of superior intelligence that it contains."[7] Verse 61 presents an excellent description of the gift of the Holy Ghost.

Adam was told also that the name of the Only Begotten Son was *"Jesus Christ, the only name which shall be given under heaven, whereby salvation shall come unto the children of men."* The Ancient of Days also learned that Christ would come to earth in the meridian of time to teach the gospel to the human family. Verse 54 points out the fact that the Son of God would atone for the fall and give to all mortals resurrection or immortality; also, as the second article of faith states, "Men will be punished for their own sins, and not for Adam's transgression." Finally, following His resurrection, Christ, as a glorified God, would be the Judge of the world.

No better explanation regarding the symbolism in baptism, confirmation, and the atoning blood of Jesus Christ is found in any of the scriptures than the one given in verses 59 and 60. The symbolism is a perfect comparison of birth into mortality and into the kingdom of God. Immersion is the only mode of

[7]John A. Widtsoe, *Rational Theology*, pp. 38-42.

baptism that could fit this symbolism. Also, these verses point out the two important phases of the atonement, namely: the contribution made by Jesus Christ—represented by the blood—and the contribution that each of us must make by repenting of all our sins and actually being born again and then making our lives conform to the gospel plan thereafter. Only by a combination of these two factors will mortals ever be able to come back into the presence of God.

CHILDREN CONCEIVED IN SIN

God's statement to Adam:

55. And the Lord spake unto Adam, saying: Inasmuch as thy children are conceived in sin, even so when they begin to grow up, sin conceiveth in their hearts, and they taste the bitter, that they may know to prize the good.

Moses 6:55.

The foregoing scripture states: "Inasmuch as thy children are conceived in sin, . . ." This statement probably means, "Inasmuch as thy children are born into a sinful, mortal world." As was pointed out in a previous chapter, it is not sinful to bear children when men and women are properly married; but it is the opposite of being sinful to rear large families. This is especially true when men and women are abiding by the law of celestial marriage and their children are born under the covenant. The law of celestial marriage is accounted to be the crowning principle of the Gospel of Jesus Christ; therefore, to live in harmony with that law is one of the greatest virtues that men and women can attain. In fact, procreation was God's first great commandment to Adam and Eve.

In modern revelation, the Lord has declared that little children are born into this world innocent and during their early years they cannot sin. To quote:

Every spirit of man was innocent in the beginning, and God having redeemed man from the fall, men became again in their infant state, innocent before God.[8] But, behold, I say unto you, that little children are redeemed from the foundation of the world through mine Only Begotten: wherefore, they cannot sin, for power is not given unto Satan to tempt little children, until they begin to become accountable before me.[9]

The most forceful discourse recorded in any of the scriptures on the subject of the innocence of little children is found in the eighth chapter of Moroni. It is an epistle written by Mormon to his son Moroni in which he strongly condemns

[8]*Doctrine and Covenants* 93:38.
[9]*Ibid.*, 29:46-47.

the wicked practice of infant baptism. Mormon's epistle could be read at this point with profit. While living in mortality, Christ sustained the foregoing doctrine by claiming that the kingdom of heaven is composed of people who have become as little children.[10]

ADAM'S BAPTISM AND CONFIRMATION

Description of Adam's baptism and confirmation:

64. And it came to pass, when the Lord had spoken with Adam, our father, that Adam cried unto the Lord, and he was caught away by the Spirit of the Lord, and was carried down into the water, and was laid under the water, and was brought forth out of the water.

65. And thus he was baptized, and the Spirit of God descended upon him, and thus he was born of the Spirit, and became quickened in the inner man.

66. And he heard a voice out of heaven, saying: Thou are baptized with fire, and with the Holy Ghost. This is the record of the Father, and the Son, from henceforth and forever;

67. And thou art after the order of him who was without beginning of days or end of years, from all eternity to all eternity.

68. Behold, thou art one in me, a son of God; and thus may all become my sons. Amen. Moses 6:64-68.

Thus through faith, repentance, baptism by immersion and confirmation, the Father of the human family received a spiritual rebirth and was initiated into the kingdom of God; and the eternal decree was given to the human family that only by following the example set by Adam can any mortal become a son or daughter of Jesus Christ and a member of the kingdom of God.

The meaning of verse 67 is that the Ancient of Days held the Holy Priesthood after the Order of the Son of God.

GOSPEL THROUGH THE AGES

Gospel was preached from the beginning:

14. And the Lord God called upon men by the Holy Ghost everywhere and commanded them that they should repent;

15. And as many as believed in the Son, and repented of their sins, should be saved; and as many as believed not and repented not, should be damned; and the words went forth out of the mouth of God in a firm decree; wherefore they must be fulfilled.

16. And Adam and Eve, his wife, ceased not to call upon God. . . .

1. And Adam hearkened unto the voice of God, and called upon his sons to repent.

1. And it came to pass that Enoch continued his speech, saying: Behold, our father Adam taught these things, and many have believed and become the sons of God, and many have believed not, and have perished in their sins, and are looking forth with fear, in torment, for the fiery indignation of the wrath of God to be poured out upon them.

58. And thus the Gospel began to be preached, from the beginning, being declared by holy angels sent forth from the presence of God, and by his own voice, and by the gift of the Holy Ghost.

[10]Matthew 19:14; Mark 10:14; Luke 18:16.

59. And thus all things were con- | the world, until the end thereof; and
firmed unto Adam, by an holy ordi- | thus it was. Amen.
nance, and the Gospel preached, and a | Moses 5:14-16a; 6:1; 7:1; 5:58-59.
decree sent forth, that it should be in |

The preceding scripture gives the firm decree from "the mouth of God" that all men must repent of their sins in order to be saved, and if they fail to repent they will be damned. The eternal command to the righteous people was for them to continue to teach the plan of salvation to their associates.

In the quotation from the *Pearl of Great Price* (verses 58-59) is recorded a strong statement to the effect that through divers methods Father Adam was given the gospel in the beginning and an "holy ordinance" (baptism); and the prediction was made that gospel doctrines and truths would be in the world until the end thereof. The other holy scriptures—*Book of Mormon* and *Doctrine and Covenants*— as well as the teachings of the Prophet Joseph Smith and many other Latter-day Saint prophets and apostles bear witness to the truth of the foregoing prophecy.

The Nephite prophets maintained that God has given to all peoples, regardless of their race, color, or creed, the amount of religious truth that they were able to receive and willing to obey. They have been given these gospel truths according to their needs and ability to harmonize their lives with the Divine Will. In the words of King Benjamin: *"And the Lord God hath sent his holy prophets among all the children of men, to declare these things to every kindred, nation, and tongue."*[11] Alma stated that God is mindful of every people. To quote: *"For behold, the Lord does grant unto all nations, of their own nation and tongue, to teach his word, yea, in wisdom, all that He seeth fit that they should have."*[12] Orson F. Whitney wrote the following under the title, "Of Their Own Nation and Tongue:"

God's truth has been taught all down the ages by men bearing the authority to represent Deity. But other men, not bearing that authority, wise teachers, auxiliaries to the Priesthood, have been raised up in various nations to give them that measure of truth which they are able to receive. Hence, such men as Confucius, the Chinese sage; Zoroaster, the Persian; and Gautama of the Hindus; men not wielding divine authority, not empowered to present the Gospel, nor to officiate in its ordinances; but nevertheless endowed with wisdom, with profundity of thought and learning, to deliver, each to his own people, that portion of truth which the

---
[11]Mosiah 3:12-13.
[12]Alma 29:8.

all-wise Dispenser sees fit that they should have; people who, if given a fulness of the truth, might trample it under foot to their condemnation. Therefore they "die without law" (D. & C. 76:72); that is, without the higher law, the Gospel, which, however, will reach after them in a future life.

The world's poets and philosophers, artists and musicians, scientists and discoverers, warriors and statesmen, with good and great characters in general—all have their work and mission under an over-ruling Providence. If some of God's children are not worthy of the fulness of truth, and would not make a wise use of it were it sent to them, that is no reason why they should not be given as much truth as they can wisely use.[13]

REPENTANCE AND BAPTISM TAUGHT BY ENOCH

Enoch lived hundreds of years after the gospel was first given to Father Adam, and, according to the following scripture, he taught repentance to the people and performed the ordinance of baptism exactly as Adam had done:

Enoch's teachings regarding repentance and baptism:

10. And the Lord said unto me: Go to this people, and say unto them—Repent, lest I come out and smite them with a curse, and they die.
11. And he gave unto me a commandment that I should baptize in the name of the Father, and of the Son, which is full of grace and truth, and of the Holy Ghost, which beareth record of the Father and the Son.

Moses 7:10-11.

OTHER SCRIPTURES ON THE GOSPEL PLAN

Since the principal purpose of this chapter is to study the "Gospel Plan of Salvation," it would be advisable at this point to compare the revelations regarding the gospel and the plan of salvation as given by the Savior in other scriptures with the revelations given to Father Adam. After Christ's resurrection He appeared to the Nephites and explained unto them the following regarding His gospel:

Behold I have given unto you my gospel, and this is my gospel which I have given unto you—that I came into the world to do the will of my Father, because my Father sent me. And my Father sent me that I might be lifted up upon the cross; and after that I had been lifted up upon the cross, that I might draw all men unto me, that as I have been lifted up by men even so should men be lifted up by the Father, to stand before me, to be judged of their works, whether they be good or whether they be evil—and for this cause have I been lifted up; therefore, according to the power of the Father I will draw all men unto me, that they may be judged according to their works.

---

[13]Orson F. Whitney, *The Strength of the Moromn Position,* pp. 22-23.

And it shall come to pass that whoso repenteth and is baptized in my name shall be filled; and if he endureth to the end, behold, him will I hold guiltless before my Father at that day when I shall stand to judge the world. And he that endureth not unto the end, the same is he that is also hewn down and cast into the fire, from whence they can no more return, because of the justice of the Father.

And this is the word which he hath given unto the children of men. And for this cause he fulfilleth the words which he hath given, and he lieth not, but fulfilleth all his words.

And no unclean thing can enter into his kingdom: therefore nothing entereth into his rest save it be those who have washed their garments in my blood, because of their faith, and the repentance of all their sins, and their faithfulness unto the end.

Now this is the commandment: Repent, all ye ends of the earth, and come unto me and be baptized in my name, that ye may be sanctified by the reception of the Holy Ghost, that ye may stand spotless before me at the last day. Verily, verily, I say unto you, this is my gospel.[14]

In the latter days, Jesus Christ declared the following to the Prophet Joseph Smith:

Hearken and listen to the voice of him who is from all eternity to all eternity, the Great I AM, even Jesus Christ. . . . But to as many as received me, gave I power to become my sons, and even so will I give unto as many as will receive me, power to become my sons. And verily, verily, I say unto you, he that receiveth my gospel, receiveth me; and he that receiveth not my gospel receiveth not me.

And this is my gospel: repentance and baptism by water, and then cometh the baptism of fire and the Holy Ghost, even the Comforter, which showeth all things, and teacheth the peaceable things of the kingdom.[15]

The foregoing scriptures from the *Book of Mormon* and the *Doctrine and Covenants,* and numerous others which could be cited, attest that the gospel plan of salvation given to Father Adam, as recorded in the *Pearl of Great Price,* was the same as Christ gave to the Nephites and as He brought back to earth in the latter days—in the Dispensation of the Fulness of Times.

---

[14]3 Nephi 27:13-21.
[15]*Doctrine and Covenants* 39:1, 4-6.

Chapter 24

ADAMIC LANGUAGE AND BOOK OF REMEMBRANCE

ADAMIC LANGUAGE

When Father Adam was placed in the Garden of Eden, God the Eternal Father and His Only Begotten Son visited him often and gave him instructions. The *Pearl of Great Price* informs us that the Lord spoke to Adam and gave him commandments; therefore, they talked with each other. It is evident that they could not have conversed if Adam had no language.

We read in the Book of Moses that after God had "formed every beast of the field and every fowl of the air" out of the ground and had "breathed into them the breath of life" that He brought them to Adam "and commanded that whatsoever Adam called every living creature, that should be the name thereof. And Adam gave names to all cattle, and to the fowls of the air, and to every beast of the field."[1] From this scripture it is very evident that the Father of the human family was an unusually intelligent man and had an extensive vocabulary.

After Adam and Eve were driven from the Garden of Eden and became mortal beings, the *Pearl of Great Price* declares that God continued to speak to Adam and holy angels also came and conversed with him. Our first parents, therefore, retained the language of the angels and the Gods when they became mortals following the fall. In regard to the language of Adam, Elder Joseph Fielding Smith wrote:

What would be more natural than to believe that the Father would speak to him [Adam] in his own language, and that the language used was perfect, for it was the language of celestial beings? We are informed that Adam and the Lord carried on conversations. How was this done unless Adam had been taught to speak? Therefore, all who have faith in the word of the Lord must know that Adam had a language; that his

[1]Moses 3:19-20.

161

language was pure and perfect for it came from the Lord. All Latter-day Saints know this to be the case, for the Lord revealed to Moses, and later to Joseph Smith in the writings of Moses, that not only did Adam have the power of speech but he was taught also to read and write, and records were kept by him and by his posterity.[2]

The ancient record bears witness to the fact that Adam and his posterity had "a language which was pure and undefiled."[3]

Language of Adam and Book of Remembrance

Adam and his descendants kept a book of remembrance and had a pure and undefiled language:

5. And a book of remembrance was kept, in the which was recorded, in the language of Adam, for it was given unto as many as called upon God to write by the spirit of inspiration;

6. And by them their children were taught to read and write, having a language which was pure and undefiled.

8. . . . and a genealogy was kept of the children of God. And this was the book of the generations of Adam, saying: In the day that God created man, in the likeness of God made he him.   Moses 6:5-6, 8b.

Teachings of Enoch:

45. And death hath come upon our fathers; nevertheless we know them, and cannot deny, and even the first of all we know, even Adam.

46. For a book of remembrance we have written among us, according to the pattern given by the finger of God; and it is given in our own language.
                    Moses 6:45-46.

The ancient records came into the hands of Father Abraham:

28. But I shall endeavor, hereafter, to delineate the chonology running back from myself to the beginning of the creation, for the records have come into my hands, which I hold unto this present time.

31. But the records of the fathers, even the patriarchs, concerning the right of Priesthood, the Lord my God preserved in mine own hands; therefore a knowledge of the beginning of the creation, and also of the planets, and of the stars, as they were made known unto the fathers, have I kept even unto this day, and I shall endeavor to write some of these things upon this record, for the benefit of my posterity that shall come after me.
                    Abraham 1:28, 31.

The foregoing scriptures declare that Adam and his posterity were taught through the spirit of inspiration to read and write, and they in turn taught their children. This statement has reference to what occurred after the fall. Also, the fact is made known that the early inhabitants of the earth utilized their knowledge of writing by keeping a record of the gospel teachings, revelations from God, and history and genealogy of the people. These things were kept in a book which the ancient ones called the "Book of Remembrance." Copies of

[2]Joseph Fielding Smith, *The Way to Perfection*, p. 67.
[3]Moses 6:6.

this holy record were handed down from generation to generation. Abraham claimed to possess "the records of the fathers" running back from his day to the beginning of creation.

RECORD OF THE JAREDITES

The "Book of Ether" in the *Book of Mormon* confirms the teachings of the *Pearl of Great Price* regarding ancient records and the language of Adam. During the days of King Mosiah the second, a company of Nephites under the direction of King Limhi discovered an ancient record written on twenty-four metal plates. The record told the story of a group of people, named Jaredites, who came to America from the Tower of Babel at the time of the confusion of tongues. Moroni, the last of the Nephite prophets, translated and made an abridgment of the record of the Jaredites (Book of Ether). Toward the beginning of his abridgment, Moroni wrote:

And as I suppose that the first part of this record, which speaks concerning the creation of the world, and also of Adam, and an account from that time even to the great tower, and whatsoever things transpired among the children of men until that time, is had among the Jews— Therefore I do not write those things which transpired from the days of Adam until that time; but they are had upon the plates; and whoso findeth them, the same will have power that he may get the full account.[4]

The first prophets and leaders of the ancient Jaredites were Jared and his brother, Mahonri Moriancumer.[5] The record states that at the time of the confusion of tongues at the Tower of Babel, the brother of Jared requested of the Lord that He would not confound the language of Jared, his brother, their families, and their friends and families. The Lord granted this request. Thus they were permitted to carry with them to America the speech of their fathers—the Adamic language—which was very powerful even in its written form. Moroni reported that the things that the brother of Jared wrote "were mighty even as thou [God] art, unto the overpowering of man to read them."[6] That is the kind of language that Adam, Seth, Enoch, and the other ancient patriarchs used in conversing with the Lord during the period when they accomplished many mighty works.

---

[4]Ether 1:3-4.
[5]*Improvement Era*, vol. 8, p. 705; *Juvenile Instructor*, vol. 27, p. 282.
[6]Ether 12:24.

Chapter 25

SECRET COMBINATIONS AND WORKS
OF DARKNESS

SATAN'S WORK

In the chapter on the "Grand Council in Heaven," the story was told of the revolt of Satan against the Eternal Father and the Only Begotten Son and the subsequent war in heaven. The Lord showed Moses a vision of the foregoing event and declared: "By the power of mine Only Begotten, I caused that he should be cast down; and he became Satan, yea, even the devil, the father of all lies, to deceive and to blind men, and to lead them captive at his will, even as many as would not hearken unto my voice."[1] This statement gives us a clear understanding regarding Satan's work among the children of men here in mortality. Following Lucifer's banishment from heaven, he immediately began his evil work in this world by tempting Mother Eve. In due course of time after Adam and Eve became mortal beings, sons and daughters were born unto them. According to the following scripture quoted from the *Pearl of Great Price*, Lucifer and his angels exerted every effort possible to lead Adam's posterity into sin and thereby destroy the work and kingdom of the Lord:

First apostasy in history:

12. And Adam and Eve blessed the name of God, and they made all things known unto their sons and their daughters.
13. And Satan came among them, saying: I am also a son of God; and he commanded them, saying: Believe it not; and they believed it not, and they loved Satan more than God. And men began from that time forth to be carnal, sensual, and devilish.   Moses 5:12-13.

GOOD AND EVIL

There are two forces in the world—the force for good and the force for evil. God the Eternal Father and His Only

---
[1]Moses 4:3b-4.

Begotten Son sustain all that is good. In fact, the ancient prophets proclaimed that all that is good emanates from Them. On the other hand, Lucifer, or the devil, and his angels sustain all that is evil and wicked. They are the expression of the powers of darkness; therefore, all that is evil comes from them. This doctrine was expressed by Alma, the ancient Nephite prophet, as follows:

> For I say unto you that whatsoever is good cometh from God, and whatsoever is evil cometh from the devil. Therefore, if a man bringeth forth good works he hearkeneth unto the voice of the good shepherd, and he doth follow him; but whosoever bringeth forth evil works, the same becometh a child of the devil, for he hearkeneth unto his voice, and doth follow him.[2]

Regarding this subject, Mormon, the ancient prophet after whom the *Book of Mormon* was named, made the following pertinent statement:

> Wherefore, all things which are good cometh of God; and that which is evil cometh of the devil; for the devil is an enemy unto God, and fighteth against him continually, and inviteth and enticeth to sin, and to do that which is evil continually. But behold, that which is of God inviteth and enticeth to do good continually; wherefore, every thing which inviteth and enticeth to do good, and to love God, and to serve him, is inspired of God.[3]

Thus from the very beginning the devil has put forth every effort possible to further his works of darkness and thereby destroy the souls of men, as the following scriptures will show:

CAIN AND ABEL AND BEGINNING OF SECRET COMBINATIONS

Cain rejects God, enters into a covenant with Satan, and slays Abel:

16. And Adam and Eve, his wife, ceased not to call upon God. And Adam knew Eve his wife, and she conceived and bare Cain, and said: I have gotten a man from the Lord; wherefore he may not reject his words. But behold, Cain hearkened not, saying: Who is the Lord, that I should know him?

17. And she again conceived and bare his brother Abel. And Abel hearkened unto the voice of the Lord. And Abel was a keeper of sheep, but Cain was a tiller of the ground.

18. And Cain loved Satan more than God. And Satan commanded him, saying: Make an offering unto the Lord.

19. And in process of time it came to pass that Cain brought of the fruit of the ground an offering unto the Lord.

20. And Abel he also brought of the firstlings of his flock, and of the fat thereof. And the Lord had respect unto Abel, and to his offering;

21. But unto Cain, and to his offering, he had not respect. Now Satan

[2]Alma 5:40-42; Ether 4:12; 2 Nephi 26:33; Omni 1:25.
[3]Moroni 7:12-17, 24; 10:18; 2 Nephi 2:18, 23-25.

knew this, and it pleased him. And Cain was very wroth, and his countenance fell.

22. And the Lord said unto Cain: Why art thou wroth? Why is thy countenance fallen?

23. If thou doest well, thou shalt be accepted. And if thou doest not well, sin lieth at the door, and Satan desireth to have thee; and except thou shalt hearken unto my commandments, I will deliver thee up, and it shall be unto thee according to his desire. And thou shalt rule over him;

24. For from this time forth thou shalt be the father of his lies; thou shalt be called Perdition; for thou wast also before the world.

25. And it shall be said in time to come—That these abominations were had from Cain; for he rejected the greater counsel which was had from God; and this is a cursing which I will put upon thee, except thou repent.

26. And Cain was wroth, and listened not any more to the voice of the Lord, neither to Abel, his brother, who walked in holiness before the Lord.

27. And Adam and his wife mourned before the Lord, because of Cain and his brethren.

28. And it came to pass that Cain took one of his brothers' daughters to wife, and they loved Satan more than God.

29. And Satan said unto Cain, Swear unto me by thy throat, and if thou tell it thou shalt die; and swear thy brethren by their heads, and by the living God, that they tell it not; for if they tell it, they shall surely die; and this that thy father may not know it; and this day I will deliver thy brother Abel into thine hands.

30. And Satan sware unto Cain that he would do according to his commands. And all these things were done in secret.

31. And Cain said: Truly I am Mahan, the master of this great secret, that I may murder and get gain. Wherefore Cain was called Master Mahan, and he gloried in his wickedness.

32. And Cain went into the field, and Cain talked with Abel, his brother. And it came to pass that while they were in the field, Cain rose up against Abel, his brother, and slew him.

33. And Cain gloried in that which he had done, saying: I am free; surely the flocks of my brother falleth into my hands.   Moses 5:16-33.

This story of Cain and Abel is much more detailed and far superior to the account in Genesis 4:1-16. The story of Satan and the covenant that Cain made with him are not mentioned in the *Bible*. Compare the two accounts.

At the birth of Cain, Mother Eve said, "I have gotten a man from the Lord." That was the hope that she had in her heart when she looked upon her new, beautiful baby, and that hope was very strong within her because of the effective work that Satan had performed in deceiving her older children and helping to cause them to be "carnal, sensual, and devilish." But as Cain grew to manhood, he rejected the Lord, ceased to hearken to Him, and declared: "Who is the Lord, that I should know him?" But the Lord loved Cain and desired to save him from dying the second death and receiving eternal damnation. In fact, He plead with Cain in the hope of getting him to repent, proclaiming the following unto him:

Satan desireth to have thee; and except thou shalt hearken unto my commandments, I will deliver thee up, and it shall be unto thee according to his desire. And thou shalt rule over him; for from this time forth thou shalt be the father of his lies; thou shalt be called Perdition.[4]

In spite of all of this, Cain rejoiced in his own wickedness. He entered into a secret covenant with Lucifer and obeyed his commandments, saying: "Truly, I am Mahan, the master of this great secret" (verse 31). (Verse 29 gives the oath and covenant that were administered to Cain by Satan). As the story proceeds, we learn that Cain slew his brother Abel. Thus Cain not only became the father of all lies, but he also became the father of secret combinations. God declared that throughout the ages *"it shall be said . . . that these abominations were had from Cain"* (verse 25). This prediction was fulfilled many times from Cain's day to the flood and also throughout much of *Book of Mormon* history, as shall be pointed out later.

Sons of Perdition

In Moses 5:24, the Lord told Cain that "thou shalt be called Perdition." Why should Cain become Perdition? He committed murder, but there have been thousands and thousands of murders committed since his day and God has not pronounced the murderers sons of Perdition. The answer to this question lies in the fact that Cain must have held the Holy Priesthood, because the *Pearl of Great Price* account infers that the Lord appeared unto him. At least it is certain that he received direct communication from the heavens and talked with the Lord. On this subject, Elder Joseph Fielding Smith said: "No doubt he held the Priesthood; otherwise his sin could not make of him Perdition."[5]

When a man receives the Holy Priesthood after the Order of the Son of God, he receives it with an oath and a covenant. The oath and covenant is that God promises him exaltation in His kingdom, even eternal life in celestial glory, on condition that he magnifies his calling and obeys all the principles and ordinances of the Gospel of Jesus Christ. In the words of the Son of Man:

All that my Father hath shall be given unto him. And this is according to the oath and covenant which belongeth to the Priesthood.

[4]Moses 5:23-24.
[5]Joseph Fielding Smith, *The Way to Perfection*, p. 98.

Therefore, all those who receive the Priesthood, receive this oath and covenant of my Father, which he cannot break, neither can it be moved.

But whoso breaketh this covenant after he hath received it, and altogether turneth therefrom, shall not have forgiveness of sins in this world nor in the world to come.[6]

This modern revelation throws much light upon the gravity of Cain's crimes and the reasons for his becoming Perdition.

Another fact in the *Pearl of Great Price* account should be mentioned, because it helps us to understand more clearly why Cain was "called Perdition." It is the fact that Cain carefully planned his crime and did not sin in ignorance. Even before he killed his righteous brother, Abel, Cain loved Satan more than he loved the Lord and obeyed him instead of rendering obedience to God. He even offered sacrifice to the Lord because Satan had commanded him, not because his Eternal Father had given the commandment. Furthermore, according to the word of the Lord (Moses 5:25), Cain became Perdition because *"he rejected the greater counsel which was had from God."* In modern revelation, the Lord declared the following in regard to mortals who sin sufficiently to become sons of Perdition:

Thus saith the Lord concerning all those who know my power, and have been made partakers thereof, and suffered themselves through the power of the devil to be overcome, and to deny the truth and defy my power—they are they who are the sons of perdition, of whom I say that it had been better for them never to have been born; for they are vessels of wrath, doomed to suffer the wrath of God, with the devil and his angels in eternity; concerning whom I have said there is no forgiveness in this world nor in the world to come—having denied the Holy Spirit after having received it, and having denied the Only Begotten Son of the Father, having crucified him unto themselves and put him to open shame. These are they who shall go away into the lake of fire and brimstone, with the devil and his angels—and the only ones on whom the second death shall have any power; yea, verily, the only ones who shall not be redeemed in the due time of the Lord, after the sufferings of his wrath.[7]

Cain fits in well with the foregoing description of those who become sons of Perdition. Even before he committed murder, Cain "gloried in his wickedness;" and after he had killed Abel "Cain gloried in that which he had done."

---

[6]*Doctrine and Covenants* 84:32-41; 93:3.
[7]*Ibid.*, 76:30-38.

CAIN'S MARRIAGE

The *Bible* gives an account of Cain's murdering Abel and God's placing a curse on Cain, and then the statement is made:

And Cain went out from the presence of the Lord, and dwelt in the land of Nod, on the east of Eden. And Cain knew his wife; and she conceived, and bare Enoch.[8]

Suddenly in the foregoing manner the fact that Cain is married is mentioned in Genesis. This statement has caused much speculation among various Christian teachers regarding where Cain got his wife and whom he married. Many of them have taught that there were other people on the earth at that time besides Adam and Eve, since Cain is their first child mentioned in the *Bible*. This concept is against the revelation that Adam was the first man. *The Pearl of Great Price*, however, throws great light on this subject. As previously mentioned, from that record we learn that Adam and Eve had children and grandchildren before Cain was born.[9] Regarding Cain's marriage, this record states: "And it came to pass that Cain took one of his brothers' daughters to wife, and they loved Satan more than God" (verse 28).

CURSE ON CAIN AND HIS POSTERITY

Account of the Lord placing a curse on Cain:

34. And the Lord said unto Cain: Where is Abel, thy brother? And he said: I know not. Am I my brother's keeper?

35. And the Lord said: What hast thou done? The voice of thy brother's blood cries unto me from the ground.

36. And now thou shalt be cursed from the earth which hath opened her mouth to receive thy brother's blood from thy hand.

37. When thou tillest the ground it shall not henceforth yield unto thee her strength. A fugitive and a vagabond shalt thou be in the earth.

38. And Cain said unto the Lord: Satan tempted me because of my brother's flocks. And I was wroth also; for his offering thou didst accept and

Enoch's vision and prophecy regarding the land of Canaan and the curse of black skins on Cain's descendants:

6. And again the Lord said unto me: Look; and I looked towards the north, and I beheld the people of Canaan, which dwelt in tents.

7. And the Lord said unto me: Prophesy; and I prophesied, saying: Behold the people of Canaan, which are numerous, shall go forth in battle array against the people of Shum, and shall slay them that they shall utterly be destroyed; and the people of Canaan shall divide themselves in the land, and the land shall be barren and unfruitful, and none other people shall dwell there but the people of Canaan;

8. For behold, the Lord shall curse the land with much heat, and the barrenness thereof shall go forth forever; and there was a blackness came upon all the children of Canaan, that they were despised among all people.

[8]Genesis 4:16-17.
[9]Moses 5:1-16.

not mine; my punishment is greater than I can bear.

39. Behold thou hast driven me out this day from the face of the Lord, and from thy face shall I be hid; and I shall be a fugitive and a vagabond in the earth; and it shall come to pass, that he that findeth me will slay me, because of mine iniquities, for these things are not hid from the Lord.

40. And I the Lord said unto him: Whosoever slayeth thee, vengeance shall be taken on him sevenfold. And I the Lord set a mark upon Cain, lest any finding him should kill him.

41. And Cain was shut out from the presence of the Lord, and with his wife and many of his brethren dwelt in the land of Nod, on the east of Eden.

Moses 5:34-41.

22. And Enoch also beheld the residue of the people which were the sons of Adam; and they were a mixture of all the seed of Adam save it were the seed of Cain, for the seed of Cain were black, and had not place among them.

Moses 7:6-8, 22.

Abraham's statement that Cain's descendants were cursed as to the rights of the Priesthood:

21. Now this king of Egypt was a descendant from the loins of Ham, and was partaker of the blood of the Canaanites by birth.

27. Now, Pharaoh being of that lineage by which he could not have the right of Priesthood, notwithstanding the Pharaohs would fain claim it from Noah, through Ham, therefore my father was led away by their idolatry.

Abraham 1:21, 27.

In Moses 5:34-41 (quoted above), the story is told of the Lord's placing the following curses on Cain; first, the earth would not yield abundantly for him; second, he would be a fugitive and vagabond in the earth; third, a mark was placed on him; and fourth, he was shut out from the presence of the Lord.

The Prophet Enoch testified to the fulfillment of these curses (Moses 7:6-8, 22). In fact, the *Pearl of Great Price* also records the fact that "Enoch continued to call upon all the people, save it were the people of Canaan [Cain's descendants], to repent;"[10] thus they were definitely shut out from the presence of the Lord and deprived from hearing the gospel plan of salvation.

In addition to the four curses placed on Cain and his descendants as accounted in the Book of Moses, Father Abraham made definite mention of a fifth curse which was the most grievous of all the curses. It was that Cain lost his Priesthood and his descendants "could not have the right of Priesthood;" in other words, they were cursed "as pertaining to the Priesthood" (Abraham 1:21,27). This item was discussed in the chapter entitled "Divine Authority;" therefore, no further details will need be presented here.

---

[10]*Ibid.*, 7:12.

"My Brother's Keeper"

(It is evident that a discussion of the statement "Am I my brother's keeper?" does not fit logically under the chapter title of "Secret Combinations and Works of Darkness;" however, the justification for discussing that statement at this point is that an attempt is being made to cover all of the teachings of the *Pearl of Great Price* in this book and the problem of "my brother's keeper" comes into the story in the foregoing quotation, Moses 5:34.)

The question "Am I my brother's keeper?" which Cain asked the Lord has been answered in revelations time and time again during the various gospel dispensations. The answer is—"Yes." Each of us is responsible for the example he sets and the teachings he gives his associates. After the Lord had revealed the gospel to Adam, He said: "I give unto you a commandment, to teach these things freely unto your children."[11] While Jesus was living in mortality, He taught the people as follows: "Let your light so shine before men, that they may see your good works, and glorify your Father which is in heaven."[12] Also, "Whosoever therefore shall break one of these least commandments, and shall teach men so, he shall be called the least in the kingdom of heaven: but whosoever shall do and teach them, the same shall be called great in the kingdom of heaven."[13] Jesus also taught: "But whoso shall offend one of these little ones which believes in me, it were better for him that a millstone were hanged about his neck, and that he were drowned in the depth of the sea."[14] In modern revelation, the Lord gave the following commandment to the Latter-day Saints: "Behold, I send you out to testify and warn the people, and it becometh every man who hath been warned to warn his neighbor. Therefore, they are left without excuse, and their sins are upon their own heads."[15] Thus the Lord made known in the very beginning that man had a moral responsibility toward his neighbor—in other words, he was "his brother's keeper"—and God has reiterated His will regarding man's responsibility to his fellow men from age to age during the various gospel dispensations even to the present day.

[11]*Ibid.*, 6:58.
[12]*Matthew* 5:16.
[13]*Ibid.*, 5:19.
[14]*Ibid.*, 18:6; Mark 9:42; Luke 17:2.
[15]*Doctrine and Covenants* 88:81-82; 68:25-29.

CAIN'S POSTERITY

In the Book of Moses is recorded the following brief account of Cain's posterity:

Cain's posterity from Enoch to Lamech:

42. And Cain knew his wife, and she conceived and bare Enoch, and he also begat many sons and daughters. And he builded a city, and he called the name of the city after the name of his son, Enoch.

43. And unto Enoch was born Irad, and other sons and daughters. And Irad begat Mahujael, and other sons and daughters. And Mahujael begat Methusael, and other sons and daughters. And Methusael begat Lamech.

44. And Lamech took unto himself two wives; the name of one being Adah, and the name of the other, Zillah.

45. And Adah bare Jabal; he was the father of such as dwell in tents, and they were keepers of cattle; and his brother's name was Jubal, who was the father of all such as handle the harp and organ.

46. And Zillah, she also bare Tubal Cain, an instructor of every artificer in brass and iron. And the sister of Tubal Cain was called Naamah.

Moses 5:42-46.

LAMECH AND SECRET COMBINATIONS

Lamech's secret combination with Satan and works of darkness among the "sons of men:"

47. And Lamech said unto his wives, Adah and Zillah: Hear my voice, ye wives of Lamech, hearken unto my speech; for I have slain a man to my wounding, and a young man to my hurt.

48. If Cain shall be avenged sevenfold, truly Lamech shall be seventy and seven fold;

49. For Lamech having entered into a covenant with Satan, after the manner of Cain, wherein he became Master Mahan, master of that great secret which was administered unto Cain by Satan; and Irad, the son of Enoch, having known their secret, began to reveal it unto the sons of Adam;

50. Wherefore Lamech, being angry, slew him, not like unto Cain, his brother Abel, for the sake of getting gain, but he slew him for the oath's sake.

51. For, from the days of Cain, there was a secret combination, and their works were in the dark, and they knew every man his brother.

52. Wherefore the Lord cursed Lamech, and his house, and all them that had covenanted with Satan; for they kept not the commandments of God, and it displeased God, and he ministered not unto them, and their works were abominations, and began to spread among all the sons of men.

53. And it was among the sons of men, and among the daughters of men these things were not spoken, because that Lamech had spoken the secret unto his wives, and they rebelled against him, and declared these things abroad, and had not compassion;

54. Wherefore Lamech was despised, and cast out, and came not among the sons of men, lest he should die.

55. And thus the works of darkness began to prevail among all the sons of men.

56. And God cursed the earth with a sore curse, and was angry with the wicked, with all the sons of men whom he had made;

57. For they would not hearken unto his voice, nor believe on his Only Begotten Son, even him whom he declared should come in the meridian of time, who was prepared from before the foundation of the world.

Moses 5:47-57.

Verses 47 and 48 are poetry. The first of these reads as if Lamech killed two men, but he killed only one. That verse serves as a good example of parallelism, which is an outstanding characteristic in Hebrew poetry. Parellelism means that there is a repetition of ideas. There are three main types of parallelism in Hebrew poetry, namely, synonymous, antithetic, and synthetic. Verse 47 illustrates the synonymous type, i.e., the second line, or *stichos*, repeats the thought of the first line.

The foregoing scripture makes it clear that "secret combinations" (works of darkness) continued among the "sons of men" from the time of Cain and that they were patterned after the oath and covenant made by Cain and Satan (verses 47-51), thereby fulfilling God's prediction wherein He declared that *"it shall be said in time to come—That these abominations were had from Cain."*[16] Lamech's sin differed from Cain's in that Lamech committed murder merely for the oath's sake (verse 50). Thus wickedness and great works of darkness spread among the "sons of men"—non-church members—and God was grieved because they would not accept the Gospel of Jesus Christ (verses 52-57).

SECRET COMBINATIONS IN ANCIENT AMERICA

The *Book of Mormon* tells the story of secret combinations and works of darkness flourishing in ancient America, first in the days of the Jaredites and later during the period of Nephite history. Thus God's prophecy to Cain was fulfilled time and time again. In fact, it was those secret combinations which brought about the destruction of the Jaredites and later the complete annihilation of the Nephites.

In regard to the establishing of secret combinations among the Jaredites, the *Book of Mormon* record states:

And it came to pass that . . . Akish did administer unto them the oaths which were given by them of old who also sought power, *which had been handed down even from Cain,* who was a murderer from the beginning. And they were kept up by the power of the devil to administer these oaths unto the people, to keep them in darkness, to help such as sought power to gain power, and to murder, and to plunder, and to lie, and to commit all manner of wickedness and whoredoms. . . .

And it came to pass that they formed a secret combination, even as they of old; which combination is most abominable and wicked above all, in the sight of God; for the Lord worketh not in secret combinations,

---
[16]Moses 5:25.

neither doth he will that man should shed blood, but in all things hath
forbidden it, from the beginning of man.[17]

During the days of the Nephites, the following is recorded
regarding the origin of secret combinations and works of darkness among this people:

> For there was one Gadianton, who was exceedingly expert in many
> works, and also in his craft, to carry on the secret works of murder and
> of robbery; therefore he became the leader of the band of Kishkumen, . . .
> and they all entered into a covenant, yea, swearing by their everlasting
> Maker; that they would tell no man that Kishkumen had murdered
> Pahoran.[18]

> But behold, Satan did stir up the hearts of the more part of the peo-
> ple of the Nephites, insomuch that they did unite with those bands of
> [Gadianton] robbers, and did enter into their covenants and their oaths,
> that they would protect and preserve one another in whatsoever difficult
> circumstances they should be placed, that they should not suffer for their
> murders, and their plunderings, and their stealings, and it came to pass
> that they did have their signs, yea, their secret signs, and their secret
> words; and this that they might distinguish a brother who had entered
> into the covenant, that whatsoever wickedness his brother should do he
> should not be injured by his brother, nor by those who did belong to
> his band, who had taken this covenant. And thus they might murder,
> and plunder, and steal, and commit whoredoms and all manner of
> wickedness, contrary to the laws of their country and also the laws of
> their God. . . .

> Now behold, those secret oaths and covenants . . . were put into
> the heart of Gadianton by that same being who did entice our first par-
> ents to partake of the forbidden fruit—yea, *that same being who did plot*
> *with Cain,* that if he would murder his brother Abel it should not be
> known unto the world. And he did plot with Cain and his followers
> from that time on.[19]

SECRET COMBINATIONS IN THE LATTER DAYS

Approximately 600 B. C. the Prophet Nephi predicted
that in the latter days secret combinations would be established
in America. He warned the people of our day regarding these
works of darkness. To quote the words of Nephi:

> And there are also secret combinations, even as in times of old, ac-
> cording to the combinations of the devil, for he is the foundation of these
> things; yea, the foundation of murder, and works of darkness; yea, and
> he leadeth them by the neck with a flaxen cord, until he bindeth them

---

[17]Ether 8:7-19. Read the entire reference in Ether.
[18]Alma 37:21-32; Helaman 2:4; 1:1-12; 2:1-14.
[19]*Ibid.*, 6:15-41; 3:23; 7:1-6, 25-39; 8:1-4, 26-28; 11:1-2, 9-10, 24-38; 3 Nephi 1:27-30; 2:11-13,
    17-19; 3:1, 9-10; 4:1-29; 5:4-7; 4 Nephi 1:40-46; Mormon 1:18-19; 2:8, 27-29; 8:7-9.

with his strong cords forever. For behold, my beloved brethren, I say unto you that the Lord God worketh not in darkness.[20]

One thousand years later, Moroni, the last writer on the ancient *Book of Mormon* records, confirmed Nephi's prediction and gave a warning to the people who should live in America in the latter days.[21] His final injunction to the inhabitants of this land was that the Lord commanded them to be awake to the awful situation which should exist among them when secret combinations should be established. They were to stamp them out in order that the people might maintain their liberties and preserve America forever as a chosen and blessed land.

[20]2 Nephi 26:22-23.
[21]Ether 8:22-23.

Chapter 26

ENOCH AND THE CITY OF ZION

ENOCH'S CALL TO BE A PROPHET

Enoch, the son of Jared, was the seventh great Patriarch and prophet from Adam through the line of Seth. The *Pearl of Great Price* reports the following in regard to the training that he received while in his youth: "And Jared taught Enoch in all the ways of God."[1] In referring to the line of patriarchs through whom Enoch descended, the same record states: "And this is the genealogy of the sons of Adam, who was the son of God, with whom God, himself, conversed. And they were preachers of righteousness, and spake and prophesied, and called upon men, everywhere, to repent; and faith was taught unto the children of men."[2]

In this book up to this point, we have already discussed a number of Enoch's teachings. It now becomes our purpose in this chapter to present his missionary call, the doctrine he taught, and the success he attained at establishing a righteous society.

Enoch called by the Lord to preach the gospel and endowed with the power of God:

26. And it came to pass that Enoch journeyed in the land, among the people; and as he journeyed, the Spirit of God descended out of heaven, and abode upon him.

27. And he heard a voice from heaven, saying: Enoch, my son, prophesy unto this people, and say unto them— Repent, for thus saith the Lord: I am angry with this people, and my fierce anger is kindled against them; for their hearts have waxed hard, and their ears are dull of hearing, and their eyes cannot see afar off;

28. And for these many generations, ever since the day that I created them,

have they gone astray, and have denied me, and have sought their own counsels in the dark; and in their own abominations have they devised murder, and have not kept the commandments, which I gave unto their father, Adam.

29. Wherefore, they have foresworn themselves, and, by their oaths, they have brought upon themselves death; and a hell I have prepared for them, if they repent not;

30. And this is a decree, which I have sent forth in the beginning of the world, from my own mouth, from the foundation thereof, and by the mouths of my servants, thy fathers, have I de-

[1]Moses 6:21.
[2]*Ibid.*, 6:22-23.

creed it, even as it shall be sent forth in the world, unto the ends thereof.

31. And when Enoch had heard these words, he bowed himself to the earth, before the Lord, and spake before the Lord, saying: Why is it that I have found favor in thy sight, and am but a lad, and all the people hate me; for I am slow of speech; wherefore am I thy servant?

32. And the Lord said unto Enoch: Go forth and do as I have commanded thee, and no man shall pierce thee. Open thy mouth, and it shall be filled, and I will give thee utterance, for all flesh is in my hands, and I will do as seemeth me good.

33. Say unto this people: Choose ye this day, to serve the Lord God who made you.

34. Behold my Spirit is upon you, wherefore all thy words will I justify; and the mountains shall flee before you, and the rivers shall turn from their course; and thou shalt abide in me, and I in you; therefore walk with me.

Moses 6:26-34.

According to the foregoing scripture, Enoch was called by the Lord through revelation to be a prophet and a preacher of righteousness. In the description of the wickedness of the people (verses 27-29), the Lord inferred that these sinful people belonged to the secret combinations that were discussed in the last chapter; and He proclaimed that if they did not repent they would experience a spiritual death and be confined to hell. Verse 30 makes reference to the fact that the gospel was given to Father Adam in the beginning, as previously discussed, and its truths would be in the world until the end thereof.

Enoch's humility is plainly shown in verse 31. His reply to the Lord reminds one of Moses' attitude when God spoke to him from the burning bush and assigned him to deliver the Israelites from the Egyptian bondage. Regarding this event, the following is recorded in the *Bible:*

And Moses said unto the Lord, O my Lord, I am not eloquent, neither heretofore, nor since thou hast spoken unto thy servant: but I am slow of speech, and of a slow tongue.

And the Lord said unto him, Who hath made man's mouth? or who maketh the dumb, or deaf, or the seeing, or the blind? have not I the Lord? Now therefore go, and I will be with thy mouth, and teach thee what thou shalt say.[3]

The marvelous promises made to Enoch in verses 32-34 were all fulfilled, as will be shown in the topic "Enoch's Faith."

ENOCH, A SEER

Enoch's vision of the spirit world and his powers of seership:

35. And the Lord spake unto Enoch, and said unto him: Anoint thine eyes with clay, and wash them, and thou shalt see. And he did so.

36. And he beheld the spirits that God had created; and he beheld also things which were not visible to the natural eye; and from thenceforth came the saying abroad in the land: A seer hath the Lord raised up unto his people.

Moses 6:35-36.

---

[3]Exodus 4:10-12; 3:1-22; 4:1-17.

In the foregoing scripture, Enoch is proclaimed to be a "seer," because he was permitted by the Lord to look into the unseen world and behold the things "which were not visible to the natural eye." The meaning of the term "seer" was aptly explained in the *Book of Mormon* record by a man named Ammon. He told King Limhi, who resided in the city of Nephi, that King Mosiah at Zarehemla possessed a gift from God which enabled him to translate records that were of ancient date. This he accomplished by making use of intsruments known as "interpreters" or "Urim and Thummim" which were endowed with miraculous powers. Ammon explained that "Whosoever is commanded to look in them, the same is called seer. . . . A seer is greater than a prophet." To continue by quoting his exact words:

A seer is a revelator and a prophet also; and a gift which is greater can no man have, except he should possess the power of God, which no man can; yet a man may have great power given him from God. But a seer can know of things which are past, and also of things which are to come, and by them shall all things be revealed, or, rather, shall secret things be made manifest, and hidden things shall come to light, and things which are not known shall be made known by them, and also things shall be made known by them which otherwise could not be known. Thus God has provided a means that man, through faith, might work mighty miracles; therefore he becometh a great benefit to his fellow beings.[4]

ENOCH'S MISSIONARY WORK

Enoch's powers as a missionary and his message:

37. And it came to pass that Enoch went forth in the land, among the people, standing upon the hills and the high places, and cried with a loud voice, testifying against their works; and all men were offended because of him.

38. And they came forth to hear him, upon the high places, saying unto the tent-keepers: Tarry ye here and keep the tents, while we go yonder to behold the seer, for he prophesieth, and there is a strange thing in the land; a wild man hath come among us.

39. And it came to pass when they heard him, no man laid hands on him; for fear came on all them that heard him; for he walked with God.

40. And there came a man unto him,

whose name was Mahijah, and said unto him: Tell us plainly who thou art, and from whence thou comest?

41. And he said unto them: I came out from the land of Cainan, the land of my fathers, a land of righteousness unto this day. And my father taught me in all the ways of God.

42. And it came to pass, as I journeyed from the land of Cainan by the sea east, I beheld a vision; and lo, the heavens I saw, and the Lord spake with me, and gave me commandment; wherefore, for this cause, to keep the commandment, I speak forth these words.

43. And Enoch continued his speech, saying: The Lord which spake with me,

---

[4]Mosiah 8:13-18.

the same is the God of heaven, and he is my God, and your God, and ye are my brethren, and why counsel ye yourselves, and deny the God of heaven?

44. The heavens he made; the earth is his footstool; and the foundation thereof is his. Behold, he laid it, an host of men hath he brought, in upon the face thereof.

48. And he said unto them: Because that Adam fell, we are; and by his fall came death; and we are made partakers of misery and woe.

49. Behold Satan hath come among the children of men, and tempteth them to worship him; and men have become carnal, sensual, and devilish, and are shut out from the presence of God.

Moses 6:37-44, 48-49.

In verses 37 and 38 we learn that Enoch pursued his missionary work with great vigor, testifying against the wickedness of the people as the Lord had commanded him and prophesying many things which would come to pass. The inhabitants of the land were astonished and offended at his teachings, but were afraid to harm him "for he walked with God."

In verses 42-44, Enoch describes the vision of the Lord which he had had and presented to the people his knowledge of God's personality and powers. Then, in his statement "Because that Adam fell, we are," Enoch echoed a divine truth which was earlier uttered by Mother Eve, wherein she said "Were it not for our transgression we never should have had seed."[5] Hundreds of years later, Father Lehi confirmed that doctrine in his statement which has in our day become famous: *"Adam fell that men might be; and men are, that they might have joy."*[6] The foregoing scripture closes with Enoch's description of the first apostasy which took place among Adam's descendants. It was discussed in the chapter "Secret Combinations and Works of Darkness."[7]

LAND OF CAINAN

In verse 41, the fact is pointed out that Enoch's home was "the land of Cainan." This land is not the same country that was known as "the land of Canaan" in the Old Testament record and Palestine in the New Testament. The land of Cainan was given that name by Adam's grandson, Enos. Regarding this event, the *Pearl of Great Price* states:

And Enos lived ninety years, and begat Cainan. And Enos and the residue of the people of God came out from the land, which was called

[5]Moses 5:11.
[6]2 Nephi 2:25.
[7]Moses 5:13.

Shulon, and dwelt in a land of promise, which he called after his own son, whom he had named Cainan.[8]

According to verse 42 the land of Cainan was by "the sea east." In an earlier chapter the fact was pointed out that following their expulsion from Eden, Adam and Eve lived north of the Garden at a place known as Adam-ondi-Ahman. It seems from the scripture under consideration at this point that Enos moved from the home of his fathers and located near "the sea east;" therefore, the land of Cainan—his new home—probably was located somewhere in what today is known as eastern United States.

ENOCH'S FAITH AND POWER

Enoch's faith and the power of God that was with him:

12. And it came to pass that Enoch continued to call upon all the people, save it were the people of Canaan, to repent;
47. And as Enoch spake forth the words of God, the people trembled, and could not stand in his presence.
13. And so great was the faith of Enoch, that he led the people of God, and their enemies came to battle against them; and he spake the word of the Lord, and the earth trembled, and the mountains fled, even according to his command; and the rivers of water were turned out of their course; and the roar of the lions was heard out of the wilderness; and all nations feared greatly, so powerful was the word of Enoch, and so great was the power of the language which God had given him.
14. There also came up a land out of the depth of the sea, and so great was the fear of the enemies of the people of God, that they fled and stood afar off and went upon the land which came up out of the depth of the sea.
15. And the giants of the land, also, stood afar off; and there went forth a curse upon all people that fought against God;
16. And from that time forth there were wars and bloodshed among them;
...   Moses 7:12; 6:47; 7:13-16a.

This scripture (verse 12) points out that Enoch preached to all the people "save it were the people of Canaan" and called upon them to repent. We have already learned that he did not preach to the people of Canaan because they were descendants of Cain, had black skins, and were not permitted to hold the Priesthood.[9]

The marvelous powers possessed by Enoch, as described in verses 13-15, 47, are the powers of God expressed through the Holy Priesthood and they operate through faith. There have been many prophets of God throughout the ages who have possessed faith and Priesthood powers similar to Enoch's. For example, "the brother of Jared said unto the mountain Zerin,

[8]*Ibid.*, 6:17.
[9]Abraham 1:21-26; Moses 7:8, 12, 22.

Remove—and it was removed."[10] Also, through faith and
through the powers of the Priesthood Moses brought forth
water from the rock and parted the waters of the Red Sea. In
the *Inspired Version* of the *Bible,* the following description of
Enoch's power is recorded:

> For God having sworn unto Enoch and unto his seed with an oath
> by himself; that everyone being ordained after this order [Holy Priest-
> hood after the Order of the Son of God] and calling should have power,
> by faith, to break mountains, divide the seas, to dry up waters, to turn
> them out of their courses; to put at defiance the armies of nations, to
> divide the earth, to break every band, to stand in the presence of God;
> to do all things according to his will, according to his command, subdue
> principalities and powers; and this by the will of the Son of God which
> was from before the foundation of the world.[11]

The Lord revealed to the Prophet Joseph Smith the fact
that Enoch received the Priesthood directly from Father Adam.
To quote: "Enoch was twenty-five years old when he was ordained under the hand of Adam; and he was sixty-five and
Adam blessed him,"[12] that is, gave him a patriarchal blessing.
Three years prior to his death, Father Adam gave Enoch and
the other great high priests his last blessings.[13]

GIANTS

In verse 15 of the foregoing scripture the statement is
made: "And the giants of the land, also, stood afar off." In
the writings of a number of the ancient peoples, such as those
of the Greeks, the Romans, the Mexicans, as well as the *Bible,*
frequent references are made to giants who lived during the
early periods of human history. In the *Bible* the following is
recorded in reference to the days of Enoch, Lamech, and
Noah:

> There were giants in the earth in those days; and also after that,
> when the sons of God came in unto the daughters of men, and they
> bare children to them, the same became mighty men which were of old,
> men of renown.[14]

And the following statement appears in the *Pearl of
Great Price:*

[10]Ether 12:30; 12:6-38.
[11]*Inspired Version, Bible,* Genesis 14:30-31.
[12]*Doctrine and Covenants* 107:48.
[13]*Ibid.,* 107:53.
[14]Genesis 6:4.

And in those days there were giants on the earth, and they sought Noah to take away his life; but the Lord was with Noah, and the power of the Lord was upon him.[15]

Even as late in history as the days of Moses and Joshua, the following is recorded regarding the giants:

And the coast of Og king of Bashan, which was of the *remnant of the giants,* that dwelt at Ashtaroth and at Edrei.[16]

All the kingdom of Og in Bashan, which reigned in Ashtaroth and in Edrei, who remained of the *remnant of the giants*: for these did Moses smite, and cast them out.[17]

The teachings of the *Pearl of Great Price,* confirmed by a number of other sources, definitely point out that there lived in ancient times a group of people known as the "giants." Just why they were called giants is not made clear, but it may have been that the members of this race were exceptionally large in stature. For this reason they could have received the name of the "giants." It is certain that during various periods in history individuals, and at times, groups of people, have lived who were exceptionally large in stature. For example, Goliath, whom David slew, was purported to have been "six cubits and a span" in height, which is approximately ten feet.

An article entitled "Fairy Tale Giants May Have Been Real," taken and condensed from the *American Weekly* of September 17, 1944, appeared in the *Science Digest* (pp. 15-16) in December of that same year. In it is pointed out that in ancient times there were men of gigantic size who lived upon this earth whom we could call giants. The following is quoted from that article:

At last science has proved what it long suspected—that those fairy tale giants really and truly did exist, "once upon a time." . . . These two-legged powerhouses were the normal type for their day.

Gigantopithecus, whose early existence recently was reported by Dr. Franz Weidenreich of the New York Museum of Natural History—co-discoverer of the giant with Dr. R. von Koenigswald of the Geological Survey of Netherlands Indies—averaged seven to nine feet tall, weighed 500 to 600 pounds and had teeth six times the size of modern man's and twice that of a gorilla. It is possible that an oversized Gigantopithecus may have stood 12 feet tall and weighed at least a half ton. . . .

The first clue to Gigantopithecus appeared in the shop of an herb doctor in Hong Kong who had three "giant's teeth" for sale. . . . He [Dr.

---

[15]Moses 8:18.
[16]Joshua 12:4; Numbers 13:26-33.
[17]*Ibid.,* 13:12; Deuteronomy 3:1-3.

von Koenigswald] and Doctor Weidenreich were convinced that these were human teeth. This seemed preposterous, because they were twice the size even of the biggest ape teeth. . . . In 1941, a jawbone was found in Java, unquestionably human, but of such gigantic size that it could have held those "giant teeth." . . .

Mr. Henry Wysham Lanier published a book in 1922, entitled *A Book of Giants*. On pages 306 to 314, he pointed out that in our day there are a good many people who live, or who have lived recently, who are large enough to be classed as giants. To quote a portion of his discussion:

During the last two hundred years there have been over a hundred men and women, figuring in the public eye, who have exceeded seven feet. Probably twenty-five of these have had a height of eight feet or over. . . .

Apparently the tallest man on record was Machnow, a Russian, who was born at Witebsk about 1882, was exhibited in London in 1905, in the United States, Germany, Holland, and elsewhere, and died around the age of thirty.

None of his family was exceptionally tall, and he himself was a normal child up to the age of four. Then he began to grow very rapidly, not eating a great deal, but sometimes sleeping for twenty-four hours at a time. At fifteen he was about five feet two; at twenty-two, according to Professors Luschau and Lisauer he was seven feet and ten inches. When he appeared in London next year, he was credited with nine feet three inches, and the most conservative of British encyclopaedias accepts this figure. . . . His weight was given as 360 pounds.

The champion in 1920 was George Auger, credited with eight feet four inches, who is an American and affects frontier costume. Then there was the famous smiling Chinaman, Chang, who exhibited his eight feet or so to nearly the whole world for a long period beginning about the end of the American Civil War.

A generation back there were in the eight-foot class the Austrian Winkelmeier; Paule Marie Elizabeth Wehde, born at Ben-Rendorft in Thuringia, who was called "The Queen of the Amazons" and was handsome enough to appear with success at the London Alhambra in a review called "Babil and Bijou"; Ben Hicks, "the Denver Steeple"; and, a little smaller, Captain Martin Van Buren Bates of Kentucky, who married in London in 1871 Miss Anna Swan, of Nova Scotia, who was three inches taller than himself—they were celebrated as the tallest bride and groom in the world—scoring fourteen feet eight inches between them, while the captain's weight of 450 pounds made him a notable figure.

At Ruanda in the Belgian Congo there lives a group of people at the present time who are large in stature, averaging approximately seven feet in height. These people could rightly termed giants. An interesting short article by Leonard

Lyons appeared in the *Salt Lake Tribune* (p. 7) on September 28, 1948, in regard to them. In that article the following statement is made:

> Arch Oboler has been in the Belgian Congo for a year, filming shorts for television. Last week in Ruanda he photographed the *giant king* of the Batutsis and his high jumpers. Two of them, using the old-fashioned feet-first method of jumping, broke the Olympic record for Oboler's camera. . . . Then the six-foot seven king asked the camera crew if Americans had any athletic specializations.

ZION—THE CITY OF HOLINESS

Among all the dispensations of the Gospel of Jesus Christ committed to man, the dispensation given to Enoch was one of the most glorious, as the following scripture attests:

Zion—the City of Holiness—and the translation of Enoch and his people:

16. . . . but the Lord came and dwelt with his people, and they dwelt in righteousness.

17. The fear of the Lord was upon all nations, so great was the glory of the Lord, which was upon his people. And the Lord blessed the land, and they were blessed upon the mountains, and upon the high places, and did flourish.

18. And the Lord called his people Zion, because they were of one heart and one mind, and dwelt in righteousness; and there was no poor among them.

19. And Enoch continued his preaching in righteousness unto the people of God. And it came to pass in his days, that he built a city that was called the City of Holiness, even Zion.

20. And it came to pass that Enoch talked with the Lord! and he said unto the Lord: Surely Zion shall dwell in safety forever. But the Lord said unto Enoch: Zion have I blessed, but the residue of the people have I cursed.

21. And it came to pass that the Lord showed unto Enoch all the inhabitants of the earth; and he beheld, and lo, Zion, in process of time, was taken up into heaven. And the Lord said unto Enoch: Behold mine abode forever.

27. And Enoch beheld angels descending out of heaven, bearing testimony of the Father and Son; and the Holy Ghost fell on many, and they were caught up by the powers of heaven into Zion.

68. And all the days of Zion, in the days of Enoch, were three hundred and sixty-five years.

69. And Enoch and all his people walked with God, and he dwelt in the midst of Zion; and it came to pass that Zion was not, for God received it up into his own bosom; and from thence went forth the saying, ZION IS FLED.

Moses 7:16b-21, 27, 68-69.

The foregoing scripture gives a description of a perfect social and economic order that God established upon the earth through the instrumentality of His prophet Enoch. Elder James E. Talmage gives the location of Enoch's "City of Holiness" as follows: "We have already spoken of the Zion of Enoch, a city once situated on the North American continent, whose inhabitants were so righteous that they too were called

Zion, 'because they were of one heart and one mind.' "[18] Finally, the ancient Patriarch and his city were taken to heaven and the Lord declared that the City of Enoch had become His abode forever.

In a meagre account, the *Bible* bears testimony to the teachings of the *Pearl of Great Price* in regard to Enoch:

And Jared lived an hundred sixty and two years, and he begat Enoch. . . . And Enoch lived sixty and five years, and begat Methuselah: and Enoch walked with God after he begat Methuselah three hundred years, and begat sons and daughters: and all the days of Enoch were three hundred sixty and five years: and Enoch walked with God: and he was not; for God took him.[19]

The Works of Flavius Josephus contain even a more meagre description of this ancient man of God, than does the *Bible*, but his statement is significant corroborative evidence. To quote:

He [Jared] lived nine hundred and sixty-two years; and then his son Enoch succeeded him, who was born when his father was one hundred and sixty-two years old. Now he, when he had lived three hundred and sixty-five years departed, and went to God; whence it is that they have not written down his death.[20]

ENOCH AND LATTER-DAY REVELATION

On several different occasions the Lord revealed pertinent information to the Prophet Joseph Smith regarding Enoch, his people, and the city Zion. To quote:

And he [Enoch] saw the Lord, and he walked with him, and was before his face continually; and he walked with God three hundred and sixty-five years, making him four hundred and thirty years old when he was translated.[21]

The foregoing revelation from the Lord to the Prophet Joseph Smith which states that Enoch was four hundred thirty year of age when he was translated helps to clarify the statement regarding Enoch's age as biven in the *Pearl of Great Price*. That record states: "And Enoch lived sixty-five years and begat Methuselah."[22] A little further along in the same record the following statement is recorded: "And all the days of Zion, in the days of Enoch, were three hundred and sixty-

[18]James E. Talmage, *The Articles of Faith*, p. 362.
[19]Genesis 5:21-24.
[20]Flavius Josephus, *The Works of Flavius Josephus*, translated by William Whiston, p. 28.
[21]*Doctrine and Covenants* 107:49.
[22]Moses 6:25

five years."[23] Therefore, Enoch was sixty-five years of age when he begat Methuselah and began his missionary work, and he lived three hundred sixty-five additional years with the people of Zion, making a total of four hundred thirty years. Thus the *Pearl of Great Price* and modern revelation to the Prophet Joseph Smith are in harmony with each other.

And again we read:

I am the same which have taken the Zion of Enoch into mine own bosom;[24] . . . Wherefore, hearken ye together and let me show unto you even my wisdom—the wisdom of him whom you say is the God of Enoch, and his brethren, who were separated from the earth, and were received unto myself—a city reserved until a day of righteousness shall come—a day which was sought for by all holy men, and they found it not because of wickedness and abominations.[25]

Therefore, Enoch and his associates, the people who created one of the most perfect human societies—if not the most perfect—that has ever existed on this earth, were translated and caught up into heaven; and Jesus Christ declared that He would make His abode with those righteous people forever. There they shall remain until the Lord transfers his abode to this earth to reign here for one thousand years as Lord of lords and King of kings.

---

[23]*Ibid.*, 7:68.
[24]*Doctrine and Covenants* 38:4.
[25]*Ibid.*, 45:11-12.

Chapter 27

ENOCH'S MARVELOUS VISION

Vision of Enoch's Day

Enoch was privileged by the Lord to see in vision the major events in the history of the world from his time down to the second coming of the Son of Man and the millennial reign. A number of these events have been discussed in previous chapters and some of them will be presented in the pages that follow; however, this chapter will be devoted to Enoch's vision of the conditions that prevailed during his day and during the time of Noah, including the covenant that the Lord made with Enoch regarding Noah's posterity.

Enoch's vision of the people of the world during his time:

2. And from that time forth Enoch began to prophesy, saying unto the people, that: As I was journeying, and stood upon the place Mahujah, and cried unto the Lord, there came a voice out of heaven, saying—Turn ye, and get ye upon the mount Simeon.

3. And it came to pass that I turned and went up on the mount; and as I stood upon the mount, I beheld the heavens open, and I was clothed upon with glory;

4. And I saw the Lord; and he stood before my face, and he talked with me, even as a man talketh one with another, face to face; and he said unto me: Look, and I will show unto thee the world for the space of many generations.

5. And it came to pass that I beheld in the valley of Shum, and lo, a great people which dwelt in tents, which were the people of Shum.

6. And again the Lord said unto me: Look; and I looked towards the north, and I beheld the people of Canaan, which dwelt in tents.

7. And the Lord said unto me: Prophesy; and I prophesied, saying: Behold the people of Canaan, which are numerous, shall go forth in battle array against the people of Shum, and shall slay them that they shall utterly be destroyed; and the people of Canaan shall divide themselves in the land, and the land shall be barren and unfruitful, and none other people shall dwell there but the people of Canaan;

8. For behold, the Lord shall curse the land with much heat, and the barrenness thereof shall go forth forever; and there was a blackness came upon all the children of Canaan, that they were despised among all people.

9. And it came to pass that the Lord said unto me: Look; and I looked, and I beheld the land of Sharon, and the land of Enoch, and the land of Omner, and the land of Heni, and the land of Shem, and the land of Haner, and the land of Hanannihah, and all the inhabitants thereof;

10. And the Lord said unto me: Go to this people, and say unto them—Repent, lest I come out and smite them with a curse, and they die.

Moses 7:2-10.

According to verses 2-3 of the foregoing scripture, Enoch received his marvelous vision as an immediate result of prayer. The fact that he talked with the Lord face to face, the description of the barrenness and unfruitfulness of the land of Canaan, and the blackness which came upon the children of that land, have been discussed in earlier chapters. Probably the major purpose of God's showing Enoch the countries and peoples of the world at his time was to more strongly impress on the Prophet's mind the vital necessity of preaching repentance to them (verse 9-10).

VISION OF NOAH'S DAY

Enoch's vision of the wickedness of the people in the days of Noah:

21. And it came to pass that the Lord showed unto Enoch all the inhabitants of the earth; and he beheld, and lo, Zion, in process of time, was taken up into heaven. And the Lord said unto Enoch: Behold mine abode forever.

22. And Enoch also beheld the residue of the people which were the sons of Adam; and they were a mixture of all the seed of Adam save it were the seed of Cain, for the seed of Cain were black, and had not place among them.

23. And after that Zion was taken up into heaven, Enoch beheld, and lo, all the nations of the earth were before him;

24. And there came generation upon generation; and Enoch was high and lifted up, even in the bosom of the Father, and of the Son of Man; and behold, the power of Satan was upon all the face of the earth.

25. And he saw angels descending out of heaven; and he heard a loud voice saying: Wo, wo be unto the inhabitants of the earth.

26. And he beheld Satan; and he had a great chain in his hand, and it veiled the whole face of the earth with darkness; and he looked up and laughed, and his angels rejoiced.

Moses 7:21-26.

In the chapter "Enoch and the City of Zion," the fact was pointed out that the City of Enoch was taken into heaven and all the righteous people of the earth, except one family through whom Noah would be born, were picked up also and taken to the City of Zion in heaven. Verse 21 of the foregoing scripture repeats that idea. The next several verses describe the extreme wickedness that prevailed upon the face of the entire earth following the translation of the people of Enoch down to the time of Noah. Satan was reigning supreme, as the description indicates, the "great chain in his hand" being symbolical of the spiritual darkness and bondage of the people. The fact that Cain's descendants were black and did not intermarry with the other people of the earth (verse 22) was discussed in an earlier chapter.

God Wept

When God showed unto Enoch the vision of the gross iniquity that would prevail throughout the entire earth at the time of Noah, so great was the grief of the Lord over His sinful children that He wept, as the following scriptures will show:

God wept because of the wickedness of the inhabitants of the earth in the days of Noah and He explained to Enoch the reasons for His grief:

28. And it came to pass that the God of heaven looked upon the residue of the people, and he wept; and Enoch bore record of it, saying: How is it that the heavens weep, and shed forth their tears as the rain upon the mountains?

29. And Enoch said unto the Lord: How is it that thou canst weep, seeing thou art holy, and from all eternity to all eternity?

30. And were it possible that man could number the particles of the earth, yea millions of earths like this, it would not be a beginning to the number of thy creations; and thy curtains are stretched out still; and yet thou art there, and thy bosom is there; and also thou art just; thou art merciful and kind forever;

31. And thou hast taken Zion to thine own bosom, from all thy creations, from all eternity to all eternity; and naught but peace, justice, and truth is the habitation of thy throne; and mercy shall go before thy face and have no end; how is it thou canst weep?

32. The Lord said unto Enoch: Behold these thy brethren; they are the workmanship of mine own hands, and I gave unto them their knowledge, in the day I created them; and in the Garden of Eden, gave I unto man his agency;

33. And unto thy brethren have I said, and also given commandment, that they should love one another, and that they should choose me, their Father;

but behold, they are without affection, and they hate their own blood;

34. And the fire of mine indignation is kindled against them; and in my hot displeasure will I send in the floods upon them, for my fierce anger is kindled against them.

36. Wherefore, I can stretch forth mine hands and hold all the creations which I have made; and mine eye can pierce them also, and among all the workmanship of mine hands there has not been so great wickedness as among thy brethren.

37. But behold, their sins shall be upon the heads of their fathers; Satan shall be their father, and misery shall be their doom; and the whole heavens shall weep over them, even all the workmanship of mine hands; wherefore should not the heavens weep, seeing these shall suffer?

38. But behold, these which thine eyes are upon shall perish in the floods; and behold, I will shut them up; a prison I have prepared for them.

39. And That which I have chosen hath plead before my face. Wherefore, he suffereth for their sins; inasmuch as they will repent in the day that my Chosen shall return unto me, and until that day they shall be in torment;

40. Wherefore, for this shall the heavens weep, yea, and all the workmanship of mine hands.

Moses 7:28-40.

The foregoing scripture contains a very unusual and interesting description of the great concern and deep love that God had for the inhabitants of this earth and the sorrow that it caused Him when mortal beings sinned. God's great concern for mortals represents the full and deepest expression of love that an infinite and divine Heavenly Father is capable of bestowing upon His own offspring; and that love and concern is far superior and much more complete than any mortal father is capable of experiencing.

Verses 30 and 31 give Enoch's description of the majesty, power, justice, and love of God, pointing out the millions of worlds that He has created, and the adoration and worship that He receives from His righteous children that dwell upon those worlds. The facts that when God placed Adam and Eve in the Garden of Eden He gave them knowledge and their free agency and the two great commandments of love (verses 32-33) have been discussed in an earlier chapter. Even after the Divine Being had done all of these things for His children, Enoch saw that they would completely reject all gospel truths which would make it necessary for God to destroy the inhabitants of the earth with a flood. In verse 36, the Lord points out the very significant fact that of all the worlds that He has created this earth holds the record in wickedness.

In Chapter 30 will be discussed the topic of the spirits which were shut up in prison at the time of the flood, as pointed out in verses 38-40; therefore, we need not go into that subject at this time.

ENOCH'S GRIEF

Enoch grieved and was comforted:

41. And it came to pass that the Lord spake unto Enoch, and told Enoch all the doings of the children of men; wherefore Enoch knew, and looked upon their wickedness, and their misery, and wept and stretched forth his arms, and his heart swelled wide as eternity; and his bowels yearned; and all eternity shook.

42. And Enoch also saw Noah, and his family; that the posterity of all the sons of Noah should be saved with a temporal salvation;

43. Wherefore Enoch saw that Noah built an ark; and that the Lord smiled upon it, and held it in his own hand; but upon the residue of the wicked the floods came and swallowed them up.

44. And as Enoch saw this, he had bitterness of soul, and wept over his brethren, and said unto the heavens: I will refuse to be comforted; but the Lord said unto Enoch: Lift up your heart, and be glad; and look.

45. And it came to pass that Enoch looked; and from Noah, he beheld all the families of the earth; . . .

Moses 7:41-45a.

Enoch's vision of the gross and extreme wickedness which prevailed throughout the entire earth during the days of Noah had such an overwhelming effect upon him, as the foregoing scriptures indicate, that his soul was engulfed in grief and he refused to be comforted. However, when the Lord continued the vision and showed Enoch the righteous people of the earth who were Noah's descendants, then Enoch's heart became glad and he was comforted.

GOD'S COVENANT REGARDING NOAH'S POSTERITY

The earth is to be sanctified and is to be cleansed but once by water:

48. And it came to pass that Enoch looked upon the earth; and he heard a voice from the bowels thereof, saying: Wo, wo is me, the mother of men; I am pained, I am weary, because of the wickedness of my children. When shall I rest, and be cleansed from the filthiness which is gone forth out of me? When will my Creator sanctify me, that I may rest, and righteousness for a season abide upon my face?

49. And when Enoch heard the earth mourn, he wept, and cried unto the Lord, saying: O Lord, wilt thou not have compassion upon the earth? Wilt thou not bless the children of Noah?

50. And it came to pass that Enoch continued his cry unto the Lord, saying: I ask thee, O Lord, in the name of thine Only Begotten, even Jesus Christ, that thou wilt have mercy upon Noah and his seed, that the earth might never more be covered by the floods.

51. And the Lord could not withhold; and he covenanted with Enoch, and sware unto him with an oath, that he would stay the floods; that he would call upon the children of Noah;

52. And he sent forth an unalterable decree, that a remnant of his seed should always be found among all nations, while the earth should stand.

Moses 7:48-52.

Verse 48 contains a very interesting statement to the effect that "Mother Earth" is grieved and weighted down with the sins of the people that live upon her and longs for the day when she shall be sanctified. The doctrine of the Church of Jesus Christ proclaims that the earth will be renewed and sanctified and "receive its paradisiacal glory."[1] The earth has been a telestial world since the time that Adam and Eve partook of the forbidden fruit. The *Pearl of Great Price* story which we have been studying pointed out the fact that at the time that Adam and Eve were cast from the Garden of Eden and became mortal beings "God cursed the ground for their sakes and it brought forth thorns and thistles and all kinds of noxious weeds," thereby telestializing "Mother Earth." Man and beast ceased to be friends. Many among Adam's posterity rejected the gospel and the earth became corrupted by the wickedness of the children of men. In the foregoing scripture, this doctrine is beautifully expressed. Then, as we have learned in this chapter, the Lord decreed that He would cleanse the earth with a great flood or deluge which would destroy all of the human race but one family. In this way the earth would receive its baptism in water. In verses 50-52 the Lord made a covenant with Enoch that the inhabitants of the earth would

[1]"Tenth Article of Faith."

be destroyed but that one time by floods. In the days of Noah, after the flood had cleansed the earth of its wickedness, the *Bible* states that God placed a rainbow in the heavens as a sign that He would never again destroy the world by floods.[2] This sign was given to Noah and his posterity and it confirms the covenant made by the Lord with His ancient Prophet Enoch.

The other holy scriptures confirm the teachings of the *Pearl of Great Price* by proclaiming that the earth will be sanctified (verse 48). In addition to being cleansed by water (representing her baptism), eventually the earth will receive her cleansing by fire (representing baptism by fire or confirmation); therefore, in order to be renewed and sanctified, the earth must pass through experiences comparable to the baptism and reception of the Holy Ghost by mortals.[3] When Christ comes to earth to dwell, then the time will have arrived when the earth will be renewed, or terrestrialized, and receive its paradisiacal glory.[4] Drastic physical changes will be brought about at that time. The Lord has declared: "For, behold, I create a new heaven and a new earth; and the former shall not be remembered, nor come in mind. But be ye glad and rejoice forever in that which I create."[5] Thus this world will be sanctified and be a terrestrial orb for one thousand years; and during that time Christ shall reign upon the earth as the Lord of lords and the King of kings.

The status of the earth even beyond the end of the millennial reign of the Son of Man was made known to the Prophet Joseph Smith. To quote:

Therefore, it [the earth] must needs be sanctified from all unrighteousness, that it may be prepared for the celestial glory; for after it hath filled the measure of its creation, it shall be crowned with glory, even with the presence of God the Father; that bodies who are of the celestial kingdom may possess it forever and ever; . . . [6]

The final status of the earth, therefore, is not only for it to ". . . rest and be cleansed from the filthiness; . . . and righteousness for a season to abide upon my [her] face," but Mother Earth will eventually become a celestial world. Jesus Christ and the former inhabitants of this earth who have merited celestial glory will live here throughout the eternities.

---

[2]Genesis 9:8-17.
[3]Malachi 4:1-2; Joseph Fielding Smith, *The Signs of the Times*, p. 38; *Doctrine and Covenants* 101:23-25.
[4]"Tenth Article of Faith"; *Doctrine and Covenants* 45:39-75; Matthew 24:1-51; Isaiah 65:17-18.
[5]Isaiah 65:17-18; 51:3; Revelation 21:1-5.
[6]*Doctrine and Covenants* 88:18-20, 25-26.

Chapter 28

THE GOSPEL OF JESUS CHRIST
AS TAUGHT BY NOAH

INTRODUCTORY STATEMENT

Only a brief story of Noah's life and activities appears in the *Pearl of Great Price;* but this account contains excellent evidence that Noah had the same gospel which was revealed in the beginning to Father Adam and also which was taught by Enoch to his people. This plan of salvation is the true Gospel of Jesus Christ, the one and only plan which has been ordained by God the Eternal Father through His Only Begotten Son for the salvation and exaltation of the human family.

RIGHTEOUSNESS OF NOAH AND HIS SONS

Noah's birth, his sons, their righteousness, and the "floods":

8. And Lamech lived one hundred and eighty-two years, and begat a son,

9. And he called his name Noah, saying: This son shall comfort us concerning our work and toil of our hands, because of the ground which the Lord hath cursed.

12. And Noah was four hundred and fifty years old, and begat Japheth; and forty-two years afterward he begat Shem of her who was the mother of Japheth, and when he was five hundred years old he begat Ham.

27. And thus Noah found grace in the eyes of the Lord; for Noah was a just man, and perfect in his generation; and he walked with God, as did also his three sons, Shem, Ham, and Japheth.

16. And it came to pass that Noah prophesied and taught the things of God, even as it was in the beginning.

17. And the Lord said unto Noah: My Spirit shall not always strive with man, for he shall know that all flesh shall die; yet his days shall be an hundred and twenty years; and if men do not repent, I will send in the floods upon them.

18. And in those days there were giants on the earth, and they sought Noah to take away his life; but the Lord was with Noah, and the power of the Lord was upon him.

Moses 8:8-9, 12, 27, 16-18.

This scripture points out that Noah and his three sons were very righteous and infers that the rest of the inhabitants of the earth were wicked. We learn, however, from the more complete story in Genesis that Noah's wife and the wives of the three sons also accepted the Gospel of Jesus Christ and were righteous along with their husbands; therefore, these eight people were the only members of the human family at their time who were not engrossed in extreme wickedness.

The statement made in verse 16 is very significant. It means that Noah received the same Gospel of Jesus Christ which had been revealed to Father Adam. The next verse in the foregoing scripture points out that the Lord decided, because of the wickedness of the inhabitants of the earth, to send in the floods and destroy all flesh. Some people have concluded from God's statement that man's "days shall be an hundred and twenty years" (verse 17) that Noah preached the gospel a hundred twenty years. That conclusion seems not to be justified, for that statement seems to indicate that the span of man's life from the time of the flood would be cut down to a hundred and twenty years. The scriptures claim that prior to the flood mortals lived many hundreds of years but following the flood such characters as Father Abraham, Sarah, Isaac, Jacob, Joseph, Moses, and others, lived slightly over a hundred years. In fact, Moses died exactly at the time that he was 120 years of age.

NOAH'S MISSIONARY WORK

Noah's Priesthood, missionary work, and the people's reaction:

19. And the Lord ordained Noah after his own order, and commanded him that he should go forth and declare his Gospel unto the children of men, even as it was given unto Enoch.

20. And it came to pass that Noah called upon the children of men that they should repent; but they hearkened not unto his words;

21. And also, after that they had heard him, they came up before him, saying: Behold, we are the sons of God; have we not taken unto ourselves the daughters of men? And are we not eating and drinking, and marrying and giving in marriage? And our wives bear unto us children, and the same are mighty men, which are like unto men of old, men of great renown. And they hearkened not unto the words of Noah.

22. And God saw that the wicked-ness of men had become great in the earth; and every man was lifted up in the imagination of the thoughts of his heart, being only evil continually.

23. And it came to pass that Noah continued his preaching unto the people, saying: Hearken, and give heed unto my words;

24. Believe and repent of your sins and be baptized in the name of Jesus Christ, the Son of God, even as our fathers, and ye shall receive the Holy Ghost, that ye may have all things made manifest; and if ye do not this, the floods will come in upon you; nevertheless they hearkened not.

25. And it repented Noah, and his heart was pained that the Lord had made man on the earth, and it grieved him at the heart.   Moses 8:19-25.

Verse 19 states that "the Lord ordained Noah after his own order," which declaration means that he received "the

Holy Priesthood after the Order of the Son of God." In the chapter entitled "The Holy Priesthood," Noah's position as the third great High Priest of the human family and the keys that he held, were discussed. That chapter could be referred to with profit at this point.

The most vital statements sustaining the title of this chapter are found in verses 20, 23-26. Therein we learn that Noah taught faith, repentance, baptism, confirmation (receiving the Holy Ghost), and belief in Jesus Christ, which were the vital principles and ordinances of the gospel as given to Father Adam, and as discussed in the chapter on "The Plan of Salvation." The people to whom Noah preached reacted to that great Prophet's message by claiming that they were "sons of God," meaning members of the true Church of Jesus Christ; and yet they refused to repent and hearken unto Noah's teachings.

In the *Bible* the following statement appears: "And it repented the Lord that he had made man on the earth, and it grieved him at his heart."[1] The *Pearl of Great Price* corrects and clarifies that statement as follows: "And it repented Noah, and his heart was pained that the Lord had made man on the earth, and it grieved him at the heart" (verse 25). That interpretation seems to be an accurate description of the reaction that Noah would have experienced after preaching to the people for such a long time without making any converts save his own family.

EARTH TO BE CLEANSED BY WATER

Wickedness of humanity and God's decision to destroy the inhabitants of the earth with a flood:

26. And the Lord said: I will destroy man whom I have created, from the face of the earth, both man and beast, and the creeping things, and the fowls of the air; for it repenteth Noah that I have created them, and that I have made them; and he hath called upon me; for they have sought his life.

28. The earth was corrupt before God, and it was filled with violence.

29. And God looked upon the earth, and, behold, it was corrupt, for all flesh had corrupted its way upon the earth.

30. And God said unto Noah: The end of all flesh is come before me, for the earth is filled with violence, and behold I will destroy all flesh from off the earth.   Moses 8:26, 28-30.

From the preceding scirpture it is evident that the earth had become completely corrupted, as the Lord had shown

[1]Genesis 6:6.

Enoch (discussed in the previous chapter) that it would be. Violence and all manner of wickedness reigned in the hearts of all the inhabitants of the earth with the exception of Noah's immediate family; therefore, God decided to destroy "all flesh" from off the earth (verses 26, 28-30).

The meaning of cleansing the earth with water, or baptizing it, was discussed in the previous chapter and need not be repeated here. Chapters six to nine in Genesis could be studied with profit in connection with this chapter.

Chapter 29

ABRAHAM AND THE COVENANT

INTRODUCTORY STATEMENT

It has been pointed out previously that a vital part of the *Pearl of Great Price* is the account written by Father Abraham of his own experiences and revelations from the Lord. The principal objective of this chapter is to study the contents of the first two chapters of the *Book of Abraham,* placing special emphasis on the covenant that God made with the Father of the Faithful. It would be well to observe the part he played in that covenant, and all of the promises given him by the Lord. In addition to this principal purpose, it is considered advisable to study the story of the ancient Patriarch's life presented in his own words.

BIBLE LANDS FOLLOWING THE FLOOD

The fact has been pointed out that the antediluvian patriarchs from Father Adam to Noah lived in North America; but before proceeding with the story of Abraham's life, the fact should be mentioned that following the flood the *Bible* peoples lived in western Asia. It is generally accepted that Noah's ark landed on Mount Ararat, north of the Mesopotamia Valley, and that the people whose story is recorded in the *Bible* resided in western Asia from that time forward.

Father Abraham was born and reared in the lower Mesopotamia Valley not a great distance north of the Persian Gulf. From his own story we learn that the land of his nativity was called Chaldea and the town in which he lived during the early part of his life was named Ur. However, God directed the ancient Patriarch to leave Ur and migrate to a foreign land. Thereupon Abraham traveled from the land of the Chaldeans northwestward up the Euphrates River to a place called Haran and then south and southwest to the land of Canaan (Palestine), which land borders on the Mediterranean Sea. This was the section of the country that God gave to Abraham and his posterity as an everlasting inheritance as long as they served Him; and it is the land that the Jews claim today as their rightful inheritance. We shall now turn our attention to the story of Abraham, reproduced from the *Pearl of Great Price*.

ABRAHAM'S HISTORY AND THE COVENANT

Abraham's righteous desires and his part in the covenant:

1. In the land of the Chaldeans, at the residence of my father, I, Abraham, saw that it was needful for me to obtain another place of residence;

2. And, finding there was greater happiness and peace and rest for me, I sought for the blessings of the fathers, and the right whereunto I should be ordained to administer the same; having been myself a follower of righteousness, desiring also to be one who possessed great knowledge, and to be a greater follower of righteousness, and to possess a greater knowledge, and to be a father of many nations, a prince of peace, and desiring to receive instructions, and to keep the commandments of God, I became a rightful heir, a High Priest, holding the right belonging to the fathers.

3. It was conferred upon me from the fathers; it came down from the fathers, from the beginning of time, yea, even from the beginning, or before the foundations of the earth to the present time, even the right of the firstborn, on the first man, who is Adam, our first father, through the fathers, unto me.

4. I sought for mine appointment ment unto the Priesthood according to the appointment of God unto the fathers concerning the seed.

Abraham 1:1-4.

Apostate conditions of Abraham's "fathers":

5. My fathers having turned from their righteousness, and from the holy commandments which the Lord their God had given unto them, unto the worshiping of the gods of the heathen, utterly refused to hearken to my voice;

6. For their hearts were set to do evil, and were wholly turned to the god of Elkenah, and the god of Libnah, and the god of Mahmackrah, and the god of Korash, and the god of Pharaoh, king of Egypt;

7. Therefore they turned their hearts to the sacrifice of the heathen in offering up their children unto their dumb idols, and hearkened not unto my voice, but endeavored to take away my life by the hand of the priest of Elkenah. The priest of Elkenah was also the priest of Pharaoh.

8. Now, at this time it was the custom of the priest of Pharaoh, the king of Egypt, to offer up upon the altar which was built in the land of Chaldea, for the offering unto these strange gods, men, women, and children.

9. And it came to pass that the priest made an offering unto the god of Pharaoh, and also unto the god of Shagreel, even after the manner of the Egyptians. Now the god of Shagreel was the sun.

10. Even the thank-offering of a child did the priest of Pharaoh offer upon the altar which stood by the hill called Potiphar's Hill, at the head of the plain of Olishem.

11. Now, this priest had offered upon this altar three virgins at one time, who were the daughters of Onitah, one of the royal descent directly from the loins of Ham. These virgins were offered up because of their virtue; they would not bow down to worship gods of wood or of stone, therefore they were killed upon this altar, and it was done after the manner of the Egyptians.

Abraham 1:5-11.

Attempt to sacrifice Abraham and his deliverance:

12. And it came to pass that the priests laid violence upon me, that they might slay me also, as they did those virgins upon this altar; and that you may have a knowledge of this altar, I will refer you to the representation at the commencement of this record.

13. It was made after the form of a bedstead, such as was had among the Chaldeans, and it stood before the gods of Elkenah, Libnah, Mahmackrah, Korash, and also a god like unto that of Pharaoh, king of Egypt.

14. That you may have an understanding of these gods, I have given you the fashion of them in the figures at the beginning, which manner of the figures is called by the Chaldeans Rahleenos, which signifies hieroglyphics.

15. And as they lifted up their hands upon me, that they might offer me up and take away my life, behold, I lifted up my voice unto the Lord my God, and the Lord hearkened and heard, and he filled me with the vision of the Al-mighty, and the angel of his presence stood by me, and immediately unloosed my bands;

20. The Lord thy God sent his angel to deliver thee from the hands of the priest of Elkenah.

16. And his voice was unto me: Abraham, Abraham, behold, my name is Jehovah, and I have heard thee, and have come down to deliver thee, and to take thee away from thy father's house, and from all thy kins-folk, into a strange land which thou knowest not of;

17. And this because they have turned their hearts away from me, to worship the god of Elkenah, and the god of Libnah, and the god of Mahmackrah, and the god of Korash, and the god of Pharaoh, king of Egypt; therefore I have come down to visit them, and to destroy him who hath lifted up his hand against thee, Abraham, my son, to take away thy life.

Abraham 1:12-15; 3:20; 1:16-17.

God's promises to Abraham as factors of the covenant:

18. Behold, I will lead thee by my hand, and I will take thee, to put upon thee my name, even the Priesthood of thy father, and my power shall be over thee.

19. As it was with Noah so shall it be with thee; but through thy ministry my name shall be known in the earth forever, for I am God.

Abraham 1:18-19.

The Lord destroyed the pagan idols:

20. Behold, Potiphar's Hill was in the land of Ur, of Chaldea. And the Lord broke down the altar of Elkenah, and of the gods of the land, and utterly destroyed them, and smote the priest that he died; and there was great mourning in Chaldea, and also in the court of Pharaoh; which Pharaoh signifies king by royal blood.

Abraham 1:20.

Famine in Chaldea:

29. Now, after the priest of Elkenah was smitten that he died, there came a fulfilment of those things which were said unto me concerning the land of Chaldea, that there should be a famine in the land.

30. Accordingly a famine prevailed throughout all the land of Chaldea, and my father was sorely tormented be-cause of the famine, and he repented of the evil which he had determined against me, to take away my life.

1. Now the Lord God caused the famine to wax sore in the land of Ur, insomuch that Haran, my brother, died; but Terah, my father, yet lived in the land of Ur, of the Chaldees.

Abraham 1:29-30; 2:1.

The Lord commanded Abraham to migrate from Ur of the Chaldees to the land of Canaan. Abraham goes via Haran:

2. And it came to pass that I, Abraham, took Sarai to wife, and Nehor, my brother, took Milcah to wife, who were the daughters of Haran.

3. Now the Lord had said unto me: Abraham, get thee out of thy country, and from thy kindred, and from thy father's house, unto a land that I will show thee.

4. Therefore I left the land of Ur, of the Chaldees, to go into the land of Canaan; and I took Lot, my brother's son, and his wife, and Sarai my wife;

and also my father followed after me, unto the land which we denominated Haran.

5. And the famine abated; and my father tarried in Haran and dwelt there, as there were many flocks in Haran; and my father turned again unto his idolatry, therefore he continued in Haran.   Abraham 2:2-5.

More of the covenant given to Abraham:

6. But I, Abraham, and Lot, my brother's son, prayed unto the Lord, and the Lord appeared unto me, and said unto me: Arise, and take Lot with thee; for I have purposed to take thee away out of Haran, and to make of thee a minister to bear my name in a strange land which I will give unto thy seed after thee for an everlasting possession, when they hearken to my voice.

9. And I will make of thee a great nation, and I will bless thee above measure, and make thy name great among all nations, and thou shalt be a blessing unto thy seed after thee, that in their hands they shall bear this ministry and Priesthood unto all nations;

10. And I will bless them through

thy name; for as many as receive this Gospel shall be called after thy name, and shall be accounted thy seed, and shall rise up and bless thee, as their father;

11. And I will bless them that bless thee, and curse them that curse thee; and in thee (that is, in thy Priesthood) and in thy seed (that is, thy Priesthood), for I give unto thee a promise that this right shall continue in thee, and in thy seed after thee (that is to say, the literal seed, or the seed of the body) shall all the families of the earth be blessed, even with the blessings of the gospel, which are the blessings of salvation, even of life eternal.

Abraham 2:6, 9-11.

Abraham continues the journey from Haran to Canaan:

12. Now, after the Lord had withdrawn from speaking to me, and withdrawn his face from me, I said in my heart: Thy servant has sought thee earnestly; now I have found thee;

13. Thou didst send thine angel to deliver me from the gods of Elkenah, and I will do well to hearken unto thy voice, therefore let thy servant rise up and depart in peace.

14. So I, Abraham, departed as the Lord had said unto me, and Lot with me; and I, Abraham, was sixty and two years old when I departed out of Haran.

15. And I took Sarai, whom I took to wife when I was in Ur, in Chaldea, and Lot, my brother's son, and all our substance that we had gathered, and the souls that we had won in Haran, and came forth in the way to the land of Canaan, and dwelt in tents as we came on our way;

16. Therefore, eternity was our covering and our rock and our salvation, as we journeyed from Haran by the way of Jershon, to come to the land of Canaan.   Abraham 2:12-16.

Abraham offers sacrifice and prays and receives from the Lord additions to the covenant:

17. Now I, Abraham, built an altar in the land of Jershon, and made an offering unto the Lord, and prayed that the famine might be turned away from my father's house, that they might not perish.

18. And then we passed from Jershon through the land unto the place of

Sechem; it was situated in the plains of Moreh, and we had already come into the borders of the land of the Canaanites, and I offered sacrifice there in the plains of Moreh, and called on the Lord devoutly, because we had already come into the land of this idolatrous nation.

19. And the Lord appeared unto me in answer to my prayers, and said unto me: Unto thy seed will I give this land.

20. And I, Abraham, arose from the place of the altar which I had built unto the Lord, and removed from thence unto a mountain on the east of Bethel, and pitched my tent there, Bethel on the west, and Hai on the east; and there I built another altar unto the Lord, and called again upon the name of the Lord.

14. And it was in the night time when the Lord spake these words unto me: I will multiply thee, and thy seed after thee, like unto these [the stars]; and if thou canst count the number of sands, so shall be the number of thy seeds.   Abraham 2:17-20; 3:14.

Abraham decides to go into Egypt, and God commands him to say that Sarai is his sister:

21. And I, Abraham, journeyed, going on still towards the south; and there was a continuation of a famine in the land; and I, Abraham, concluded to go down into Egypt, to sojourn there, for the famine became very grievous.

22. And it came to pass when I was come near to enter into Egypt, the Lord said unto me: Behold, Sarai, thy wife, is a very fair woman to look upon;

23. Therefore it shall come to pass, when the Egyptians shall see her, they will say—She is his wife; and they will kill you, but they will save her alive; therefore see that ye do on this wise:

24. Let her say unto the Egyptians, she is thy sister, and thy soul shall live.

25. And it came to pass that I, Abraham, told Sarai, my wife, all that the Lord had said unto me—Therefore say unto them, I pray thee, thou art my sister, that it may be well with me for thy sake, and my soul shall live because of thee.   Abraham 2:21-25.

THE COVENANT

The most important item to be considered in this chapter is the covenant which was entered into between the Lord and the ancient Patriarch, Abraham. The *Bible* declares that God reconfirmed this holy covenant with Isaac, Jacob, and Joseph; therefore, the most far-reaching event in the Abrahamic Dispensation of the gospel was the covenant. Following are the main points of the covenant: (1) Abraham was to be a minister of the Gospel of Jesus Christ to a strange nation (Abr. 2:6); (2) he was to be the father of a great nation (Abr. 2:9); (3) his name would be great among all nations (*ibid.*); (4) Abraham and his posterity would be given a land which would be unto them an everlasting inheritance as long as they served God (Abr. 2:6, 19); (5) Abraham's posterity would be as numerous as the stars of the heavens and the sands of the sea (Abr. 3:14); (6) many of his descendants would bear the name of God, even the Holy Priesthood (Abr. 2:9); in fact, Abraham's posterity would be a nation of Priesthood holders (Abr. 2:11); (7) in Abraham and that Priesthood all families of the earth would be blessed (*ibid.*; Gen. 12:3); (8) those throughout the world from Abraham's time forward who received the Gospel of Jesus Christ would be accounted as the seed of Abraham (Abr. 2:10); (9) Christ would come through Abraham's seed (Abr. 2:11); (10) God promised to bless them that blessed Abraham and curse them that cursed Abraham (Abr. 2:11); (11) circumcision was to be the sign of the covenant (Gen. 17:10-14); (12) the covenant was to be an everlasting one, or a gospel covenant (Gen. 17:7); (13) in return for all of the foregoing blessings, Father Abraham and his posterity were to serve the Lord their God and keep all of His commandments.

It should be observed at this point that on April 3, 1836, a heavenly messenger bestowed upon modern Israel through Joseph Smith and Oliver Cowdery the same blessings, covenants, and promises which had been made approximately 4,000 years ago to Father Abraham. The revelation states that: "Elias appeared and committed the dispensation of the gospel of Abraham, saying, that in us and our seed, all generations after us should be blessed."[1]

One of the most vital forces that has ever been inculcated in any race of people was the covenant concept which exerted its influence in every generation of Jewish history and is exerting a powerful influence on the members of the Church of Jesus Christ of Latter-day Saints today.

---

[1]*Doctrine and Covenants* 110:12

Chapter 30

CRUCIFIXION AND RESURRECTION OF CHRIST AND SPIRITS IN PRISON

INTRODUCTORY STATEMENT

As previously mentioned, the Lord showed Enoch a vision of the history of the world from his day to the end thereof, the account of which is recorded in the *Pearl of Great Price*. The portion of that vision which deals with the first coming of Jesus Christ, His crucifixion and resurrection, and the conditions which Enoch learned would prevail at that time will be presented in this chapter. Also, a discussion will be given of the "spirits in prison."

ENOCH'S VISION REGARDING THE SON OF MAN

Enoch's vision of the crucifixion of the Son of Man, resurrection, and Spirits in prison:

45. . . . And he [Enoch] cried unto the Lord, saying: When shall the day of the Lord come? When shall the blood of the Righteous be shed, that all they that mourn may be sanctified and have eternal life?

46. And the Lord said: It shall be in the meridian of time, in the days of wickedness and vengeance.

47. And behold, Enoch saw the day of the coming of the Son of Man, even in the flesh; and his soul rejoiced, saying: The Righteous is lifted up, and the Lamb is slain from the foundation of the world; and through faith I am in the bosom of the Father, and behold, Zion is with me.

53. And the Lord said: Blessed is he through whose seed Messiah shall come; for he saith—I am Messiah, the King of Zion, the Rock of Heaven, which is broad as eternity; whoso cometh in at the gate and climbeth up by me shall never fall; wherefore, blessed are they of whom I have spoken, for they shall come forth with songs of everlasting joy.

54. And it came to pass that Enoch cried unto the Lord, saying: When the Son of Man cometh in the flesh, shall the earth rest? I pray thee, show me these things.

55. And the Lord said unto Enoch: Look, and he looked and beheld the Son of Man lifted up on the cross, after the manner of men;

56. And he heard a loud voice; and the heavens were veiled, and all the creations of God mourned, and the earth groaned; and the rocks were rent; and the saints arose, and were crowned at the right hand of the Son of Man, with crowns of glory;

57. And as many of the spirits as were in prison came forth, and stood on the right hand of God; and the remainder were reserved in chains of darkness until the judgment of the great day.

58. And again Enoch wept and cried unto the Lord, saying: When shall the earth rest?   Moses 7:45b-47, 53-58.

203

In the portion of Enoch's vision just quoted, the ancient prophet saw that Christ's blood would be shed for the sins of the world and that He would be killed by the method of crucifixion. This vision came to Enoch many years before any people in the world adopted crucifixion as their common method of execution.

CRUCIFIXION OF JESUS CHRIST

Enoch also saw that the "heavens were veiled; and all the creations of God mourned; and the earth groaned; and the rocks were rent" at the time of the crucifixion of the Lord (verse 56). God revealed the same facts to other prophets during later ages, and the testimonies of those prophets sustain the teachings of the *Pearl of Great Price*. For example, about 600 B. C. the Prophet Nephi saw in vision the same events that Enoch had seen and described them as follows:

> And it came to pass that I saw a mist of darkness on the face of the land of promise; and I saw lightnings, and I heard thunderings, and earthquakes, and all manner of tumultuous noises; and I saw the earth and the rocks, that they rent; and I saw mountains tumbling into pieces; and I saw the plains of the earth, that they were broken up; and I saw many cities that they were sunk; and I saw many that they were burned with fire; and I saw many that did tumble to the earth, because of the quaking thereof.[1]

Five years B. C. an angel of the Lord appeared unto Samuel the Lamanite and told him of the signs of the death of the Son of Man. Samuel's testimony also verifies Enoch's vision. To quote the words of Samuel:

> But behold, as I said unto you concerning another sign, a sign of his death, behold, in that day that he shall suffer death the sun shall be darkened and refuse to give his light unto you; and also the moon and the stars; and there shall be no light upon the face of this land, even from the time that he shall suffer death, for the space of three days, to the time that he shall rise again from the dead.
>
> Yea, at the time that he shall yield up the ghost there shall be thunderings and lightnings for the space of many hours, and the earth shall shake and tremble; and the rocks which are upon the face of this earth, which are both above the earth and beneath, which ye know at this time are solid, or the more part of it is one solid mass, shall be broken up; yea, they shall be rent in twain, and shall ever after be found in seams and in cracks, and in broken fragments upon the face of the whole earth, yea, both above the earth and beneath.

[1] Nephi 12:4.

And behold, there shall be great tempests, and there shall be many mountains laid low, like unto a valley, and there shall be many places which are now called valleys which shall become mountains, whose height is great. And many highways shall be broken up, and many cities shall become desolate.[2]

The *Book of Mormon* records the fulfillment of the fore-going prophecies which occurred at the time of the crucifixion of the Lord. The following scripture tells that story and it could be studied with profit at this point: 3 Nephi 8:5-25; 9:1-19.

THE FIRST RESURRECTION

Enoch also beheld in his vision that at the time of the resurrection of Christ "the saints arose, and were crowned at the right hand of the Son of Man, with crowns of glory" (verse 56). And again, Enoch's vision, as recorded in the *Pearl of Great Price,* was verified by the testimonies of prophets who lived many years after his time. For example, Samuel the Lamanite was told by the angel the same facts which Enoch had seen in vision. To quote: "And many graves shall be opened, and shall yield up their dead; and many saints shall appear unto many. And behold, thus hath the angel spoken unto me."[3] Both the *New Testament* and the *Book of Mormon* testify to the fulfillment of Enoch's vision. The following is recorded in Matthew:

Jesus, when he had cried again with a loud voice, yielded up the ghost. And, behold, the veil of the temple was rent in twain from the top to the bottom; and the earth did quake, and the rocks rent; and the graves were opened; and many bodies of the saints which slept arose, and came out of the graves after his resurrection, and went into the holy city, and appeared unto many.[4]

After the resurrection of the Lord, He appeared unto the Nephites. The *Book of Mormon* states:

And it came to pass that he [Jesus Christ] said unto Nephi: Bring forth the record which ye have kept. And when Nephi had brought forth the records, and laid them before him, he cast his eyes upon them and said: Verily I say unto you, I commanded my servant Samuel, the Lamanite, that he should testify unto this people that at the day that the Father should glorify his name in me that there were many saints who

[2]Helaman 14:20-24, 26-31.
[3]Helaman 14:25-26.
[4]Matthew 27:50-53.

should arise from the dead, and should appear unto many, and should minister unto them. And he said unto them: Was it not so?

And his disciples answered him and said: Yea, Lord, Samuel did prophesy according to thy words, and they were all fulfilled.

And Jesus said unto them: How be it that ye have not written this thing, that many saints did arise and appear unto many and did minister unto them. . . . And it came to pass that Jesus commanded that it should be written; therefore it, was written according as he commanded.[5]

Jesus Christ was the first fruits of the resurrection and those who rose from the grave at the time of His resurrection were the Saints who had lived righteous lives prior to the coming of Christ. The group would include such great men of God as Adam, Noah, Abraham, Isaac, Jacob, Moses, Nephi, Alma, and all other holy prophets of antiquity and all the saints who lived according to the gospel plan. They came forth in the "first resurrection" or "the resurrection of the just."

SPIRITS IN PRISON

In Enoch's vision (verse 57) he saw that "as many of the spirits as were in prison came forth, and stood on the right hand of God; and the remainder were reserved in chains of darkness until the judgment of the great day." From another part of Enoch's vision which was quoted in chapter 27, but is not discussed, it is made clear that the spirits in prison were the men and women who were destroyed at the time of the great flood in the days of Noah. The Lord said unto the ancient Prophet Enoch:

> But behold, these which thine eyes are upon shall perish in the floods; and behold, I will shut them up; a prison have I prepared for them. And That which I have chosen hath plead before my face. Wherefore, he suffereth for their sins; inasmuch as they will repent in the day that my Chosen shall return unto me, and until that day they shall be in torment.[6]

The *Bible* and the *Doctrine and Covenants* can be referred to with profit for sustaining evidence, proving the validity of the truths proclaimed in the great vision had by Enoch as recorded in the *Pearl of Great Price*. For example, in the course of his writings the Prophet Isaiah made reference several times to the spirits in prison and the work of the Master

---

[5]3Nephi 23:7-13.
[6]Moses 7:38-39.

for them. These scriptures are regarded as referring to the Messiah:

The Spirit of the Lord God is upon me; because the Lord hath anointed me to preach good tidings unto the meek; he hath sent me to bind up the brokenhearted, to proclaim liberty to the captives, and the *opening of the prison to them that are bound.*[7]

Also,

To open the blind eyes, *to bring out the prisoners from the prison, and them that sit in darkness out of the prison house.*[8]

And on another occasion the Prophet Isaiah declared:

Thus saith the Lord, the Redeemer of Israel, and His Holy One, to him whom man despiseth, to him whom the nation abhorreth, . . . That thou mayest say to the prisoners, Go forth; to them that are in darkness, Shew yourselves.[9]

According to the teachings of Peter, the prophecies made by Enoch and Isaiah were fulfilled during the three days while Christ's body lay in the tomb. In the words of the ancient apostle of the Lord:

For Christ also hath once suffered for sins, the just for the unjust, that he might bring us to God, being put to death in the flesh, but quickened by the Spirit: by which also he went and preached unto the spirits in prison; which sometime were disobedient, when once the longsuffering of God waited in the days of Noah, while the ark was a preparing, wherein few, that is, eight souls were saved by water.[10]

In modern revelation the Lord gives additional information regarding the spirits in prison. After "they who are Christ's, the first fruits," descend with Him at His coming, the following will take place:

And after this another angel shall sound, which is the second trump; and then cometh the redemption of those who are Christ's at his coming; who have received their part in that prison which is prepared for them, that they might receive the gospel, and be judged according to men in the flesh.[11]

In the vision of the three degrees of glory, the Lord showed the Prophet Joseph Smith and Sidney Rigdon the final reward of the spirits in prison who accepted the Gospel of Jesus Christ. To quote the words of the vision:

[7]Isaiah 61:1. The italics were supplied by the author.
[8]*Ibid.*, 42:7.
[9]*Ibid.*, 49:7a, 9.
[10]1 Peter 3:18-20.
[11]*Doctrine and Covenants* 88:99.

And again, we saw the terrestrial world, and behold and lo, these are they who are of the terrestrial, whose glory differs from that of the church of the Firstborn who have received the fulness of the Father, . . . And also they who are the spirits of men kept in prison, whom the Son visited, and preached the gospel unto them, that they might be judged according to men in the flesh; who received not the testimony of Jesus in the flesh, but afterwards received it.[12]

On October 3, 1918, President Joseph F. Smith beheld a vision of the spirit world which he termed a "Vision of the Redemption of the Dead".[13] This marvelous vision gives the most comprehensive and clearly defined description of the "spirits in prison" and the visit of Jesus Christ to the spirit world while His body lay in the tomb that is known to the author. It would be advisable to study President Smith's vision in connection with this topic.

Thus the Lord revealed to Enoch, as recorded in the *Pearl of Great Price,* the vital points regarding the "spirits in prison"; and many of the great prophets since Enoch's day (including the late President Joseph F. Smith) have born testimony to the truths beheld in vision by that ancient holy man of God.

[12]*Ibid.,* 76:71, 73.
[13]Joseph F. Smith, *Gospel Doctrine,* pp 596-602; *Improvement Era,* vol. 22, pp. 166-170.

Chapter 31

THE LAST DAYS AND SECOND COMING OF CHRIST

Enoch's Vision of the Last Days and Second Coming of Christ

The ancient Patriarch Enoch saw in vision the second coming of the Son of Man and the conditions that would prevail in the latter days prior to His coming to usher in the Millennium.

The last days, restoration of the gospel, second coming of Christ, and the Millennium:

59. And Enoch beheld the Son of Man ascend up unto the Father; and he called unto the Lord, saying: Wilt thou not come again upon the earth? Forasmuch as thou art God, and I know thee, and thou hast sworn unto me, and commanded me that I should ask in the name of thine Only Begotten; thou hast made me, and given unto me a right to thy throne, and not of myself, but through thine own grace; wherefore, I ask thee if thou wilt not come again on the earth.

60. And the Lord said unto Enoch: As I live, even so will I come in the last days, in the days of wickedness and vengeance, to fulfil the oath which I have made unto you concerning the children of Noah.

61. And the day shall come that the earth shall rest, but before that day the heavens shall be darkened, and a veil of darkness shall cover the earth; and the heavens shall shake, and also the earth; and great tribulations shall be among the children of men, but my people I will preserve;

62. And righteousness will I send down out of heaven; and truth will I send forth out of the earth, to bear testimony of mine Only Begotten; his resurrection from the dead; yea, and also the resurrection of all men; and righteousness and truth will I cause to sweep the earth as with a flood, to gather out mine elect from the four quarters of the earth, unto a place which I shall prepare, an Holy City, that my people may gird up their loins, and be looking forth for the time of my coming; for there shall be my tabernacle, and it shall be called Zion, a New Jerusalem.

63. And the Lord said unto Enoch: Then shalt thou and all thy city meet them there, and we will receive them into our bosom, and they shall see us; and we will fall upon their necks, and they shall fall upon our necks, and we will kiss each other.

64. And there shall be mine abode, and it shall be Zion, which shall come forth out of all the creations which I have made; and for the space of a thousand years the earth shall rest.

65. And it came to pass that Enoch saw the day of the coming of the Son of Man, in the last days, to dwell on the earth in righteousness for the space of a thousand years;

66. But before that day he saw great tribulations among the wicked; and he also saw the sea, that it was troubled, and men's hearts failing them, looking forth with fear for the judgments of the Almighty God, which should come upon the wicked.

67. And the Lord showed Enoch all things, even unto the end of the world; and he saw the day of the righteous, the hour of their redemption; and received a fulness of joy.

Moses 7:59-67.

WORLD CONDITIONS AND SECOND COMING OF CHRIST

The description of what would prevail in the world at the time of and prior to the second coming of Jesus Christ, as presented in the foregoing scripture (verses 59-61, 66), is in complete harmony with numerous predictions made by *Book of Mormon* prophets, by Jesus to His apostles shortly before His crucifixion, and by the Lord to the Prophet Joseph Smith as recorded in the *Doctrine and Covenants.*[1] Thus the holy scriptures bear testimony to the truthfulness of Enoch's vision. We should be aware that we are living in the last days and have seen and are seeing the fulfillment of Enoch's vision as recorded in the *Pearl of Great Price.*

RESTORATION OF THE GOSPEL AND BOOK OF MORMON

Verse 62 in Enoch's vision is a prediction of the coming forth of the *Book of Mormon,* the restoration of the Gospel of Jesus Christ, the carrying of the message of truth throughout the earth, the establishment of Zion, and the building of the New Jerusalem. Several prophets of God during the various gospel dispensations have looked down through the stream of time and described the same events that Enoch saw in vision.[2]

For convenience in making a comparison, the Lord's statement to Enoch regarding the coming forth of the *Book of Mormon* in the latter days is quoted as follows: *"And righteousness will I send down out of heaven; and truth will I send forth out of the earth, to bear testimony of mine Only Begotten."* The Psalmist declared: "Truth shall spring out of the earth and righteousness shall look down from heaven,"[3] which declaration is almost exactly like the foregoing statement quoted from the *Pearl of Great Price.* Also, God's statement to Enoch was echoed time and time again by the writers of the ancient Nephite records from the days of Nephi to Moroni, i.e., from the first to the last prophet-writer. For example, Nephi prophesied regarding the coming forth of that record (the *Book of Mormon*) to the Gentiles in the last days as follows:

[1] Nephi 22:15-29; 2 Nephi 27:1-5, 23-35; 28:1-32; 30:1-18; 3 Nephi 21:1-29; Matthew 23:39; 24:1-51 Mormon 8:1-41; *Doctrine and Covenants* 5:18-20; 29:7-37; 45:16-75.
[2] Ether 13:3-12; Revelation 3:12; 21:1-27; Hebrews 12:22; Galatians 4:26; *Doctrine and Covenants* 42:35, 62, 67; 45:64-71; 52:2-5; 57; 58:6-14; 68:24-36; 84:1-4; 133:56.
[3] Psalms 85:11.

And it shall come to pass that the Lord God shall bring forth unto you the words of a book, and they shall be the words of them which have slumbered. . . . For those who shall be destroyed shall speak unto them out of the ground, and their speech shall be low out of the dust, and their voice shall be as one who hath a familiar spirit.[4]

On another occasion the Prophet Nephi declared:

And it shall be as if the fruit of thy loins had cried unto them from the dust; for I know their fate and they shall cry from the dust; yea, even repentance unto their brethren, even after many generations have gone by.[5]

Moroni, the last of the Nephite prophets, when he was completing the sacred records given him by his father, Mormon, wrote the following regarding their coming forth in the latter days:

And no one need say, They shall not come, for they surely shall, for the Lord hath spoken it; for out of the earth shall they come by the hand of the Lord, and none can stay it; and it shall come in a day when it shall be said that miracles are done away; and it shall come even as if one should speak from the dead.[6]

Thus we see from the words of the *Book of Mormon* prophets that the statement of the Lord to Enoch certainly referred definitely to the coming forth of the Nephite record to the Prophet Joseph Smith in the latter days.

Their statements also make it clear that the purpose of writing the *Book of Mormon* was exactly the same as the Lord had proclaimed to Enoch nearly 3,000 years before the time of the Nephite nation. That purpose was made known to Nephi, the first record-keeper of his people. When the angel from God appeared to him and instructed him regarding the keeping of a religious record, the angel declared that the purpose of making such a record was to "make known to all kindreds, tongues, and people, that the Lamb of God is the Son of the Eternal Father, and the Savior of the world; and that all men must come unto Him or they cannot be saved."[7] Therefore, the purpose of writing the *Book of Mormon* fits in exactly with the words of the Lord to the ancient prophet Enoch, previously quoted.

This purpose of convincing all of the people in the world in the latter days of the divinity of Jesus Christ and of return-

[4]2 Nephi 27:6; 26:16.
[5]*Ibid.*, 3:19.
[6]*Mormon* 8:26.
[7]1 Nephi 13:40-41; Jacob 4:4.

ing to them the gospel plan was proclaimed time and time again by the writers of the Nephite record to be the purpose of the *Book of Mormon*. For example, in Moroni's preface to the book he states the following:

> Written and sealed up and hid up unto the Gentiles, . . . to come forth in due time by way of the Gentiles. . . . and also to the convincing of the Jew and Gentile that Jesus is the Christ, the eternal God, manifesting himself to all nations.[8]

ZION OR THE NEW JERUSALEM

It now becomes necessary to refer again to verse 62 of Enoch's vision of the last days wherein God pointed out to the ancient Patriarch that a "Holy City" would be established which would "be called Zion, a New Jerusalem." The *Book of Mormon* prophets also verified the words of the Lord to Enoch regarding this great event. They declared that America was a "land of promise, a land choice above all other lands" upon the face of the earth.[9] The land had been blessed by the Lord and dedicated for the gathering of Israel and the building of Zion in the latter days. Ether, the last of the Jaredite prophets, predicted that America was to be the land upon which the New Jerusalem was to be built and that it should be "the Holy Sanctuary of the Lord."[10] Those who dwell in this "Holy City," he explained, will be "they whose garments are white through the blood of the Lamb; and they who are numbered among the remnant of the seed of Joseph who are of the house of Israel."[11]

Modern revelation also confirms Enoch's vision. The Lord revealed to the Prophet Joseph Smith the exact spot where the New Jerusalem will be built and that the members of the Church of Jesus Christ of Latter-day Saints are the people of Zion who will be the principal ones in building it.[12]

CITY OF ENOCH TO RETURN TO EARTH

In Chapter 26 the fact was pointed out that Enoch and his city, known as Zion, were translated and the Lord declared that that city had become His abode forever. In verse 63 of Enoch's

---

[8]Moroni "Preface," *Book of Mormon.*
[9]Ether 1:42-43; 2:5-12; 1 Nephi 2:20-21; 2 Nephi 1:5-12; 10:10-20.
[10]Ether 13:3-6.
[11]*Ibid.,* 13:10-11.
[12]*Doctrine and Covenants* 84:1-4.

vision of the latter days (quoted above), the Lord told the ancient Patriarch that when He came to earth to usher in the Millennium that Enoch and his people would return with Him. There they would meet with the Saints of God who had established a New Jerusalem. Also, according to verse 64, the "Holy City," known as Zion, would be the abode of the Lord during the Millennium. Other prophets saw in vision the return to the earth of the City of Enoch. For example, Ether, the last of the Jaredite prophets, spoke "of the New Jerusalem, which should come down out of heaven, and the Holy Sanctuary of the Lord."[13] Also, John the Revelator saw the return of the City of Enoch; and of this event, he wrote:

And I John saw the holy city, new Jerusalem, coming down from God out of heaven, prepared as a bride adorned for her husband and I heard a great voice out of heaven saying, Behold, the tabernacle of God is with men, and he will dwell with them, and they shall be his people, and God himself shall be with them, and be their God.[14]

In the words of Dr. James E. Talmage:

The Church in this day teaches that the New Jerusalem seen by John, and by the Prophet Ether, as descending from the heavens in glory, is the return of exalted Enoch and his righteous people; and that the people or Zion of Enoch, and the modern Zion, or the gathered elect on the western continent, will become one people.[15]

MILLENNIAL REIGN OF JESUS CHRIST

In verses 61, 64-66, the Lord showed Enoch the conditions which would prevail in the world at the time of His second coming and described to him the millennial reign of the Son of Man which should last for one thousand years. All of the events shown Enoch in his great vision have been verified by other prophets, such as Isaiah, Joseph Smith, and even by the Lord Himself.[16]

Also, Enoch's testimony of the righteous reign of Christ on earth for one thousand years has been verified by many prophets, especially Isaiah and Joseph Smith.[17] Therefore, it is marvelous to us to learn from the *Pearl of Great Price* of the many wonderful things which were shown Enoch by the Lord

---

[13]Ether 13:3-7.
[14]Revelation 21:2-3.
[15]James E. Talmage, *The Articles of Faith*, p. 363.
[16]Matthew 24:1-51; Isaiah 13:9-16; *Doctrine and Covenants* 1:10-14; 5:18-20; 29:7-37, 41; 34:6-10; 38:4-11; 43:28-35; 45:16-75; 49:5-7, 22-25; 63:32-37, 49-54; 88:87-116, 97:22-27; 101:11-14, 24-38; 106:4-5; 112:23-29; 130:1-3, 6-11, 14-19; 133:1-3, 17-74.
[17]Isaiah 9:6-7; 11:1-7; 16:5; 32:1-7; 25:8; 65:17-25; 11:6-9; 2:2-5; *Doctrine and Covenants* 101:26; 58:6-14;133:16-35, 46-47, 54-56; 45:58-59; 101:24-34; Revelation 1:1-27; 22:1-21.

regarding our day and also the fact that those truths were verified by the other prophets down through the ages.

JUDE'S TESTIMONY

From a statement made by Jude as recorded in the New Testament, it is evident that the Jews in the days of the sojourn of the Son of God on the earth knew a great deal more regarding the teachings of Enoch than we find recorded in the Old Testament at the present time. To quote the words of Jude:

> And Enoch, also, the seventh from Adam, prophesied of these, saying, Behold, the Lord cometh with ten thousand of his saints, to execute judgment upon all, and to convince all that are ungodly among them of all their ungodly deeds which they have ungodly committed, and of all their hard speeches which ungodly sinners have spoken against him.[18]

Therefore, Jude's significant statement bears witness to the marvelous vision and teachings of Enoch regarding the second coming of the Son of Man to reign in righteousness upon this earth.

ONE LIKE UNTO MOSES

Not only did Enoch behold in vision the great events which should transpire in the latter days, but in the account of Moses' vision which he beheld upon the mount a very significant statement appears regarding the Lord's promise to raise up another like unto him in the latter days. This great prophet that the Lord predicted He would raise up is none other than Joseph Smith.

The words of the Lord to Moses regarding the coming and work of Jesus Christ:

41. And in a day when the children of men shall esteem my words as naught and take many of them from the book which thou shalt write, behold, I will raise up another like unto thee; and they shall be had again among the children of men—among as many as shall believe.

Moses 1:41.

In the *Inspired Version* of the *Bible,* the Lord made it clear that the prophet whom He should raise up in the latter days to do His work, or the "one like unto Moses," was indeed the Prophet Joseph. Shortly before his death, Joseph, the ancient Patriarch, told his family of a promise that he had

---

[18]Jude 1:14-15.

received from the Lord of that great latter-day prophet. To quote his words:

And Joseph said unto his brethren, I die, and go unto my fathers; and I go down to my grave with joy. The God of my father Jacob be with you to deliver you out of affliction in the days of your bondage; for the Lord hath visited me, and I have obtained a promise of the Lord, that out of the fruit of my loins, the Lord God will raise up a righteous branch out of my loins; and unto thee, whom my father Jacob hath named Israel, a prophet; (not the Messiah who is called Shilo); and this prophet shall deliver my people out of Egypt in the days of thy bondage.

And it shall come to pass that they shall be scattered again; and a branch shall be broken off, and shall be carried into a far country; nevertheless they shall be remembered in the covenants of the Lord, when the Messiah cometh; for he shall be made manifest unto them in the latter days, in the Spirit of power; and shall bring them out of darkness into light; out of hidden darkness, and out of captivity unto freedom.

And a seer shall the Lord my God raise up, who shall be a choice seer unto the fruit of my loins. Thus saith the Lord God of my fathers unto me. A choice seer will I raise up out of the fruit of thy loins, and he shall be esteemed highly among the fruit of thy loins, his brethren; and unto him will I give commandments that he shall do a work for the fruit of thy loins. And he shall bring them to the knowledge of the covenants which I have made with thy father; and he shall do whatsoever work I shall command him.

And I will make him great in mine eyes, for he shall do my work; *and he shall be great like unto him whom I have said I would raise up unto you, to deliver my people, O house of Israel, out of the land of Egypt; for a seer will I raise up to deliver my people out of the land of Egypt; and he shall be called Moses.* And by this name he shall know that he is of thy house; for he shall be nursed by the king's daughter, and shall be called her son.

And again, a seer will I raise up out of the fruit of thy loins, and unto him will I give power to bring forth my word unto the seed of thy loins; and not to the bringing forth of my word only, said the Lord, but to the convincing them of my word, which shall have already gone forth among them in *the last days;* wherefore the fruit of thy loins shall write, and the fruit of the loins of Judah shall write and that which shall be written by the fruit of thy loins, and also that which shall be written by the fruit of the loins of Judah, shall grow together unto the confounding of false doctrines, and laying down of contentions, and establishing peace among the fruit of thy loins, and bringing them to a knowledge of their fathers *in the latter days;* and also to the knowledge of my covenants, saith the Lord. And out of weakness shall·he be made strong, in that day when my work shall go forth among all my people,which shall restore them, who are of the house of Israel, in the last days.

And that seer will I bless, and they that seek to destroy him shall be confounded; for this promise I give unto you; for I will remember you from generation to generation; and *his name shall be called Joseph, and it shall be after the name of his father;* and he shall be like unto you; for the thing which the Lord shall bring forth by his hand shall bring my people unto salvation.[19]

Shortly before his death, Father Lehi was giving his last instructions and blessings to his children. While speaking to his son Joseph, he pointed out that he had named his son after Joseph, the ancient Patriarch who was sold into Egyptian bondage. He also told his son that that Joseph had prophesied regarding a great prophet whom the Lord should raise up in the latter days. A portion of the teachings of Lehi are as follows:

For Joseph truly testified, saying: A seer shall the Lord my God raise up, who shall be a choice seer unto the fruit of my loins. Yea, Joseph truly said: Thus saith the Lord unto me: A choice seer will I raise up out of the fruit of thy loins; and he shall be esteemed highly among the fruit of thy loins. And unto him will I give commandment that he shall do a work for the fruit of thy loins, his brethren, which shall be of great worth unto them, even to the bringing of them to the knowledge of the covenants which I have made with thy fathers. And I will give unto him a commandment that he shall do none other work, save the work which I shall command him. And I will make him great in mine eyes; for he shall do my work. *And he shall be great like unto Moses,* whom I have said I would raise up unto you, to deliver my people, O house of Israel. . . .

And thus prophesied Joseph, saying: Behold, that seer will the Lord bless; and they that seek to destroy him shall be confounded; for this promise, which I have obtained of the Lord, of the fruit of my loins, shall be fulfilled. Behold, I am sure of the fulfilling of this promise; and his name shall be called after me [Joseph]; and it shall be after the name of his father [Joseph Smith, Sr.]. And he shall be like unto me; for the thing, which the Lord shall bring forth by his hand, by the power of the Lord shall bring my people unto salvation.

Yea, thus prophesied Joseph: . . . And there shall rise up one mighty among them, who shall do much good, both in word and in deed, being an instrument in the hands of God, with exceeding faith, to work mighty wonders, and do that thing which is great in the sight of God, unto the bringing to pass much restoration unto the house of Israel, and unto the seed of thy brethren.[20]

---

[19]*Inspired Version, Bible,* Genesis 50:24-33.
[20]2 Nephi 3:6-16a, 24.

Chapter 32

WRITINGS OF JOSEPH SMITH
1.

AN EXTRACT FROM A TRANSLATION OF THE BIBLE

*Being the twenty-fourth chapter of Matthew, commencing with the
last verse of the twenty-third chapter, King James' Version.*

SIGNS AND PREDICTIONS OF THE SECOND
COMING OF CHRIST

INSPIRED VERSION OF THE HOLY SCRIPTURES

Beginning in 1831, after arriving in Ohio, Joseph Smith undertook through divine inspiration and revelation the work of correcting the errors in the *Bible*. Whenever occasion permitted, he pursued that work until July 2, 1833. However, he never completed the translation of all parts of the *Bible* and never authorized it to be published; and yet his translation is one of the most accurate versions of the Holy Scriptures in existence. In the second series of *Church History and Modern Revelation*, 1948, on page 15, Elder Joseph Fielding Smith made the following explanation in regard to Joseph Smith's translation of the Old and New Testaments:

It has been thought of some, that the Prophet went through the *Bible* beginning with the first chapter of Genesis and continued through to the book of Revelation, but this was not the case. He went through the *Bible* topic by topic, and revising as the Spirit of the Lord indicated to him where changes and additions should be made. There are many parts of the *Bible* that the Prophet did not touch, because the Lord did not direct him to do so. Therefore, there are many places in the Scriptures where errors still are found. This work was never fully completed, but the Prophet did as much as the Lord commanded him to do before the days of Nauvoo. February 2, 1833, he finished the revision of the New Testament, and on the second day of July that same year, he finished the Scriptures, as far as the Lord permitted him to go at that time.

In 1867, twenty-three years following his death, a copy of the manuscript containing the changes that Joseph had made was published by a group of people who had broken away from the true Church of Jesus Christ and organized a church of their own. This church they named "the Reorganized Church of Jesus Christ of Latter-day Saints," which name in itself tells the story of its origin. The Prophet Joseph Smith's translation of the *Bible* is known as the *Inspired Version* of the *Holy Scriptures*.

The material in this chapter, taken by Elder Franklin D. Richards from a copy of a manuscript of Joseph Smith's translation of the *Bible* which is in the possession of the Church of Jesus Christ of Latter-day Saints in Salt Lake City, was published in England (1851) as part of the *Pearl of Great Price*. Its contents agree in practically every detail with similar material published by the "Reorganized Church of Jesus Christ" in the *Inspired Version* of the *Bible* in 1867 from the manuscript which is owned by that church.

The writer of this book made a comparison of Joseph Smith's translation of the twenty-fourth chapter of Matthew as reproduced in the *Pearl of Great Price* with the material dealing with the same subject in the 1867 and 1944 editions of the *Inspired Version* of the *Holy Scriptures*. He found that there was a variance in punctuation in the various publications, but that practically every word—with the possible exception of three or four—in the *Pearl of Great Price* publication is identical with the text of the first edition of the *Inspired Version* (1867). However, in the edition that the "Reorganized Church of Jesus Christ" calls "A New Corrected Edition" of the *Inspired Version* of the *Holy Scriptures*, copyrighted in 1944, numerous changes have been made; therefore, the *Inspired Version* as used by that church today differs in many respects from the copy of the manuscript as it came from the hands of the Prophet Joseph Smith. The following is that church's justification for making those changes:

"Preface to 1944 Edition: This corrected edition of the *Inspired Version* of the *Holy Scriptures* was prepared under the direction of the First Presidency and the Board of Publication of the Reorganized Church of Jesus Christ of Latter-day Saints.

"The committee found some words and phrases transposed or improperly placed in the work done by Joseph Smith, Jr. These errors, together with others involving spelling, punctua-

tion, and typographical or *other omissions, were corrected, particularly in those instances where the meaning of the text had been effected. Few other corrections were required.*"[1]

If the readers of this book desire to ascertain the changes made in Matthew 23:39; 24:1-51 of the King James Version by the Prophet Joseph Smith in this particular text taken from the *Pearl of Great Price*, a comparison of the two could be made.

Jesus' Second Coming

The last chapter was devoted to a discussion of Enoch's vision of the last days and the second coming of Jesus Christ. This chapter is a continuation of the same subject; however, the discussion will center upon Jesus' prediction to His apostles relative to the last days and His second coming.

Jesus' prediction of His second coming:

1. For I say unto you, that ye shall not see me henceforth and know that I am he of whom it is written by the prophets, until ye shall say: Blessed is he who cometh in the name of the Lord, in the clouds of heaven, and all the holy angels with him. Then understood his disciples that he should come again on the earth, after he was glorified and crowned on the right hand of God.

The New Testament record indicates that several times during the Savior's ministry He predicted that He would return to earth again in His glory. For example: "For the Son of man shall come in the glory of his Father with his angels; and then he shall reward every man according to his works."[2]

And again we read:

Jesus saith unto him, Thou hast said: nevertheless I say unto you, hereafter shall ye see the Son of man sitting on the right hand of power, and coming in the clouds of heaven.[3]

Whosoever therefore shall be ashamed of me and of my words in this adulterous and sinful generation; of him also shall the Son of man be ashamed, when he cometh in the glory of his Father with the holy angels.[4]

The Acts of the Apostles declares that following the resurrection of Jesus Christ He appeared to His apostles and others many times during a period of forty days. Eventually the time

[1]*Inspired Version, the Holy Scriptures*, 1944 edition, "Preface," p. 6. The italics were supplied by the author of this book.
[2]Matthew 16:27.
[3]*Ibid.*, 26:64; 25-31.
[4]Mark 8:38.

arrived for Him to take His final departure from this earth. Luke, the author of Acts, described Christ's ascension and the promise of His return in the following words:

And when he had spoken these things, while they beheld, he was taken up; and a cloud received him out of their sight. And while they looked stedfastly toward heaven as he went up, behold, two men stood by them in white apparel; which also said, Ye men of Galilee, why stand ye gazing up into heaven? this same Jesus, which is taken up from you into heaven, shall so come in like manner as ye have see him go into heaven.[5]

John the Revelator, the last survivor of Jesus' apostles, bore fervent testimony to the second coming of the Son of Man. To quote his exact words:

Behold, he cometh with clouds; and every eye shall see him, and they also which pierced him: and all kindreds of the earth shall wail because of him.[6] . . . And I looked, and, lo, a Lamb stood on the mount Sion and with him an hundred forty and four thousand, having his Father's name written in their foreheads.[7]

To these predictions could be added the memorable statement made by Job, namely: "For I know that my redeemer liveth, and that he shall stand at the latter day upon the earth."[8]

DESTRUCTION OF THE TEMPLE

Jesus tells His apostles of the destruction of the temple at Jerusalem:

2. And Jesus went out, and departed from the temple; and his disciples came to him, for to hear him, saying: Master, show us concerning the buildings of the temple, as thou hast said—They shall be thrown down, and left unto you desolate.

3. And Jesus said unto them: See ye not all these things, and do ye not understand them? Verily I say unto you, there shall not be left here, upon this temple, one stone upon another that shall not be thrown down.

Josephus—a Jewish historian and probably an eye-witness of the destruction of Jerusalem—recorded a graphic word-picture of the capture of the "Holy City" by the Romans (led by Titus) in 70 A.D., the terrible slaughtering and scattering of the Jews, and the burning, destruction, and complete demolishing of the temple and the entire city. These events fulfilled the predictions made by the Son of Man. The following

---

[5]Acts 1:9-11.
[6]Revelation 1:7.
[7]*Ibid.*, 14:1.
[8]Job 19:25.

quotation is only a small portion of the vivid account given by Josephus:

And thus was the holy house burned down. . . . Now, although anyone would justly lament the destruction of such as this was, since it was the most admirable of all the works that we have seen or heard of, both for its curious structure and its magnitude, and also for the vast wealth bestowed upon it, as well as for the glorious reputation it had for its holiness; yet might such a one comfort himself with the thought, that it was fate that decreed it so to be, which is inevitable, both as to living creatures and as to works and places also. . . .

While the holy house was on fire, everything was plundered that came to hand, and ten thousand of those that were caught were slain; nor was there a commiseration of any age, or any reference of gravity; but children, and old men, and profane persons, and priests, were all slain in the same manner. . . .

The people also that were left above were beaten back upon the enemy, and under great consternation, and made sad moans at the calamity they were under; the multitude also that was in the city joined in this outcry with those that were upon the hill; and besides many of those that were worn away by the famine, and their mouths almost closed when they saw the fire of the holy house, they exerted their utmost strength, and broke out in groans and outcries again: Perea did also return the echo, as well as the mountains round about, [the city,] and augmented the force of the entire noise. Yet was the misery itself more terrible than this disorder; for one would have thought that the hill itself, on which the temple stood, was seething-hot, as full of fire on every part of it, that the blood was larger in quantity than the fire, and those that were slain more in number than those that slew them; for the ground did nowhere appear visible, for the dead bodies that lay on it; but the soldiers went over heaps of these bodies, as they ran upon such as fled from them.[9]

DESTRUCTION OF JERUSALEM

Jesus tells His apostles of the destruction of Jerusalem:

4. And Jesus left them, and went upon the Mount of Olives. And as he sat upon the Mount of Olives, the disciples came unto him privately, saying: Tell us when shall these things be which thou hast said concerning the destruction of the temple, and the Jews; and what is the sign of thy coming, and of the end of the world, or the destruction of the wicked, which is the end of the world?

5. And Jesus answered, and said unto them: Take heed that no man deceive you;

6. For many shall come in my name saying—I am Christ—and shall deceive many;

7. Then shall they deliver you up to be afflicted, and shall kill you, and ye shall be hated of all nations, for my name's sake;

8. And then shall many be offended, and shall betray one another;

9. And many false prophets shall arise, and shall deceive many;

10. And because iniquity shall abound, the love of many shall wax cold;

11. But he that remaineth steadfast and is not overcome, the same shall be saved.

12. When you, therefore, shall see the abomination of desolation, spoken

[9]Flavius Josephus, *The Works of Flavius Josephus,* translated by William Whiston, p. 581.

of by Daniel the prophet, concerning the destruction of Jerusalem, then you shall stand in the holy place; whoso readeth let him understand.

13. Then let them who are in Judea flee into the mountains;

14. Let him who is on the housetop flee, and not return to take anything out of his house;

15. Neither let him who is in the field return back to take his clothes;

16. And wo unto them that are with child, and unto them that give suck in those days;

17. Therefore, pray ye the Lord that your flight be not in the winter, neither on the Sabbath day;

18. For then, in those days, shall be great tribulation on the Jews, and upon the inhabitants of Jerusalem, such as was not before sent upon Israel, of God, since the beginning of their kingdom until this time; no, nor ever shall be sent again upon Israel.

19. All things which have befallen them are only the beginning of the sorrows which shall come upon them.

20. And except those days should be shortened, there should none of their flesh be saved; but for the elect's sake, according to the covenant, those days shall be shortened.

21. Behold, these things I have spoken unto you concerning the Jews.

SIGNS OF JESUS' SECOND COMING

The vivid description of the destruction of Jerusalem and the signs of His second coming given by the Savior in the following scripture quoted from Matthew should be studied carefully at this point. If the readers desire to augment what the Son of God told His apostles, these additional scriptures could be referred to with profit: Luke 21:10-17, 25-27, 35-36; 2 Thessalonians 2:1-3; Revelation 1:7; 6:12-17; *Doctrine and Covenants* 5:19-20; 29:7-28; 34:6-9; 38:8; 45:16-75; 49:6-7, 22-25; 63:32-35; 88:87-116; 97:23-27; 101:11-12, 24-28; 112:23-26; 133:2-3, 17-74.

Jesus tells his apostles of the signs of His second coming:

[Tell us . . . what is the sign of thy coming, and the end of the world . . . ? See verse 4] And again, after the tribulation of those days which shall come upon Jerusalem, if any man shall say unto you, Lo, here is Christ, or there, believe him not;

22. For in those days there shall also arise false Christs, and false prophets, and shall show great signs and wonders, insomuch, that, if possible, they shall deceive the very elect, who are the elect according to the covenant.

23. Behold, I speak these things unto you for the elect's sake; and you also shall hear of wars, and rumors of wars; see that ye be not troubled, for all I have told you must come to pass; but the end is not yet.

24. Behold, I have told you before;

25. Wherefore, if they shall say unto you: Behold, he is in the desert; go not forth; Behold, he is in the secret chambers; believe it not;

26. For as the light of the morning cometh out of the east, and shineth even unto the west, and covereth the whole earth, so shall also the coming of the Son of Man be.

27. And now I show unto you a parable. Behold, wheresoever the carcass is, there will the eagles be gathered together; so likewise shall mine elect be gathered from the four quarters of the earth.

28. And they shall hear of wars and rumors of wars.

29. Behold, I speak for mine elect's sake; for nation shall rise against nation, and kingdom against kingdom; there shall be famines, and pestilences, and earthquakes, in divers places.

30. And again, because iniquity shall abound, the love of many shall wax cold; but he that shall not be overcome, the same shall be saved.

31. And again, this Gospel of the Kingdom shall be preached in all the world, for a witness unto all nations, and then shall the end come, or the destruction of the wicked;

32. And again shall the abomination of desolation, spoken of by Daniel the prophet, be fulfilled.

33. And immediately after the tribulation of those days, the sun shall be darkened, and the moon shall not give her light, and the stars shall fall from heaven, and the powers of heaven shall be shaken.

34. Verily, I say unto you, this generation, in which these things shall be shown forth, shall not pass away until all I have told you shall be fulfilled.

35. Although, the days will come, that heaven and earth shall pass away; yet my words shall not pass away, but all shall be fulfilled.

Second Coming of Christ

Jesus predicts His second coming and describes the conditions that would prevail at that time:

36. And, as I said before, after the tribulation of those days, and the powers of the heavens shall be shaken, then shall appear the sign of the Son of Man in heaven, and then shall all the tribes of the earth mourn; and they shall see the Son of Man coming in the clouds of heaven, with power and great glory;

37. And whoso treasureth up my word, shall not be deceived, for the Son of Man shall come, and he shall send his angels before him with the great sound of a trumpet, and they shall gather together the remainder of his elect from the four winds, from one end of heaven to the other.

38. Now learn a parable of the fig-tree—When its branches are yet tender, and it begins to put forth leaves, you know that summer is nigh at hand;

39. So likewise, mine elect, when they shall see all these things, they shall know that he is near, even at the doors;

40. But of that day, and hour, no one knoweth; no, not the angels of God in heaven, but my Father only.

41. But as it was in the days of Noah, so it shall be also at the coming of the Son of Man;

42. For it shall be with them, as it was in the days which were before the flood; for until the day that Noah entered into the ark they were eating and drinking, marrying and giving in marriage;

43. And knew not until the flood came, and took them all away; so shall also the coming of the Son of Man be.

44. Then shall be fulfilled that which is written, that in the last days, two shall be in the field, the one shall be taken, and the other left;

45. Two shall be grinding at the mill, the one shall be taken, and the other left;

46. And what I say unto one, I say unto all men; watch, therefore, for you know not at what hour your Lord doth come.

47. But know this, if the good man of the house had known in what watch the thief would come, he would have watched, and would not have suffered his house to have been broken up, but would have been ready.

48. Therefore be ye also ready, for in such an hour as ye think not, the Son of Man cometh.

Wise and Evil Servants

Jesus' parable of the wise and evil servants:

49. Who, then, is a faithful and wise servant, whom his lord hath made ruler over his household, to give them meat in due season?

50. Blessed is that servant whom his lord, when he cometh, shall find so doing; and verily I say unto you, he shall make him ruler over all his goods.

51. But if that evil servant shall say in his heart: My lord delayeth his coming,

52. And shall begin to smite his fel-

low-servants, and to eat and drink with the drunken,

53. The lord of that servant shall come in a day when he looketh not for him, and in an hour that he is not aware of.

54. And shall cut him asunder, and shall appoint him his portion with the hypocrites; there shall be weeping and gnashing of teeth.

55. And thus cometh the end of the wicked, according to the prophecy of Moses, saying: They shall be cut off from among the people; but the end of the earth is not yet, but by and by.

Concluding Thought

The complete contents of this chapter impress on one's mind the absolute necessity of his living the Gospel of Jesus Christ and preparing himself for the day when the Lord shall come to dwell upon the earth. Those who cleanse themselves by living righteous lives—those whose "garments have been made white through the blood of the Lamb"—shall be caught up in the clouds of heaven to meet the Savior at His coming while all the wicked and the filthy throughout the entire earth shall be destroyed.

Chapter 33

JOSEPH SMITH, 2.

2.

EXTRACTS FROM THE HISTORY OF JOSEPH SMITH, THE PROPHET[1]

THE "FIRST VISION"

HISTORY OF JOSEPH SMITH, THE PROPHET

In the spring of 1838, the Prophet Joseph Smith began to write his history which has come to be known as the *History of the Church of Jesus Christ of Latter-day Saints, Period I, or History of Joseph Smith, the Prophet,* by himself. The first of this narrative to appear came from the press on March 15, 1842, at Nauvoo, Illinois. It was published in the *Times and Seasons,* beginning in volume 3, number 10, page 726, and continued in succeeding issues until February 15, 1846. By the latter date, the events up to August, 1834, had been printed. The publication of the *History of the Prophet Joseph Smith* was continued by the *Deseret News* (volume 2, number 1, November 15, 1851,) from the point where the *Times and Seasons* had left off and the story was carried forward to the death of the Prophet, including the succession of the Twelve Apostles to the leadership of the Church. This history was reproduced in the *Millennial Star,* a Latter-day Saint periodical begun in England in 1840.

Elder B. H. Roberts took the *History of Joseph, the Prophet* from the *Times and Seasons,* the *Deseret News,* and the *Millennial Star,* and also other journal accounts of the leaders of the Church, especially those of the Prophet Joseph Smith, and from these primary sources he published in six volumes *The History of the Church of Jesus Christ of Latter-day Saints, Period I.* These six volumes came from the press

---

[1]For the complete record see *History of the Church,* vol. 1, chaps. 1 to 5 inclusive.

during the period from 1902 to 1912. This history has ofttimes been referred to as the *Documentary History of the Church*. It covers the period of Church History from the birth of the Prophet Joseph Smith up to the time of his martyrdom.

In 1851 Franklin D. Richards took extracts from the *Times and Seasons'* account of the *History of the Prophet Joseph Smith* and published that material in the *Pearl of Great Price*. The portion of the Prophet's history reproduced by Elder Richards began prior to the "First Vision" and carried the story up to the restoration of the Aaronic Priesthood. The material presented in this chapter was first published in the *Times and Seasons,* volume 3, number 10, March 15, and number 11, April 1, 1842, appearing in that periodical on pages 726-728 and pages 748-749.

We shall now go directly to the account reproduced from the *Pearl of Great Price* and let the Prophet Joseph Smith tell his own story.

PURPOSE OF JOSEPH SMITH'S HISTORY

Joseph Smith presents his purpose in writing his history:

1. Owing to the many reports which have been put in circulation by evil-disposed and designing persons, in relation to the rise and progress of the Church of Jesus Christ of Latter-day Saints, all of which have been designed by the authors thereof to militate against its character as a Church and its progress in the world—I have been induced to write this history, to disabuse the public mind, and put all inquirers after truth in possession of the facts, as they have transpired, in relation both to myself and the Church, so far as I have such facts in my possession.

2. In this history I shall present the various events in relation to this Church, in truth and righteousness, as they have transpired, or as they at present exist, being now the eighth year since the organization of the said Church.

THE SMITH FAMILY

Joseph Smith gives an account of his birth and lists the names of his father's family:

3. I was born in the year of our Lord one thousand eight hundred and five, on the twenty-third day of December, in the town of Sharon, Windsor county, State of Vermont. . . . My father, Joseph Smith, Sen., left the State of Vermont, and moved to Palmyra, Ontario (now Wayne) county, in the State of New York, when I was in my tenth year, or thereabouts. In about four years after my father's arrival in Palmyra, he moved with his family into Manchester, in the same county of Ontario—

4. His family, consisting of eleven souls, namely, my father, Joseph Smith; my mother, Lucy Smith (whose name, previous to her marriage, was Mack, daughter of Solomon Mack); my brothers, Alvin (who died November 19th, 1824, in the 27th year of his age), Hyrum, myself, Samuel Harrison, William, Don Carlos; and my sisters, Sophronia, Catherine, and Lucy.

Religious Revival

Joseph Smith gives an account of the religious revival in New York:

5. Some time in the second year after our removal to Manchester, there was in the place where we lived an unusual excitement on the subject of religion. It commenced with the Methodists, but soon became general among all the sects in that region of country. Indeed, the whole district of country seemed affected by it, and great multitudes united themselves to the different religious parties, which created no small stir and division amongst the people, some crying, "Lo, here!" and others, "Lo, there!" Some were contending for the Methodist faith, some for the Presbyterian, and some for the Baptist.

6. For, notwithstanding the great love which the converts to these different faiths expressed at the time of their conversion, and the great zeal manifested by the respective clergy, who were active in getting up and promoting this extraordinary scene of religious feeling, in order to have everybody converted, as they were pleased to call it, let them join what sect they pleased; yet when the converts began to file off, some to one party and some to another, it was seen that the seemingly good feelings of both the priests and the converts were more pretended than real; for a scene of great confusion and bad feeling ensued—priest contending against priest, and convert against convert; so that all their good feelings one for another, if they ever had any, were entirely lost in a strife of words and a contest about opinions.

7. I was at this time in my fifteenth year. My father's family was proselyted to the Presbyterian faith, and four of them joined that church, namely, my mother, Lucy; my brothers Hyrum and Samuel Harrison; and my sister Sophronia.

"If Any of You Lack Wisdom"

Joseph decided to appeal to the Lord for wisdom:

8. During this time of great excitement my mind was called up to serious reflection and great uneasiness; but though my feelings were deep and often poignant, still I kept myself aloof from all these parties, though I attended their several meetings as often as occasion would permit. In process of time my mind became somewhat partial to the Methodist sect, and I felt some desire to be united with them; but so great were the confusion and strife among the different denominations, that it was impossible for a person young as I was, and so unacquainted with men and things, to come to any certain conclusion who was right and who was wrong.

9. My mind at times was greatly excited, the cry and tumult were so great and incessant. The Presbyterians were most decided against the Baptists and Methodists, and used all the powers of both reason and sophistry to prove their errors, or, at least, to make the people think they were in error. On the other hand, the Baptists and Methodists in their turn were equally zealous in endeavoring to establish their own tenets and disprove all others.

10. In the midst of this war of words and tumult of opinions, I often said to myself: What is to be done? Who of all these parties are right; or, are they all wrong together? If any one of them be right, which is it, and how shall I know it?

11. While I was laboring under the extreme difficulties caused by the contests of these parties of religionists, I was one day reading the Epistle of James, first chapter and fifth verse, which reads: *If any of you lack wisdom, let him ask of God, that giveth to all men liberally, and upbraideth not; and it shall be given him.*

12. Never did any passage of scripture come with more power to the heart of man than this did at this time to mine. It seemed to enter with great force into every feeling of my heart. I reflected on it again and again, knowing that if any person needed wisdom from God, I did; for how to act I did not know, and unless I could get more wisdom than I then had, I would never know; for the teachers of religion of the different sects understood the same passages of scripture so differently as to destroy all confidence in settling the question by an appeal to the Bible.

The "First Vision"

The Father and His Only Begotten Son appeared to Joseph Smith:

13. At length I came to the conclusion that I must either remain in darkness and confusion, or else I must do as James directs, that is, ask of God. I at length came to the determination to "ask of God," concluding that if he gave wisdom to them that lacked wisdom, and would give liberally, and not upbraid, I might venture.

14. So, in accordance with this, my determination to ask of God, I retired to the woods to make the attempt. It was on the morning of a beautiful, clear day, early in the spring of eighteen hundred and twenty. It was the first time in my life that I had made such an attempt, for amidst all my anxieties I had never as yet made the attempt to pray vocally.

15. After I had retired to the place where I had previously designed to go, having looked around me, and finding myself alone, I kneeled down and began to offer up the desires of my heart to God. I had scarcely done so, when immediately I was seized upon by some power which entirely overcame me, and had such an astonishing influence over me as to bind my tongue so that I could not speak. Thick darkness gathered around me, and it seemed to me for a time as if I were doomed to sudden destruction.

16. But, exerting all my powers to call upon God to deliver me out of the power of this enemy which had seized upon me, and at the very moment when I was ready to sink into despair and abandon myself to destruction—not to an imaginary ruin, but to the power of some actual being from the unseen world, who had such marvelous power as I had never before felt in any being —just at this moment of great alarm, I saw a pillar of light exactly over my head, above the brightness of the sun, which descended gradually until it fell upon me.

17. It no sooner appeared than I found myself delivered from the enemy which held me bound. When the light rested upon me I saw two Personages, whose brightness and glory defy all description, standing above me in the air. One of them spake unto me, calling me by name, and said, pointing to the other —*This is My Beloved Son. Hear Him!*

18. My object in going to inquire of the Lord was to know which of all the sects was right, that I might know which to join. No sooner, therefore, did I get possession of myself, so as to be able to speak, than I asked the Personages who stood above me in the light, which of all the sects was right—and which I should join.

19. I was answered that I must join none of them, for they were all wrong; and the Personage who addressed me said that all their creeds were an abomination in his sight; that those professors were all corrupt; that: "they draw near to me with their lips, but their hearts are far from me; they teach for doctrines the commandments of men, having a form of godliness, but they deny the power thereof."

20. He again forbade me to join with any of them; and many other things did he say unto me which I cannot write at this time. When I came to myself again, I found myself lying on my back, looking up into heaven. When the light had departed, I had no strength; but soon recovering in some degree, I went home. And as I leaned up to the fireplace, mother inquired what the matter was. I replied, "Never mind, all is well—I am well enough off." I then said to my mother, "I have learned for myself that Presbyterianism is not true."

Reactions Against Joseph and His Testimony

Joseph tells the story of the evil reactions against him and bears his testimony:

It seems as though the adversary was aware, at a very early period of my life, that I was destined to prove a disturber and an annoyer of his kingdom; else why should the powers of darkness combine against me? Why the opposition and persecution that arose against me, almost in my infancy?

21. Some few days after I had this vision, I happened to be in company

with one of the Methodist preachers, who was very active in the before mentioned religious excitement; and, conversing with him on the subject of religion, I took occasion to give him an account of the vision which I had had. I was greatly surprised at his behavior; he treated my communication not only lightly, but with great contempt, saying it was all of the devil, that there were no such things as visions or revelations in these days; that all such things had ceased with the apostles, and that there would never be any more of them.

22. I soon found, however, that my telling the story had excited a great deal of prejudice against me among the professors of religion, and was the cause of great persecution, which continued to increase; and though I was an obscure boy, only between fourteen and fifteen years of age, and my circumstances in life such as to make a boy of no consequence in the world, yet men of high standing would take notice sufficient to excite the public mind against me, and create a bitter persecution; and this was common among all the sects—all united to persecute me.

23. It caused me serious reflection then, and often has since, how very strange it was that an obscure boy, of a little over fourteen years of age, and one, too, who was doomed to the necessity of obtaining a scanty maintenance by his daily labor, should be thought a character of sufficient importance to attract the attention of the great ones of the most popular sects of the day, and in a manner to create in them a spirit of the most bitter persecution and reviling. But strange or not, so it was, and it was often the cause of great sorrow to myself.

24. However, it was nevertheless a fact that I had beheld a vision. I have thought since, that I felt much like

Paul, when he made his defense before King Agrippa, and related the account of the vision he had when he saw a light and heard a voice; but still there were but few who believed him; some said he was dishonest, others said he was mad; and he was ridiculed and reviled. But all this did not destroy the reality of his vision. He had seen a vision, he knew he had, and all the persecution under heaven could not make it otherwise; and though they should persecute him unto death, yet he knew, and would know to his latest breath, that he had both seen a light and heard a voice speaking unto him, and all the world could not make him think or believe otherwise.

25. So it was with me. I had actually seen a light, and in the midst of that light I saw two Personages, and they did in reality speak to me; and though I was hated and persecuted for saying that I had seen a vision, yet it was true; and while they were persecuting me, reviling me, and speaking all manner of evil against me falsely for so saying, I was led to say in my heart: Why persecute me for telling the truth? I have actually seen a vision; and who am I that I can withstand God, or why does the world think to make me deny what I have actually seen? For I had seen a vision; I knew it, and I knew that God knew it, and I could not deny it, neither dared I do it; at least I knew that by so doing I would offend God, and come under condemnation.

26. I had now got my mind satisfied so far as the sectarian world was concerned—that it was not my duty to join with any of them, but to continue as I was until further directed. I had found the testimony of James to be true—that a man who lacked wisdom might ask of God, and obtain, and not be upbraided.

Chapter 34

VISITATIONS OF THE ANGEL MORONI

Introductory Statement

The material which appears in this chapter was first published in the *Times and Seasons,* volume 3, number 11, page 749, April 1; number 12, pages 753-754, April 15; and number 13, pages 771-773, May 2, 1842, and it was reproduced in the *Pearl of Great Price* by Elder Franklin D. Richards in 1851. It is now our purpose to proceed with the Prophet Joseph Smith's story told in his own words.

Joseph's Life Between 1820 and 1823

Joseph gives an account of his experiences between 1820 and 1823:

27. I continued to pursue my common vocations in life until the twenty-first of September, one thousand eight hundred and twenty-three, all the time suffering severe persecution at the hands of all classes of men, both religious and irreligious, because I continued to affirm that I had seen a vision.

28. During the space of time which intervened between the time I had the vision and the year eighteen hundred and twenty-three—having been forbidden to join any of the religious sects of the day, and being of very tender years, and persecuted by those who ought to have been my friends and to have treated me kindly, and if they supposed me to be deluded to have endeavored in a proper and affectionate manner to have reclaimed me—I was left to all kinds of temptations; and, mingling with all kinds of society, I frequently fell into many foolish errors, and displayed the weakness of youth, and the foibles of human nature; which, I am sorry to say, led me into divers temptations, offensive in the sight of God. In making this confession, no one need suppose me guilty of any great or malignant sins. A disposition to commit such was never in my nature. But I was guilty of levity, and sometimes associated with jovial company, etc., not consistent with the character which ought to be maintained by one who was called of God as I had been. But this will not seem very strange to any one who recollects my youth, and is acquainted with my native cheery temperament.

First Visitation of the Angel Moroni

Joseph's account of the appearance of the Angel Moroni to him:

29. In consequence of these things, I often felt condemned for my weakness and imperfections; when, on the evening of the above-mentioned twenty-first of September, after I had retired to my bed for the night, I betook myself to prayer and supplication to Almighty God for forgiveness of all my sins and follies, and also for a manifestation to me, that I might know of my state and standing before him; for I had full confidence in obtaining a divine manifestation, as I previously had one.

30. While I was thus in the act of calling upon God, I discovered a light appearing in my room, which continued to increase until the room was lighter than at noonday, when immediately a personage appeared at my bedside, standing in the air, for his feet did not touch the floor.

31. He had on a loose robe of most exquisite whiteness. It was a whiteness beyond anything earthly I had ever seen; nor do I believe that any earthly thing could be made to appear so exceedingly white and brilliant. His hands were naked, and his arms also, a little above the wrist; so, also, were his feet naked, as were his legs, a little above the ankles. His head and neck were also bare. I could discover that he had no other clothing on but this robe, as it was open, so that I could see into his bosom.

32. Not only was his robe exceedingly white, but his whole person was glorious beyond description, and his countenance 'truly like lightning. The room was exceedingly light, but not so very bright as immediately around his person. When I first looked upon him, I was afraid; but the fear soon left me.

33. He called me by name, and said unto me that he was a messenger sent from the presence of God to me, and that his name was Moroni; that God had a work for me to do; and that my name should be had for good and evil among all nations, kindreds, and tongues, or that it should be both good and evil spoken of among all people.

34. He said there was a book deposited, written upon gold plates, giving an account of the former inhabitants of this continent, and the source from whence they sprang. He also said that the fulness of the everlasting Gospel was contained in it, as delivered by the Savior to the ancient inhabitants;

35. Also, that there were two stones in silver bows—and these stones, fastened to a breastplate, constituted what is called the Urim and Thummim—deposited with the plates; and the possession and use of these stones were what constituted "seers" in ancient or former times; and that God had prepared them for the purpose of translating the book.

Ancient Prophets Quoted

The Angel Moroni quotes prophecies from the Old and New Testament:

36. After telling me these things, he commenced quoting the prophecies of the Old Testament. He first quoted part of the third chapter of Malachi; and he quoted also the fourth or last chapter of the same prophecy, though with a little variation from the way it reads in our Bibles. Instead of quoting the first verse as it reads in our books, he quoted it thus:

37. *For behold, the day cometh that shall burn as an oven, and all the proud, yea, and all that do wickedly shall burn as stubble; for they that come shall burn them, saith the Lord of Hosts, that* *it shall leave them neither root nor branch.*

38. And again, he quoted the fifth verse thus: *Behold, I will reveal unto you the Priesthood, by the hand of Elijah the prophet, before the coming of the great and dreadful day of the Lord.*

39. He also quoted the next verse differently: *And he shall plant in the hearts of the children the promises made to the fathers, and the hearts of the children shall turn to their fathers. If it were not so, the whole earth would be utterly wasted at his coming.*

40. In addition to these, he quoted the eleventh chapter of Isaiah, saying that it was about to be fulfilled. He quoted also the third chapter of Acts, twenty-second and twenty-third verses, precisely as they stand in our New Testament. He said that that prophet was Christ; but the day had not yet come when "they who would not hear his voice should be cut off from among the people," but soon would come.

41. He also quoted the second chapter of Joel, from the twenty-eighth verse to the last. He also said that this was not yet fulfilled, but was soon to be. And he further stated that the fulness of the Gentiles was soon to come in. He quoted many other passages of scripture, and offered many explanations which cannot be mentioned here.

FURTHER INSTRUCTIONS AND ASCENSION OF MORONI

Joseph Smith receives further instructions regarding the ancient sacred relics, and the ascension of the Angel Moroni:

42. Again, he told me, that when I got those plates of which he had spoken —for the time that they should be obtained was not yet fulfilled—I should not show them to any person; neither the breastplate with the Urim and Thummim; only to those to whom I should be commanded to show them; if I did I should be destroyed. While he was conversing with me about the plates, the vision was opened to my mind that I could see the place where the plates were deposited, and that so clearly and distinctly that I knew the place again when I visited it.

43. After this communication, I saw the light in the room begin to gather immediately around the person of him who had been speaking to me, and it continued to do so until the room was again left dark, except just around him; when, instantly I saw, as it were, a conduit open right up into heaven, and he ascended till he entirely disappeared, and the room was left as it had been before this heavenly light had made its appearance.

SECOND AND THIRD VISITATIONS

Joseph's account of the second and third visitations of the Angel Moroni:

44. I lay musing on the singularity of the scene, and marveling greatly at what had been told to me by this extraordinary messenger; when, in the midst of my meditation, I suddenly discovered that my room was again beginning to get lighted, and in an instant, as it were, the same heavenly messenger was again by my bedside.

45. He commenced, and again related the very same things which he had done at his first visit, without the least variation; which having done, he informed me of great judgments which were coming upon the earth, with great desolations by famine, sword, and pestilence; and that these grievous judgments would come on the earth in this generation. Having related these things, he again ascended as he had done before.

46. By this time, so deep were the impressions made on my mind, that sleep had fled from my eyes, and I lay overwhelmed in astonishment at what I had both seen and heard. But what was my surprise when again I beheld the same messenger at my bedside, and heard him rehearse or repeat over again to me the same things as before; and added a caution to me, telling me that Satan would try to tempt me (in consequence of the indigent circumstances of my father's family), to get the plates for the purpose of getting rich. This he forbade me, saying that I must have no other object in view in getting the plates but to glorify God, and must not be influenced by any other motive than that of building his kingdom; otherwise I could not get them.

47. After his third visit, he again ascended into heaven as before, and I was again left to ponder on the strangeness of what I had just experienced; when almost immediately after this heavenly messenger had ascended from me for the third time, the cock crowed, and I found that day was approaching, so that our interviews must have occupied the whole of that night.

FOURTH VISITATION

Joseph's account of the fourth visitation of the Angel Moroni:

48. I shortly after arose from my bed, and, as usual, went to the necessary labors of the day; but, in attempting to work as at other times, I found my strength so exhausted as to render me entirely unable. My father, who was laboring along with me, discovered something to be wrong with me, and told me to go home. I started with the intention of going to the house; but, in attempting to cross the fence out of the field where we were, my strength entirely failed me, and I fell helpless on the ground, and for a time was quite unconscious of anything.

49. The first thing that I can recollect was a voice speaking unto me, calling me by name. I looked up, and beheld the same messenger standing over my head, surrounded by light as before. He then again related unto me all that he had related to me the previous night, and commanded me to go to my father and tell him of the vision and commandments which I had received.

RECORD DEPOSITORY AND FIFTH VISITATION

Joseph visits the depository of the ancient relics, and the fifth visitation of the Angel Moroni:

50. I obeyed; I returned to my father in the field, and rehearsed the whole matter to him. He replied to me that it was of God, and told me to go and do as commanded by the messenger. I left the field, and went to the place where the messenger had told me the plates were deposited; and owing to the distinctness of the vision which I had had concerning it, I knew the place the instant I arrived there.

51. Convenient to the village of Manchester, Ontario county, New York, stands a hill of considerable size, and the most elevated of any in the neighborhood. On the west side of this hill, not far from the top, under a stone of considerable size, lay the plates, deposited in a stone box. This stone was thick and rounding in the middle on the upper side, and thinner towards the edges, so that the middle part of it was visible above the ground, but the edge all around was covered with earth.

52. Having removed the earth, I obtained a lever, which I got fixed under the edge of the stone, and with a little exertion raised it up. I looked in, and there indeed did I behold the plates, the Urim and Thummim, and the breastplate, as stated by the messenger. The box in which they lay was formed by laying stones together in some kind of cement. In the bottom of the box were laid two stones crossways of the box, and on these stones lay the plates and the other things with them.

53. I made an attempt to take them out, but was forbidden by the messenger, and was again informed that the time for bringing them forth had not yet arrived, neither would it, until four years from that time; but he told me that I should come to that place precisely in one year from that time, and that he would there meet with me, and that I should continue to do so until the time should come for obtaining the plates.

YEARLY INSTRUCTIONS

Joseph receives instructions from the angel yearly for four years:

54. Accordingly, as I had been commanded, I went at the end of each year, and at each time I found the same messenger there, and received instruction and intelligence from him at each of our interviews, respecting what the Lord was going to do, and how and in what manner his kingdom was to be conducted in the last days.

Chapter 35

VITAL EVENTS FROM 1823 TO 1829

INTRODUCTORY STATEMENT

The historical account presented in this chapter was published for the first time in the *Times and Seasons,* Nauvoo, Illinois, volume 3, number 13, May 2, 1842, on pages 771-773. As we have done in the last two chapters, we shall let the Prophet Joseph Smith tell his own story.

VITAL EVENTS FROM 1824 TO 1827

The Prophet's account of Alvin's death, Joseph a "money digger," and his marriage to Emma Hale:

55. As my father's worldly circumstances were very limited, we were under the necessity of laboring with our hands, hiring out by day's work and otherwise, as we could get opportunity. Sometimes we were at home, and sometimes abroad, and by continuous labor were enabled to get a comfortable maintenance.

56. In the year 1824 my father's family met with a great affliction by the death of my eldest brother, Alvin. In the month of October, 1825, I hired with an old gentleman by the name of Josiah Stoal, who lived in Chenango county, State of New York. He had heard something of a silver mine having been opened by the Spaniards in Harmony, Susquehanna county, State of Pennsylvania; and had, previous to my hiring to him, been digging, in order, if possible, to discover the mine. After I went to live with him, he took me, with the rest of his hands, to dig for the sil-

ver mine, at which I continued to work for nearly a month, without success in our undertaking, and finally I prevailed with the old gentleman to cease digging after it. Hence arose the very prevalent story of my having been a money-digger.

57. During the time that I was thus employed, I was put to board with a Mr. Isaac Hale, of that place; it was there I first saw my wife (his daughter) Emma Hale. On the 18th of January, 1827, we were married, while I was yet employed in the service of Mr. Stoal.

58. Owing to my continuing to assert that I had seen a vision, persecution still followed me, and my wife's father's family were very much opposed to our being married. I was, therefore, under the necessity of taking her elsewhere; so we went and were married at the house of Squire Tarbill, in South Bainbridge, Chenango county, New York. Immediately after my marriage, I left Mr. Stoal's, and went to my father's, and farmed with him that season.

Plates Received by Joseph and Returned to the Angel Moroni

Joseph's account of receiving the ancient records, efforts made to wrest them from him, and his statement of returning them to the Angel Moroni:

59. At length the time arrived for obtaining the plates, the Urim and Thummim, and the breastplate. On the twenty-second day of September, one thousand eight hundred and twenty-seven, having gone as usual at the end of another year to the place where they were deposited, the same heavenly messenger delivered them up to me with this charge: that I should be responsible for them; that if I should let them go carelessly, or through any neglect of mine, I should be cut off; but that if I would use all my endeavors to preserve them, until he, the messenger, should call for them, they should be protected.

60. I soon found out the reason why I had received such strict charges to keep them safe, and why it was that the messenger had said that when I had done what was required at my hand, he would call for them. For no sooner was it known that I had them, than the most strenuous exertions were used to get them from me. Every stratagem that could be invented was resorted to for that purpose. The persecution became more bitter and severe than before, and multitudes were on the alert continually to get them from me if possible. But by the wisdom of God, they remained safe in my hands, until I had accomplished by them what was required at my hand. When, according to arrangements, the messenger called for them, I delivered them up to him; and he has them in his charge until this day, being the second day of May, one thousand eight hundred and thirty-eight.

Early Efforts at Translating

Joseph's early efforts at translating the ancient characters on the plates:

61. The excitement, however, still continued, and rumor with her thousand tongues was all the time employed in circulating falsehoods about my father's family, and about myself. If I were to relate a thousandth part of them, it would fill up volumes. The persecution, however, became so intolerable that I was under the necessity of leaving Manchester, and going with my wife to Susquehanna county, in the State of Pennsylvania. While preparing to start—being very poor, and the persecution so heavy upon us that there was no probability that we would ever be otherwise—in the midst of our afflictions we found a friend in a gentleman by the name of Martin Harris, who came to us and gave me fifty dollars to assist us on our journey. Mr. Harris was a resident of Palmyra township, Wayne county, in the State of New York, and a farmer of respectability.

62. By this timely aid was I enabled to reach the place of my destination in Pennsylvania; and immediately after my arrival there I commenced copying the characters off the plates. I copied a considerable number of them, and by means of the Urim and Thummim I translated some of them, which I did between the time I arrived at the house of my wife's father, in the month of December, and the February following.

Professor Anthon's Certificate

Martin Harris receives a certificate from Professor Charles Anthon of New York City:

63. Sometime in this month of February, the aforementioned Mr. Martin Harris came to our place, got the characters which I had drawn off the plates, and started with them to the city of New York. For what took place relative to him and the characters, I refer to his own account of the circumstances, as he related them to me after his return, which was as follows:

64. "I went to the city of New York, and presented the characters which had

been translated, with the translation thereof, to Professor Charles Anthon, a gentleman celebrated for his literary attainments. Professor Anthon stated that the translation was correct, more so than any he had before seen translated from the Egyptian. I then showed him those which were not yet translated, and he said that they were Egyptian, Chaldaic, Assyriac, and Arabic; and he said they were true characters. He gave me a certificate, certifying to the people of Palmyra that they were true characters, and that the translation of such of them as had been translated was also correct. I took the certificate and put it into my pocket, and was just leaving the house, when Mr. Anthon called me back, and asked me how the young

man found out that there were gold plates in the place where he found them. I answered that an angel of God had revealed it unto him.

65. "He then said to me, 'Let me see that certificate.' I accordingly took it out of my pocket and gave it to him, when he took it and tore it to pieces, saying that there was no such thing now as ministering of angels, and that if I would bring the plates to him he would translate them. I informed him that part of the plates were sealed, and that I was forbidden to bring them. He replied, 'I cannot read a sealed book.' I left him and went to Dr. Mitchell, who sanctioned what Professor Anthon had said respecting both the characters and the translation.

Joseph's Scribe

Oliver Cowdery becomes Joseph's scribe:

66. On the 5th day of April, 1829, Oliver Cowdery came to my house, until which time I had never seen him. He stated to me that having been teaching school in the neighborhood where my father resided, and my father being one of those who sent to the school, he went to board for a season at his house,

and while there the family related to him the circumstances of my having received the plates, and accordingly he had come to make inquiries of me.

67. Two days after the arrival of Mr. Cowdery (being the 7th of April) I commenced to translate the Book of Mormon, and he began to write for me.

Restoration of the Aaronic Priesthood

Joseph Smith's account of the restoration of the Aaronic Priesthood:

68. We still continued the work of translation, when, in the ensuing month (May, 1829), we on a certain day went into the woods to pray and inquire of the Lord respecting baptism for the remission of sins, that we found mentioned in the translation of the plates. While we were thus employed, praying and calling upon the Lord, a messenger from heaven descended in a cloud of light, and having laid his hands upon us, he ordained us, saying:

69. *Upon you my fellow servants, in the name of Messiah, I confer the Priesthood of Aaron, which holds the keys of the ministering of angels, and of the gospel of repentance, and of baptism by immersion for the remission of sins; and this shall never be taken again from the earth until the sons of Levi do offer again an offering unto the Lord in righteousness.*

70. He said this Aaronic Priesthood

had not the power of laying on hands for the gift of the Holy Ghost, but that this should be conferred on us hereafter; and he commanded us to go and be baptized, and gave us directions that I should baptize Oliver Cowdery, and that afterwards he should baptize me.

71. Accordingly we went and were baptized. I baptized him first, and afterwards he baptized me—after which I laid my hands upon his head and ordained him to the Aaronic Priesthood, and afterwards he laid his hands on me and ordained me to the same Priesthood —for so we were commanded.

72. The messenger who visited us on this occasion and conferred this Priesthood upon us, said his name was John, the same that is called John the Baptist acted under the direction of Peter, James, and John, who held the keys of the Priesthood of Melchizedek, which

Priesthood, he said, would in due time be conferred on us, and that I should be called the first Elder of the Church, and he (Oliver Cowdery) the second. It was on the fifteenth day of May, 1829, that we were ordained under the hand of this messenger, and baptized.

73. Immediatley on our coming up out of the water after we had been baptized, we experienced great and glorious blessings from our Heavenly Father. No sooner had I baptized Oliver Cowdery, than the Holy Ghost fell upon him, and he stood up and prophesied many things which should shortly come to pass. And again, so soon as I had been baptized by him, I also had the spirit of prophecy, when, standing up, I prophesied concerning the rise of this Church, and many other things connected with the Church, and this generation of children of men. We were filled with the Holy Ghost, and rejoiced in the God of our salvation.

Oliver Cowdery's description of his work with the Prophet Joseph Smith and the glorious experience of the appearance of John the Baptist and the restoration of the Aaronic Priesthood:

"These were days never to be forgotten—to sit under the sound of a voice dictated by the inspiration of heaven, awakened the utmost gratitude of this bosom! Day after day I continued, uninterrupted to write from his mouth, as he translated with the Urim and Thummim, or, as the Nephites would have said, 'Interpreters,' the history or record called 'The Book of Mormon.'

"To notice, in even few words, the interesting account given by Mormon and his faithful son Moroni, of a people once beloved and favored of heaven, would supersede my present design; I shall therefore defer this to a future period, and, as I said in the introduction, pass more directly to some few incidents immediately connected with the rise of this Church, which may be entertaining to some thousands who have stepped forward amid the frowns of bigots and the calumny of the hypocrites, and embraced the Gospel of Christ.

"No men, in their sober senses, could translate and write the directions given to the Nephites from the mouth of the Savior, of the precise manner in which men should build up His Church, and especially when corruption had spread an uncertainty over all forms and systems practiced among men, without desiring a privilege of showing the willingness of the heart by being buried in the liquid grave, to answer a 'good conscience by the resurrection of Jesus Christ.'

"After writing the account given of the Savior's ministry to the remnant of the seed of Jacob, upon this continent, it was easy to be seen, as the prophet said would be, that darkness covered the earth and gross darkness the minds of the people. On reflecting further it was easy to be seen, that amid the great strife and noise concerning religion, none had authority from God to administer the ordinances of the Gospel. For the question might be asked, have men authority to administer in the name of Christ, who deny revelations, when His testimony is no less than the spirit of prophecy, and His religion based, built, and sustained by immediate revelations, in all ages of the world when He has had a people on earth? If these facts were buried, and carefully concealed by men whose craft would have been in danger if once permitted to shine in the faces of men, they were no longer to us; and we only waited for the commandment to be given 'Arise and be baptized.'

"This was not long desired before it was realized. The Lord, who is rich in mercy, and ever willing to answer the consistent prayer of the humble, after we had called upon him in a fervent manner, aside from the abodes of men, condescended to manifest to us His will. On a sudden, as from the midst of eternity, the voice of the Redeemer spake peace to us. While the veil was parted and the angel of God came down clothed with glory, and delivered the anxiously looked for message, and the keys of the Gospel of repentance. What joy! what wonder! what amazement! While the world was racked and distracted—while millions were groping as the blind for the wall, and while all men were resting upon uncertainty, as a general mass, our eyes beheld, our ears heard, as in the 'blaze of the day'; yes, more—above the glitter of the May sunbeam, which then shed its brilliancy over the face of nature! Then his voice, though mild, pierced to the center, and his words, 'I am thy fellow-servant,' dispelled every fear. We listened, we gazed, we admired! 'Twas the voice of an angel, from glory, 'twas a message from the Most High! And as we heard we rejoiced, while His love enkindled upon our souls, and we were wrapped in the vision of the Almighty! Where was room for doubt? Nowhere; uncertainty had fled, doubt had sunk no more to rise, while fiction and deception had fled forever!

"But, dear brother, think, further think for a moment, what joy filled our hearts, and with what surprise we must have bowed, (for who would not have bowed the knee for such a blessing?) when we received under his hand the Holy Priesthood as he said, 'Upon you my fellow-servants, in the name of Messiah, I confer this Priesthood and this authority, which shall remain upon earth, that the sons of Levi may yet offer an offering unto the Lord in righteousness!'

"I shall not attempt to paint to you the feelings of this heart, nor the majestic beauty and glory which surrounded us on this occasion; but you will believe me when I say, that earth, nor men, with the eloquence of time, cannot begin to clothe language in as interesting and sublime a manner as this holy personage. No; nor has this earth power to give the joy, bestow the peace, or comprehend the wisdom which was contained in each sentence as they were delivered by the power of the Holy Spirit! Man may deceive his fellow-men, deception may follow deception, and the children of the wicked one may have power to seduce the foolish and untaught, till naught but fiction feeds the many, and the fruit of falsehood carries in its current the giddy to the grave; but one touch with the finger of his love, yes, one ray of glory from the upper world, or one word from the mouth of the Savior, from the bosom of eternity, strikes it all into insignificance, and blots it forever from the mind. The assurance that we were in the presence of an angel, the certainty that we heard the voice of Jesus, and the truth unsullied as it flowed from a pure personage, dictated by the will of God, is to me past description, and I shall ever while I am permitted to tarry; and in those mansions where perfection dwells and sin never comes, I hope to adore in that day which shall never cease."—*Times and Seasons,* Vol. 2, p. 201.

SPIRITUAL ENLIGHTENMENT AND THREATENED
MOB-VIOLENCE

The Prophet and Oliver receive spiritual enlightenment. Persecutions and threatened mob-violence at Harmony, Pennsylvania:

74. Our minds being now enlightened, we began to have the scriptures laid open to our understandings, and the true meaning and intention of their more mysterious passages revealed unto us in a manner which we never could attain to previously, nor ever before had thought of. In the meantime, we were forced to keep secret the circumstances of having received the Priesthood and our having been baptized, owing to a spirit of persecution which had already manifested itself in the neighborhood.

75. We had been threatened with being mobbed, from time to time, and this, too, by professors of religion. And their intentions of mobbing us were only counteracted by the influence of my wife's father's family (under Divine Providence), who had become very friendly to me, and who were opposed to mobs, and were willing that I should be allowed to continue the work of translation without interruption; and therefore offered and promised us protection from all unlawful proceedings, as far as in them lay.

Chapter 36

THE ARTICLES OF FAITH AND CANONIZING
THE SCRIPTURES

THE WENTWORTH LETTER

A document of great hisotrical and doctrinal importance, which was first published at the same time as the Book of Abraham, namely, on March 1, 1842, is known as *"The Wentworth Letter."* It made its first appearance in the *Times and Seasons,* volume 3, number 9, pages 706-710, published at Nauvoo, Illinois. In that periodical, it followed immediately after the Book of Abraham and comprises less than four printed pages.

This letter is not only one of the choicest documents in our church literature, but it is also the earliest published statement by the Prophet Joseph Smith in which he personally made pretension of presenting a consecutive narrative of those events in which the great latter-day work had its origin. It appears under the title of "Church History," and the Prophet introduces the account with the following paragraph:

At the request of Mr. John Wentworth, Editor, and Proprietor of the "Chicago Democrat," I have written the following sketch of the rise, progress, persecution, and faith of the Latter-day Saints, of which I have the honor, under God, of being the founder. Mr. Wentworth says, that he wishes to furnish Mr. Bastow, a friend of his, who is writing the history of New Hampshire, with this document. As Mr. Bastow has taken the proper steps to obtain correct information all that I should ask at his hands is, that he publish the account entire, ungarnished, and without misrepresentation.[1]

The Wentworth Letter begins with a brief statement of the birth of Joseph Smith in 1805. Then it traces in an admirable manner the story of the "First Vision," the appearances of the Angel Moroni, the receiving of the ancient plates and Urim and Thummim, and a short account of the translation and publication of the ancient Nephite records. This was followed

---

[1]Joseph Smith, "Church History," *Times and Seasons,* vol. 3, p. 706.

with a résumé of the contents of the *Book of Mormon*. Then a description of the organizing of the Church of Jesus Christ and the story of the persecutions of the Saints up to the settlement of Nauvoo were delineated. Also, statements of the prosperous condition and happy prospects of the Saints at that time and the missionary work that they were undertaking were included in the document. *The Wentworth Letter* closed with an epitome of the doctrines of the Church which has since been called "The Articles of Faith." In regard to these articles, Elder B. H. Roberts made the following comment:

Millions of these "Articles of Faith" have been published; they have been translated into many languages and carried to all the nations of the earth and tribes of men where the New Dispensation of the gospel has been preached. They were not produced by the labored efforts and harmonized contentions of scholastics, but were struck off by one mind at the single effort to make a declaration of that which is most assuredly believed by the Church, for one making earnest inquiry about her history and her fundamental doctrines. The combined directness, perspicuity, simplicity and comprehensiveness of this statement of the doctrine of the Church is regarded as strong evidence of a divine inspiration operating upon the mind of Joseph Smith.[2]

THE ARTICLES OF FAITH
OF THE CHURCH OF JESUS CHRIST OF LATTER-DAY SAINTS

1. We believe in God, the Eternal Father, and in His Son, Jesus Christ, and in the Holy Ghost.

2. We believe that men will be punished for their own sins, and not for Adam's transgression.

3. We believe that through the Atonement of Christ, all mankind may be saved, by obedience to the laws and ordinances of the Gospel.

4. We believe that the first principles and ordinances of the Gospel are: first, Faith in the Lord Jesus Christ; second, Repentance; third, Baptism by immersion for the remission of sins; fourth, Laying on of hands for the gift of the Holy Ghost.

5. We believe that a man must be called of God, by prophecy, and by the laying on of hands, by those who are in authority to preach the Gospel and administer in the ordinances thereof.

6. We believe in the same organization that existed in the Primitive Church, viz., apostles, prophets, pastors, teachers, evangelists, etc.

7. We believe in the gift of tongues, prophecy, revelation, visions, healing, interpretation of tongues, etc.

8. We believe the Bible to be the word of God as far as it is translated correctly; we also believe the Book of Mormon to be the word of God.

9. We believe all that God has revealed, all that He does now reveal, and we believe that He will yet reveal many great and important things pertaining to the Kingdom of God.

10. We believe in the literal gathering of Israel and in the restoration of the Ten Tribes; that Zion will be built upon this [the American] continent; that Christ will reign personally upon the earth; and, that the earth will be renewed and receive its paradisiacal glory.

[2]B. H. Roberts, *A Comprehensive History of the Church*, vol. 2, pp. 130-131.

11. We claim the privilege of worshiping Almighty God according to the dictates of our own conscience, and allow all men the same privilege, let them worship how, where, or what they may.

12. We believe in being subject to kings, presidents, rulers, and magistrates, in obeying, honoring, and sustaining the law.

13. We believe in being honest, true, chaste, benevolent, virtuous, and in doing good to all men; indeed, we may say that we follow the admonition of Paul—We believe all things, we hope all things, we have endured many things, and hope to be able to endure all things. If there is anything virtuous, lovely, or of good report or praiseworthy, we seek after these things.—JOSEPH SMITH.

The author thinks that it will not be necessary for him to discuss in this book each of the thirteen articles but would suggest that if the readers desire to make a detailed study of the Latter-day Saints' beliefs in regard to these subjects, they could refer to Dr. James E. Talmage's outstanding work entitled *The Articles of Faith*. That book is devoted entirely to a masterful discussion of each of the thirteen articles.

CANON DEFINED

When a group of people vote to accept a book as having been Divinely inspired, hence authoritative, and binding upon each of them, they canonize it and proclaim it to be their scripture. According to Dr. George L. Robinson, the origin of canonized writings is as follows:

The word "Canon" is of Christian origin, from the Greek word *kanon,* which in turn was probably borrowed from the Hebrew word *kane,* meaning a reed or measuring rod, hence norm or rule. Later it came to mean a rule of faith, and eventually a catalogue or list. In present usage it signifies a collection of religious writings Divinely inspired, and hence authoritative, normative, sacred, and binding.[3]

CANONIZING THE OLD TESTAMENT

The Old Testament was canonized by the Jews. The thirty-nine books which it contains today were not all canonized at one time, but they became canonical (or holy scripture) gradually as the people accepted each of them as authoritative. By the time that Christ came into the world, most of them were completely canonized and all of them were regarded with high respect. However, it was not until the end of the first century A. D. and beginning of the second that Jewish councils met and officially sanctioned the canonization of these books. In the words of Dr. George L. Robinson:

---

[3]George L. Robinson, *Where Did We Get Our Bible?* p. 1.

According to certain traditions preserved in the Mishna, two councils of Jewish rabbis were held in 90 and 118 A. D., respectively, at Jabne, or Jamnia, not far south of Joppa, near the Mediterranean coast, at which the books of the Old Testament, notably Ecclesiastes and Canticles, were discussed and their canonicity ratified. . . . In these councils the canon was formally and officially restricted to our thirty-nine books. It is, therefore, possible that at Jamnia the limits of the Hebrew canon were officially and finally determined by Jewish authority; not, however, that official sanction created public opinion, but rather only confirmed it.[4]

The Church of Jesus Christ of Latter-day Saints accepts as canonical writings the Old Testament exactly as it was canonized by the Hebrews; but Catholics accept a "larger canon of scripture," namely, the apocryphal books in addition to the thirty-nine in our Old Testament. These seven books deal with Jewish history and doctrine written between the Old and New Testaments. In this "larger canon" there are seven complete books and portions of two others in addition to the "smaller canon." These books are as follows: Tobit, Judith, Wisdom, Ecclesiasticus, Baruch, First and Second Maccabees, together with certain additions to Esther and to Daniel. When St. Jerome translated the Hebrew scriptures into Latin about 400 A. D., he translated these extra books. They were not accepted immediately by the Catholic Church, however, as holy scripture but as time passed they gradually won universal approval. The final and absolute seal of the Catholic Church was placed upon the apocryphal books at two councils, one held in the fifteenth century and the other in the sixteenth. We shall quote from an account given by Dr. Robinson:

At the Council of Florence (1442), however, a new step was taken in the direction of their [apocryphal books] canonization, when "Eugenius IV, with the approval of the Fathers of that august assembly, declared all the books found in the Latin Bibles then in use to be inspired by the same Holy Spirit, without distinguishing them into classes or categories." Though this bull of Pope Eugenius IV did not deal with the *canonicity* of the apocryphal books, it did proclaim their *inspiration;* so that men ever afterwards were able to claim that all of the books of the Old Testament, the apocryphal as well as the canonical were equally inspired. Nevertheless, down to the Council of Trent (1546), the apocryphal books possessed only inferior canonical authority; and when men spoke of canonical scripture in the strict sense, these were not included. . . .

Accordingly, the Council of Trent . . . decreed at their fourth sitting, April 8, 1546, that the apocryphal books were equal in authority and canonical value to the other books of sacred Scripture.[5]

---

[4]*Ibid.,* pp. 45-46.
[5]*Ibid.,* pp. 57-60.

The Apocrypha was included in the early editions of the *King James Version* of the *Bible*, but later editions omitted it. Finally, after the Protestant Reformation had been consummated, the Protestant churches rejected the Apocrypha as scripture and accepted the size of the Old Testament canon as thirty-nine books, the exact books that the Jews had canonized back near the time of the days of the Lord.

The Prophet Joseph Smith asked the Lord if the Apocrypha contained His holy word. On March 9, 1833, he received the following reply: "Verily, thus saith the Lord unto you concerning the Apocrypha—There are many things contained therein that are true, and it is mostly translated correctly; there are many things contained therein that are not true, which are interpolations by the hands of men."[6] And then the Lord advised the Prophet not to translate the Apocrypha. The Church of Jesus Christ of Latter-day Saints does not accept the Apocrypha as scripture.

CANONIZING THE NEW TESTAMENT

A number of books were written during the early Christian period, and as time passed the people accepted many of them as being equal in authority with the writings found in the Old Testament; in other words, they were gradually becoming canonical. In some Christian communities, as many as forty books came to be regarded as scripture while in other communities the number was only half as great. In order to establish an uniformity throughout the Christian world regarding the books that Catholics should accept as scripture, Athanasius, one of the bishops of the Church, wrote a letter at Easter-time to the churches in his diocese in which he listed twenty-seven books which should be accepted by the church as New Testament scripture on the grounds that they were written either by Jesus' apostles or associates of the apostles.[7] This letter was written in 367 A.D., and exerted a marked influence in helping to establish the New Testament canon. Gradually the list of books by Athanasius became universally accepted by Christians as the New Testament canon, or scripture, and the other Christian writings were regarded as apocryphal works. Many of these writings, however, maintained a marked influence on

---

[6]*Doctrine and Covenants* 91:1-2.
[7]Edgar J. Goodspeed, *The Formation of the New Testament*, pp. 106-110, 130-134, 138, 142, 159-165, 177, 192.

the thinking of the church during much of the Middle Ages. Finally, the Athanasius list of twenty-seven books won a permanent place as canonical, being accepted by the people as the word of the Lord. Later church councils gave their official approval to that list. Thus the New Testament became canonized. Catholics, Protestants, and Latter-day Saints accept exactly the same New Testament canon.

The Church of Jesus Christ of Latter-day Saints inherited the *Bible* many years after it had been canonized; and, as previously suggested this Church accepts as scripture the "smaller canon."

Canonizing the Book of Mormon

The story of the canonizing of the *Book of Mormon* differs greatly from the story of the canonizing of the *Bible*. Shortly after Joseph Smith completed his work of translating the ancient Nephite record, the voice of God came from heaven to the "Three Special Witnesses" (Oliver Cowdery, David Whitmer, and Martin Harris), declaring: *"These plates have been revealed by the power of God, and they have been translated by the power of God. The translation of them which you have seen is correct, and I command you to bear record of what you now see and hear."*[8] In modern revelation, the Lord confirmed His declaration to the "Three Special Witnesses." He proclaimed: *"The Book of Mormon . . . contains the truth and the word of God."*[9] *"And again, the elders, priests and teachers of this church shall teach the principles of my gospel, which are in the Bible and the Book of Mormon, in the which is the fulness of the gospel."*[10] Thus the Church claims that *through Divine proclamation the Lord canonized the Book of Mormon,* thereby declaring it to be holy scripture to all the members of the true Church of Jesus Christ in the latter days. Therefore, every person who becomes affiliated with the Church of Jesus Christ of Latter-day Saints must accept the *Book of Mormon* to be the word, the will, and the mind of God, hence authoritative and binding upon them.

---

[8]Joseph Smith, *History of the Church*, Period I, vol. 1, p. 55.
[9]*Doctrine and Covenants* 19:26.
[10]*Ibid.*, 42:12. The italics in 8 to 10 were supplied by the author.

CANONIZING THE DOCTRINE AND COVENANTS

The canonizing of the *Doctirne and Covenants* occurred as follows: On August 17, 1835, a general conference of the church members was held at Kirtland, Ohio. At this time Joseph Smith and Frederick G. Williams were on a visit to Michigan; therefore, Oliver Cowdery and Sidney Rigdon presided over the conference. All the quorums of the Priesthood were arranged in order. In the afternoon session, Oliver Cowdery presented a collection of latter-day revelations to the general assembly of the Church for acceptance. By vote of the Saints, the revelations were to be published in a book under the name of *Book of Doctrine and Covenants of the Church,* later shortened to *Doctrine and Covenants.* Sidney Rigdon conducted the voting by which they obtained the voice of the assembly. Each of the church councils and quorums of the Priesthood voted separately, acknowledging the revelations which had been selected for publication as from the Lord and acceptable to them as a "law and a rule of faith and practice to the Church." Many testimonies were borne to the truth of the revelations; and a written testimony of the Twelve Apostles was read. Thus by official action the *Doctrine and Covenants* was canonized and thereby accepted by church members as a holy scripture.

CANONIZING THE PEARL OF GREAT PRICE

The fact was pointed out in the first chapter of this book that the *Pearl of Great Price* was accepted as being "the will, the word, and the mind of God, or scripture" just as definitely as were the other three volumes of scripture; but no mention was made of the exact date and occasion when the *Pearl of Great Price* was presented to the entire Church for a vote. The first mention that the author has found regarding a vote being taken by the members of the Church to accept and sustain the teachings of this book as scripture is recorded in the Semi-annual Conference Report of the Church of Jesus Christ of Latter-day Saints which was held in Salt Lake City on October 10, 1880. In that conference report the following information appears:

President George Q. Cannon said: "I hold in my hand the book of *Doctrine and Covenants* and also the book *The Pearl of Great Price,* which books contain revelations of God. In Kirtland, the *Doctrine and Covenants* in its original form, as first printed, was submitted to the officers of the Church and the members of the Church to vote upon. As there have been additions made to it by the publishing of revelations which were not contained in the original edition, it has been deemed wise to submit these books with their contents to the Conference, to see whether the Conference will vote to accept the books and their contents as from God, and binding upon us as a people and as a church."

President Joseph F. Smith said, "I move that we receive and accept the revelations contained in these books, as revelations from God to the Church of Jesus Christ of Latter-day Saints, and to all the world."

The motion was seconded and sustained by unanimous vote of the whole Conference.[11]

Thus the official act of canonizing the *Pearl of Great Price* became an accomplished fact.

The Articles of Faith, being part of the *Pearl of Great Price,* were certainly canonized by vote of the Saints on the foregoing occasion. However, ten years later, according to the journal of Marriner W. Merrill—a member of the Quorum of the Twelve Apostles—the Articles of Faith were accepted as scripture separate and apart from the *Pearl of Great Price* by a vote of the Conference. On October 6, 1890, the same date that President Wilford Woodruff's manifesto regarding the cessation of plural marriage in the Church was read and adopted, the following action was taken in regard to the Articles of Faith: "Bishop Orson F. Whitney then read the Articles of Faith, when they were adopted by the Conference by vote."[12]

CONCLUSIONS

The *Pearl of Great Price,* therefore, is indeed one of the "Holy Scriptures" and one of the great books of the world. As has been pointed out in this commentary, in many respects it holds an unique position and in all respects it supplements and sustains the other standard works of the Church of Jesus Christ. Some of the Divine truths revealed in its pages are not found in any other scripture in the world, and can be rated among the

---

[11]*Latter-day Saint Journal History,* October 10, 1880, Ms.
[12]Melvin Clarence Merrill, *Utah Pioneer and Apostle Marriner Wood Merrill and His Family,* p. 128.

most sublime doctrinal utterances ever made. A few of these statements are as follows: *"For behold, this is my work and my glory—to bring to pass the immortality and eternal life of man;"*[13] and again, in regard to the Father and the Son, *"Man of Holiness is his name, and the name of his Only Begotten is the Son of Man, even Jesus Christ;"*[14] also *"For I, the Lord God, created all things, of which I have spoken, spiritually, before they were naturally upon the earth;"*[15] and also, *"But now mine own eyes have beheld God; but not my natural, but my spiritual eyes, for my natural eyes could not have beheld; for I should have withered and died in his presence; but his glory was upon me; and I beheld his face, for I was transfigured before him;"*[16] *"And thus the Gospel began to be preached, from the beginning, being declared by holy angels sent forth from the presence of God, and by his own voice, and by the gift of the Holy Ghost; and thus all things were confirmed unto Adam, by an holy ordinance, and the Gospel preached, and a decree sent forth, that it should be in the world, until the end thereof; and thus it was. Amen."*[17]

Surely this great scripture is indeed A PEARL OF GREAT PRICE.

---

[13]Moses 1:39.
[14]*Ibid.*, 6:46.
[15]*Ibid.*, 1:11.
[16]*Ibid.*, 3:5.
[17]*Ibid.*, 5:58-59.

INDEX

A

Aaron, Priesthood of, 139-140.

Aaronic Priesthood, restoration of, 5; Joseph Smith's account of restoration of, 236; Oliver Cowdery's account of restoration of, 237-238.

Abel, birth of, 148; killed by Cain, 140, 165-166, 168.

Abraham, visions of, 4; records of, 6-7, 10; writings of preserved, 11; language used by, 20; writings of, 36; life of, 46; vision of regarding God, 55-56; vision of God's intelligence, 58; quoted—God's omnipotence & omniscience, 60; vision of Grand Council & foreordination of Christ, 67-68, 99; vision of spirit world, 71; chosen before he was born, 71; account of creation, 74-82; vision of God's creations, 87ff.; had Urim & Thummim, 89-90; knowledge of heavenly bodies, 91-96; attests Moses' vision, 98; now a God, 105; tells of creation of woman, 116; righteous desires & covenant of, 135; Priesthood of, 135; ordained by Melchizedek, 136-138; celestial marriage practiced by, 143; teachings on Book of Remembrance, 162; quoted—Pharaoh denied Priesthood, 170; lived over 100 years, 194; God's covenant with, 197; Chaldea home of, 197; desire for righteousness of, 198; idolators threatened life of, 198; God's deliverance of, 199; Terah father of, 199; migration of, 199-200; departs from Haran, 200; sacrifices at Moreh, 200; goes to Egypt, 201; calls Sarai his sister, 201; seed of to be numerous as stars, 201; in first resurrection, 206.

Abomination, creeds of men were, 228.

Acts of the Apostles, Moroni quotes from, 232.

Adam, gospel revealed to, 4, 41, 125-127, 152, 154-156, 171; is "Michael, the Ancient of Days," 5; mentioned by Josephus, 38; fall of & receiving of gospel, 46; gospel had by, 49-51; vision of God of, 55; Holy Ghost fell upon, 52, 157; part played in war in heaven by, 69-71; foreordination of, 72-73; gave names to beasts & fowls, 81-82; first mortal man, 97; in Garden of Eden, 106-110; condition of in Eden, 110; commanded to bear children, 111; not to partake of forbidden fruit, 112; God's curse upon, 119; eyes opened because of transgression, 126; Priesthood of, 131-133; a creator of earth, second High Priest, keys of, 132; prophecy of, 133-134; celestial marriage lived by, 145-148; a "son of God," 149, 151; received commandment to work, 152; received law of love, 153-154; language of pure & undefiled, 154, 161-163; procreation law given to, 156; baptism of, 157; fell that men might be, 179; lived at Adam-ondi-Ahman, 180; ordained Enoch, 181; free agency given to, 190; posterity of rejected gospel, 191; Noah had same gospel as, 193-194; North America home of, 197; in first resurrection, 206.

Adamic Language, language of Adam & Jaredites, 161-163.

Adam-ondi-Ahman, Adam lived at, 108, 180; Adam to hold council at, 180.

Age, of man prior to & after flood, 194.

Agency, Satan sought to destroy, 68; man given, 114-116.

Akish, secret combinations of, 173-174.

Alexander the Great, Egyptian dominant language until time of, 25.

Alexandria, Sebolo sailed from, 8.

Alexandria Gazette, quoted, 11, 15-16.

Alma, quoted—gospel given to Adam, 49, 126; God's glory described by, 65; quoted—gospel truths to all peoples, 158; on good comes from God & evil from the devil, 165; in first resurrection, 206.

Altar, Lord destroyed heathen, 199.

Alphabet, Egyptian, preparation of by Joseph Smith, 29-30.

Alvin, Prophet's brother, death of, 234.

America, ancient inhabitants of, 2; Chandler & mummies arrive in, 8; Garden of Eden located in, 107-109; Jaredites lived in, 163; secret combinations established in, 173-175; chosen land, 175; land of promise dedicated for gathering of Israel, 212.

E

Earth, creation of, 74; telestializing of, 191; mourns at sin of inhabitants of, 101; to be sanctified, 191; baptism of, 191; to be terrestrialized, 192; baptism of by fire, 192; cleansing of by water, 195-196.

Ecclesiasticus, apocryphal book of Old Testament, 243.

Egypt, papyrus found in, 7; Joseph sold into, 10; Latter-day Saints' interest in, 18; language of, 25; visited by Europeans, 25; Abraham goes to, 201.

Egyptian, characters in, 7; soldiers, 7; treasure of, 8; tomb, records discovered in, 11; writing or characters of, 12; record, exhibition of, 13; mummies, exhibited to non-Mormons, 16; mummies, purchased by Saints, 46; characters, engraved on brass plates, 18; used by ancient Americans, used to write Book of Abraham, read by Lehi, 18; demotic a type of, 19; altered to fit needs, 19; demotic compared to Nephite record, 19; type of characters, 19; priests, used Hieratic language, 20; dead language, 25; characters, decipherment of, 26; Champollion's knowledge of, 27; grammar & alphabet prepared, 29-30; language deciphered by inspiration, 31; relics, final disposition of, 40; plagues of, 139.

Egyptians, early scholars, 20.

Egyptus, Ham's daughter, 141.

Elder, Joseph Smith designated as first, Oliver Cowdery as second of the Church, 237.

Elect, to be gathered from four quarters, 209; days of tribulation to be shortened for sake of, 222.

Elias, committed dispensation of gospel of Abraham, 202.

Elkenah, Abraham's fathers worshiped god of, 198.

Elijah, Priesthood to be restored by hand of, 231.

Eighth Article of Faith, quoted, 1.

Embalming, orders of, 7-8.

Energy, conservation of, 82-84.

England, Pearl of Great Price published in, 43.

Enlightenment, Joseph Smith & Oliver Cowdery baptized & received spiritual, 239.

Enoch, visions of, 4; pillar of, 36-38; story of, 46; Priesthood had by, 50; vision of regarding God, 55-56; quoted—God's omnipresence, 60; vision of spirit world, 71, 177; attests Moses' vision, 98; received Priesthood, 133; statement regarding, 149; teachings of regarding "sons of God," 151; teachings of, 157; on Book of Remembrance, 162; message of, 178; testified of Cain's curses, 170; son of Jared, seventh from Adam, 176; training in youth of, 176; missionary call of, 176-177; a seer, 177-178; humility of, 177; faith & power of, 180; ordained by Adam, 181; gospel dispensation of, 184; translation of, 184; vision of world at his time, 187; vision of Noah's day of, 188; grief of at wickedness, 190; rainbow confirms covenant with, 192; had same gospel as Adam, 193-194; vision of coming & crucifixion of Son of Man, 203; foresaw resurrection of Christ, 205; foresaw to end of world, 209; city of to meet the Lord, 209-212; foresaw second coming of Christ, 209; city of identified as Zion or New Jerusalem, 213.

Enos, Priesthood had by, 50; received Priesthood, 133; birth of, 148; history of, 149; land of Cainan named by, 179.

Eternal, matter is, 82.

Eternal Father, plan of salvation presented by, 67-69; spirit-children resemble, 106; knowledge & power of, 128-129; father of spirit-children, 150; displeasure of, 151.

Eternal life, promise of, 50; Jesus quoted on, 51; to know God is, 52; gospel offers, 97; meaning of, 122-125; received in presence of God, 134; received through power of Priesthood, 136.

Eternal Mother, of spirit-children, 104; spirit-children resemble, 106.

Ether, Jaredite prophet, saw New Jerusalem come out of heaven, 213.

Eve, fall of, 46; vision of God of, 55; in Garden of Eden, 106-110; first & second great commandments received by, 111-113; creation of, 116-117; mother of all living, 118; God's curse upon, 118-119; knowledge of gospel of, 125-127; celestial marriage received by, 145-148; creation of symbolizes celestial marriage, 145-147; law of work obeyed by, 152; to bear children, 156; righteousness of, 157; driven from Eden, 161; tempted by Satan, 164; hope of for Cain's righteousness, 166; statement of regarding fall,

taught by Noah, 195; Aaronic
Priesthood had no power to bestow,
236; Joseph Smith & Oliver Cow-
dery received, 237.
Holy Priesthood, received by Noah,
194-195.
Holy Scripture, Pearl of Great Price
is, 248.
Holy Spirit of Promise, sealed by,
144, 147.
Holy Trinity, three persons in, 52-53;
Enoch to baptize in name of, 52-53.
Humility, of Enoch, 177.

I

Immortality, promise of, 50; Christ's
mission to bring to pass, 97; mean-
ing of, 122-125.
Immortals, Adam & Eve were, 119.
Indians, ill-treatment of, 141.
Inspired Version, Bible, quoted—
Enoch's power, 181; on "one like
unto Moses," 214ff.; Joseph Smith
prepared through inspiration, 217;
comparison of 1867 & 1944 editions
of, 218; published by Reorganized
Church & changes in, 218.
Intelligence, of God is supreme, 58.
Interpreters, possessed by King Mosiah, 178; Nephite name for Urim
& Thummim, 237.
Irad, killed by Lamech, 172.
Isaac, now a God, 105; celestial marriage practiced by, 143; lived over
100 years, 194; Abraham's covenant confirmed with, 201; in first
resurrection, 206.
Isaiah, quoted—fall of Lucifer, 70; on
doctrine of spirits in prison, 207;
predicts millennial reign, 213; Moroni quoted from, 232.
Israel, to be gathered on American
continent, 212.
Israelites, Moses called to deliver, 177.

J

Jacob, now a God, 105; celestial marriage practiced by, 143; lived over
100 years, 194; covenant confirmed
with, 201; in first resurrection, 206.
James, Epistle of, appealed to Joseph
Smith, 227.
Japheth, birth of, 149; son of Noah,
193.
Jared, Priesthood had by, 50; vision
of Christ had by brother of, 85;
Urim & Thummim received by
brother of, 90; received Priesthood,
133; history of, 149; father of
Enoch, 176; faith of brother of,
180-181.
Jaredites, records of, 163; secret com-

binations of, 173f.
Jehovah, name defined, 61-62; righteousness in pre-mortal life of, 70;
commands Abraham to leave Ur,
199.
Jeremiah, history of known to Nephites,
18; foreordination of, 72-73.
Jershon, Abraham built altar at, 200.
Jerusalem, destruction of, 220-221.
Jethro, Moses received Priesthood
from, 139.
Jesus Christ, teachings of in New
Testament, 1; chosen to be Savior,
4, 67-68; quoted—life eternal, 51;
described by Joseph Smith, 56;
names of, 56-57; intelligence, wisdom, prudence of, 57-58; Son of
God, 59; named Jehovah, 61-62;
heavens & earth created by, 62-63;
"light & truth," 63; appearance to
Joseph Smith of, 65-66; accepted
to be Savior, 70-71; foreordination
of, 72; appeared to brother of
Jared, 85; mortals patterned after,
104; atonement of, 121, 127; quoted
—power to rise from grave, 122;
immortality gift of, 123-124; Adam's
knowledge of, 126; a creator, 129;
Holy Priesthood after order of, 128;
first great High Priest, 132; descendant of Abraham, 136; miracles
performed in name of, 139; quoted
—Adam & marriage, 146; "sons of
God" His children, 150; Adam became son of, 151; teaching of on
love, 154; only name given for salvation & mission of, 154-156;
children of, 157; meaning of gospel
plan of salvation explained by, 159-
160; quoted—"our brother's keeper," 171; Zion abode of, 186; Noah
taught belief in, 195; Enoch's vision
of crucifixion of, 203; spirits in
prison visited by, 206-208; tells His
apostles signs of second coming, 219,
222; predicts destruction of temple,
220; predicts destruction of Jerusalem, 221-222.
Jews, learning of, 18; rulers of, 139;
Book of Mormon to show divinity
of Christ to, 212.
Job, foresaw Christ to stand upon
earth in latter days, 220.
Joel, Moroni quotes from, 232.
John, Gospel of, states Jesus Christ
is creator, 63; bore record of Jesus
as creator, 129-130.
John the Baptist, restoration of Priesthood by, 5; Aaronic Priesthood conferred on Joseph Smith & Oliver
Cowdery by, 236; Oliver Cowdery's
account of appearance of, 237.

M

Maccabees, First & Second, aprocryphal books of Old Testament, 243.

Machnow, Russian giant, 183.

Mahalaleel, Priesthood had by, 50; received Priesthood, 133; history of, 149.

Mahijah, inquired of Enoch his identity, 179.

Mahujah, place where Enoch cried to Lord, 187.

Mahmackrah, Abraham's fathers worshiped god of, 198.

Malachi, Moroni quotes from, 231.

Man, created in image of Only Begotten, 64; Satan sought to destroy agency of, 68-69; Adam is first, 96-97; dignity & eternal nature of, 99-106; creation of, 102-105; dominion of, 102, 111.

Man of Holiness, meaning of, 57; God's name is, 154, 248.

Manchester, Smith family moved to, 226.

Marriage, ordained of God, 143; law of celestial, 143ff.; Adam & patriarchs obeyed celestial, 148, 150; disregarded celestial, 150-151; law of celestial, 156.

Master Mahan, Cain became, 166-167; Lamech became, 172.

Matter, conservation of, 82-84.

McLellin, William E., mummies shown to, 13.

Mediterranean Sea, Canaan on borders of, 198.

Mehemet Ali, viceroy of Egypt, 7.

Melchizedek Priesthood, without beginning of days, 131; Peter, James, & John held keys of, 236; promised to Joseph Smith & Oliver Cowdery, 237.

Men, are because of Adam's fall, 179.

Merrill, Marriner W., journal of records canonization of Articles of Faith, 247.

Mesopotamia Valley, ark landed north of, & Chaldea located in, 197.

Messenger, Moroni sent from God as, 231-233, 235.

Messiah, coming of, 2; foreordination of, 4; called King of Zion, Rock of Heaven, 203; Priesthood conferred on Joseph Smith & Oliver Cowdery in name of, 238.

Methuselah, Priesthood had by, 50; received Priesthood, 133; history of, 149.

Mexicans, writings of mention giants, 181.

Michael, the Ancient of Days, Adam is, 5; part played in war in heaven by, 69-71; righteousness of in premortal life, 70; foreordination of, 72-73; the Archangel, at Grand Council & war in heaven, 132-133; Abraham's Priesthood descended from, 135-136.

Milcah, wife of Nehor, 199.

Millenial Star, account of mummies published in, 9; Book of Abraham published in, 34-35; Prophet's history reproduced in, 225.

Millennium, Enoch's vision of events to usher in, 209, 213.

Missionary, Enoch's work as, 178.

Mitchell, Dr., verifies Professor Anthon's certification of translation, 236.

Mob-violence, Joseph Smith & Oliver Cowdery threatened by, 239.

Moon, revolutions & rotations of, 93; will not give light in last days, 223.

Money-digger, Joseph Smith referred to as, 234.

Moreh, Abraham sacrificed in plains of, 200.

Moriancumer, Mahonri, brother of Jared named, 163; Adamic language used by, 163.

Mormon, Nephite prophet & historian, 19; abridgment of records made by, 19; epistle of to Moroni on infant baptism, 156-157; quoted— good comes from God, evil from the devil, 165.

Moroni, abridged "24 plates," 2; Mormon's epistle on infant baptism to, 156-157; Jaredite records abridged by, 163; warning to us of, 175; promise of regarding coming forth of records, 211; preface to Book of Mormon written by, 212.

Mortal, Adam & Eve not yet, 117; Adam & Eve became, 118.

Mortality, conditions of, 118-119.

Moses, visions of, 4; Joseph foresaw work of, 39; vision of regarding God, 55-56; quoted—God's omnipresence, 60; on God the creator, 62; vision of Satan had by, 63-64; God's glory beheld by, 63-64; foresaw Grand Council & Satan's plan in vision, 67-68; gives account of creation, 74-82; vision of God & His creations had by, 96-97; spiritual eyes of, 102; gives story of creation of woman, 116; quoted— God created through Priesthood, 129; Priesthood of, 138; power of